MERCHANT BANKING

GEORGE K. YOUNG

Merchant Banking

PRACTICE AND PROSPECTS

WEIDENFELD AND NICOLSON
5 Winsley Street London W1

© 1966 by George K. Young
First printed in 1966
Second edition 1971

ISBN 0 297 00475 1
Printed in Great Britain
by C. Tinling & Co. Limited
Prescot and London

Contents

Preface to Second Edition

Quite the nicest thing about the City of London is the way the people there, from the humblest senior partner or chairman of the board to the most hard-pressed-for-time office boy, seem to make it a pleasure to help the ignorant stranger upon his way; and I should like to acknowledge the immense assistance I have received from them in bringing facts and figures more up to date and in providing material for some modifications of the original text where such seemed to be called for. A large number of take-overs have taken place since the first edition was prepared but I have not changed the examples because the original selection appears to bring out the main points of the principal varieties of take-over likely to be encountered in practice.

CATERHAM, SURREY   JOHN F. RICHARDS
December 1970

Preface

I was invited to produce a book which would give a young man some idea of the kind of career offered by merchant banking and which would also make a forecast of the likely status of the profession over the next decade or so. 'Political in the widest sense of the word', was the publisher's commission. When I rather lightheartedly embarked on this undertaking, I little realized the handicap which would be imposed by the absence of any standard work on the subject. So to produce an introductory work comprehensible to the 'lay' reader, I have had to give general descriptions of the main fields in which merchant banking operates, such as the business of the money market, export credit, hire purchase and leasing finance, share issuing procedures, and investment management.

Since there is no single merchant banking activity which is not also conducted by other financial institutions or professions, it has been difficult to avoid occasionally appearing to stray from the central theme; but I trust that I always come back to it. If a forecast is to mean anything at all, it has to be presented within a framework of some general comparative statistics, international as well as national, so that the role of the accepting houses can be put in perspective. For the sake of completeness several footnotes have had to be added on Euro-dollar policy, investment analysis, etc. But I should like to think that I have thereby prepared the way for some better-qualified student or writer to embark on a much-needed definitive and authoritative work on a sector of banking which is certainly overwritten in the Press and probably underestimated by academic economists.

There is no lack of material. Indeed I am surprised that merchant bankers have acquired the reputation of being reticent about their activities. Of course the *segreto bancario* has to be observed but otherwise they are a fairly vocal crowd and there is a rich supply of information in both popular and specialist periodicals, quite apart from what is presented in the daily Press. The simplest method of imposing some limitation on my material seemed to be to make a selection from the reported activities of merchant banking during the year April 1964–April 1965 when the manuscript was being composed and, apart from a historical introduction, to go back only as far as appeared necessary for adequate explanation. This approach may mean that some merchant banks will feel that I have done less than justice to what they regard as their finest hour. I have tried to keep a balance, and specific activities and events have been selected to illustrate significant skills and procedures, not because at one time they were headline news. This applies particularly in the case of take-over bids and merger work.

Needless to say, the opinions expressed – other than where they are clearly attributed or given as quotations – are my own. I am in fact most grateful to my employers for so unhesitatingly agreeing that I should accept the commission. My thanks are also due to Messrs Peter Brackfield, Peter Cannon, Julian S. Hodge, Cyril H. Kleinwort, Gordon Richardson, Edmund L. de Rothschild, and Siegmund Warburg for submitting to interrogation. To my colleagues who helped me on innumerable points of fact I am deeply in debt, particularly to Mr W.C. Baldock of Kleinwort, Benson Ltd, who provided sage counsel and guidance on technical questions. The Secretary of the Accepting Houses Committee, Mr T.A.C.D. Stewart, put himself about most generously in suggesting historical and contemporary material, and Mr Roy Lewis took time off from other pressing preoccupations to read through the manuscript and make a number of valuable suggestions.

The outcome has been a highly interpretative work and I should not like to hazard how many of my City friends and acquaintances will agree with me. However, since the completion of the manuscript, such developments as the link-up between National and Grindlays Bank and Wm. Brandt's Sons and Co., the purchase of a stake in the Bank of London and South America by the Mellon National Bank and Trust Company of Pittsburgh, the re-entry of the Westminster Bank into issue work, the intensified activity in Europe of American investment houses, to say nothing of political happenings, do appear

3

to bear out my conclusions. In any case, one of the main characteristics of merchant bankers is their propensity for arguing what their
profession is all about. If I have given fresh impetus to the argument, I
must be on the right lines.

LONDON EC 2
December 1965

CHAPTER ONE

Waterloo and All That

Legend and History

Merchant banking suffers from its legends: Nathan Rothschild, on the first unofficial tidings of Waterloo, creating a 'bear' market on the Stock Exchange and making a killing when confirmation comes through; couriers hastening with funds to bolster Metternich's reaction or to further the intrigues of the Risorgimento; and in the Edwardian heyday, titles and grey toppers in the Enclosure as rewards for pandering to royal weakness.

None of these legends quite accord with the mood of our own time. Personal advancement too obviously associated with cunning is no recommendation in an age which professes to set store by more open ways. So perforce up-to-date legends have had to be created, and over the past decade merchant bankers have been represented as tough bargainers, practitioners in esoteric arts of share issuing and take-over bids, and specialists in the mysterious ways of foreigners. Since by the mid-sixties some subtle alchemy had brought about a change in popular attitudes to such skills, treating some of them as almost akin to the black arts, the merchant bankers now seem to be searching round – a little too anxiously – for a fresh legend.

Yet a merchant banker is still a banker, taking in other men's money and depending for his livelihood on a reputation for trustworthiness and fair dealing. While the older world of finance and commerce perhaps took its own legends with a pinch of salt, the self-conscious Englishman of today is apt to confuse his own love of play-acting with the common tasks of his daily round. That is certainly no state of mind for a banker.

What, in the nineteen-seventies do all the yesterdays of the merchant banks add up to? Have these 'houses' a role for tomorrow? They appear to do nothing which cannot be done by other banks and finance institutions. The main difference seems to be that a merchant banker does them all under one roof. For merchants can find other ways of having their bills discounted; capital can be raised without bringing in a whole panoply of issuing houses. In an age of tele-communications and jet travel are we not all becoming experts in foreign parts and foreigners' ways? As far as pure function is concerned merchant banks do not seem to be indispensable. They even look rather puny with £3,217 millions assets at the end of 1970 compared to £11,788 millions of the clearing banks. If they survive, is it only because the English have a liking for non-essential survivals such as top-hatted functionaries: or do our merchant banks fulfil a role which is more than function?

The legends hardly match history. The great growth of merchant banking business in and through London is not merely to be ascribed to some special skill brought to these shores by the Barings, Klein-worts, Hambros and Rothschilds. Some of the skills were already in existence in Britain and overseas. It was what was happening in the United Kingdom and in the lands of British settlement or ascendancy that transformed the nature of banking and enhanced the role of banking houses. The foundation on which they built their renown was the London Bill and the part it played in trade with the Americas and Asia, not the patronage of princes.

Since those days they have acquired a multitude of functions, and the term 'merchant bank' has inevitably become stretched to apply to any group engaged in any one or more of them. This is a semantic process which is inherent in human consciousness and defies the tight-lipped disapproval of the aristocrats of the profession. After all, they too became 'bankers' when they added the function to that of merchant. However, an establishment does have the right to try to define its own titles and the merchant banks who form the Accepting Houses Committee, in laying down a norm for their own existence, give the others at least a claim to a privileged existence.*

An 'Accepting House', as the name implies, is an entity whose business consists of accepting bills of exchange to finance the trade of

---

*The list of members of the Accepting Houses Committee and the representatives of each bank are given in Appendix One.

others,* whose acceptances command the finest rates in the discount market and can, if need be, be discounted by the Bank of England. The Accepting Houses are not the only ones who accept bills of exchange but, among the merchant banks, they are the only houses who meet the above description. All of them conduct banking operations of one kind or another, taking in money on current and other account for customers at home and abroad. In all matters affecting the regulation of banking, whether by law or custom, they enjoy the same rights, duties, and responsibilities as the clearing banks. Within the mechanism of the City, their place is recognized and assured. Whatever the claims of other aspirants to the status of merchant bankers, it is from the Accepting Houses that they derive their original.

The bill of exchange itself is almost as old as trade. It was the natural sequel to the custom of merchants putting their name or seal on a tablet or document when they ordered or received their goods: if for any reason payment could not be made immediately, the written proof of the transaction could serve as a means of raising credit, either against guarantee of the goods themselves or against the good name of the trader. Merchant banking began quite soberly when merchants agreed, for a consideration or commission, to lend their reputation to 'accept' the bills of other traders, thus guaranteeing that they would be met at the date of maturity.

The tablets of Ur testify to the earliest use of the practice; the Ancient Greeks, as the pre-eminent traders of the classical world, invoked the curses of the gods on those who failed to honour their bills; Rome employed them in trade throughout its empire, and during barbarian invasions and even in its decline and fall the use of bills continued without interruption, as the slender records of the trading towns and centres of the Dark Ages bear witness. In their original and simplest form they are still to be found along the caravan routes from Pakistan to Iran and Iraq. The signature of a Peshawar merchant and the endorsements of many go-betweens ensure that the Koochi trader's camel is reloaded in Isphahan with an equivalent value of

---

* Under the Bills of Exchange Act, 1882, a bill of exchange is defined as an unconditional order in writing addressed by one person to another, signed by the person giving it, requiring the person to whom it is addressed to pay on demand or at a fixed or determinable future date a sum certain in money to or to the order of a specified person, or to bearer. The person to whom it is addressed 'accepts' it by signing on the face of it, thereby undertaking an unconditional obligation to pay the amount under the terms of the wording.

goods for his return journey. A great world stretches across Asia where pieces of paper produced by brown fingers from voluminous robes, with an accompanying '*Inshallah*', are honoured at sight.

The first official mention in England of bills is in a statute of 1379, and in 1697 inland bills were made legal south of the Border. But it was not until the Bills of Exchange Act, 1882, that customary rules received full statutory backing. Long before then Britain's adherence to a gold standard, the reputation of her merchants and bankers, and the growth of international trade had made a Bill on London as good as gold. For the three decades after the passing of the Act the London Bill became the charter of world trade. The London acceptor began to lay claim to both legend and grey topper.

And so they poured into London, the merchants and bankers, not only from Central Europe but from Baltimore and New Orleans, from Cuba, Scandinavia, and India to establish themselves at the heart of the bill business. In the firms they founded, many members of the original families still play a prominent part; some are now public companies with boards of directors possessing wide connections throughout British industry and finance. 'Trade is no longer unfashionable,' *The Times* had written in a leading article on 18 April 1864:

> The present age has outlived at least one folly of past times, and nobody now imagines that he loses caste or forfeits position by going into business: 'Business', in fact, as commercially understood has pretty well driven the old 'liberal professions' from the field. The object of a man in entering life is now, we will not say merely to make money, but still to make money at a respectable rate and in a reasonable time. To these practical conditions he sacrifices without the least hesitation the old ideas of 'gentility'. He considers that a gentleman is not less a gentleman on account of his occupation, so long as it be honourable and not of a kind to induce deterioration of character. He has no idea of going for twenty years penniless in order to save his dignity.

And this remained the unquestioned and vigorous philosophy until the events of 1914 and their sequel forced other considerations into the national consciousness.

The Era of Great Loans

One fresh asset was brought to London by the immigrant European bankers which, combined with the accumulating wealth of Britain, added to the country's power and influence in the world. That was their skill in arranging large loans through issues of bonds placed internationally. The Jewish bankers had developed the technique in the fast-changing Europe of the Revolutionary and Napoleonic Wars. The eighteenth century had, until then, been an age when funds were transferred as bullion, and coins were loaded into great waggons and despatched under guard. But the wars with France changed all this, especially for the German princes anxiously weighing up the pros and cons of opposing the Corsican usurper, allying themselves with him in time to share the fruits of his military victories, or maintaining a precarious neutrality. This was the agonizing daily reappraisal of Europe's wealthiest man, the Margrave of Hesse, rich from the sale of well-trained regiments especially to his dear Hanoverian cousins in London. All rulers turned to him when they were short of funds, every great contractor borrowed from him, there was no major commercial venture where the entrepreneurs did not appeal to his avarice.

But as the pendulum of fortune swung from one side to another in the Napoleonic Wars, how was a sagacious prince to turn an honest ducat, if his compromising signature was found by Napoleon's agents on a written promise to pay, or if his specie was liable to be captured by French dragoons? The Jews of Kassel and Frankfurt with their network of correspondents throughout an embattled Europe came forward with a solution. No need for His Serene Highness' signature at all! No compromising traces! The loans will be made in the name of the banker. The books will be kept in cellars in the Frankfurt ghetto. The London proceeds of the sale of the Hanau grenadier battalion can be credited to somebody else's account in Copenhagen. A mechanism for loans and credits arranged through bankers was not new: it had been the speciality of the Dutch and Scottish banking houses of Amsterdam. Barings and Hope & Co. had arranged such facilities for the newly-born United States of America. The exigencies of war so improved and perfected the process that it could operate as fast as the horses of the Imperial postal service of the Prince of Thurn und Taxis could gallop; or if French cavalry pickets were on the look-out, a rider in hodden-grey hired in Frankfurt by the Rothschilds could slip past on his way to Berlin and Vienna. The service met the needs of the age and the rewards were high.

Thus, when Nathan Rothschild was sent to Britain by his father to operate on the other side of Napoleon's Continental Blockade, he brought with him a highly-developed technique of which the British

9

Government stood in dire need. Napoleon's paymasters could at least carry the funds for soldiers' pay, for the commissary, for the intelligence service, in horse-drawn waggons escorted by the armies. Nelson in the Mediterranean and Wellington in Spain, in between the irregular intervals of delayed frigates, could only cash bills at an exorbitant discount rate with the Spanish, Maltese, and Sicilian merchants they were protecting. The Rothschild network, operating even through Paris under the nose of Fouché, the efficient French Minister of Police, effected the cash disbursements at half price. The Lords Commissioner of H.M. Treasury, not for the first time nor, alas, for the last, discovered that old tried ways were neither the best nor the most economical.

And the war, unbeknown to the Treasury officials, was going to bring changes which would present them with tasks and responsibilities far beyond anything for which they had been equipped by status and experience. The failure of the Bank of Amsterdam in 1796, the unfortunate choice by the Dutch of the losing side in the war, and finally the Continental Blockade, had brought a general move of merchants and financiers from the Continent to London. Barings had already moved before the Revolution: as wool merchants from Bremen, they had established themselves in Exeter and, as far back as 1776, had had their own ships insured with Lloyds and maintained continental connections through the Scottish bankers, Hope & Co., who had opened their counting house in Amsterdam.*

So when peace was signed, London found that it possessed the skills and the knowledge which enabled Prussia to raise a reconstruction loan, the Allies to arrange the orderly distribution of the indemnity payments by the defeated French, and Metternich to borrow to uphold the policies of the Holy Alliance. Profits were good. In 1818 the Rothschilds persuaded the Prussians that their bonds could only be placed at a fifteen per cent discount. They reached par in 1824 thanks to Prussian hard work and careful ordering of state finances. The Rothschilds may well have been right about the market when they launched the reconstruction loan in 1818 but as underwriters they kept back sufficient of the issue to profit from the rise and arranged a conversion in 1829 at ninety-eight per cent with a commission of $1\frac{1}{2}$ per cent. As Metternich's secretary, the Austrian

---

* Hope & Co. are now merged in the Dutch banking group of Mees & Hope N.V.

state counsellor Friedrich von Gentz, wrote from the Congress of Aachen to his friend Adam Müller in 1818:

> I was delighted with your idea of a monograph on the Rothschilds. It is one of the brightest and most happy notions that I have heard for some time. The word is all the more appropriate since the Rothschilds really do constitute a special *species plantarum* with its own characteristics. They are vulgar, ignorant Jews, outwardly presentable. In their craft they act entirely in accordance with the principles of naturalism, having no suspicion of a higher order of things, but they are gifted with a remarkable instinct which causes them always to choose the right, and of two rights the better. Their enormous wealth (they are the richest people in Europe) is entirely the result of this instinct which the public are wont to call luck. Baring's most profound reasoning inspires me, now that I have seen everything at close quarters, with less confidence than the sound judgement of the less intelligent Rothschilds – for amongst the five brothers there is one whose intelligence is wanting and another whose intelligence is weak – and if Baring and Hope ever fail, I can state with confidence that it will be because they have thought themselves cleverer than Rothschild and have not followed his advice.*

Not surprisingly von Gentz finished up on the Rothschild payroll and wrote a flattering book about the family.

Just at this moment in history, however, a whole new field of human activity was being opened up for which the skill evolved to meet the needs of princely power and intrigue, seemed almost providentially to have been designed. This was the capital requirement of the New World, rhetorically summoned by Canning to redress the balance of the Old, but which in practice badly needed to balance its own books before it could move on to new endeavour. The American need for investment capital continued to make London a lure for far-seeing merchants and bankers. Alexander Kleinwort, who, a decade or so earlier had left Bremen, came from Cuba to find fresh uses for the profits made from running sugar through the Continental blockade in the expanding banking centre of London. The Browns, who had sailed from Ulster to Baltimore to sell their Irish linen, sent a son back to Liverpool to organize the business of King Cotton. In the United States, moreover, there were railways to be built from Baltimore to Ohio and beyond, while on the other side of the Alleghenies new industries were growing up with the prospect of more even further afield. While young men obeyed the injunction to go West, some at least of the merchants were coming East. From 1804

---

* *The Rise of the House of Rothschild,* Count Corti (Gollancz, 1928), p. 228.

onwards the order of battle of London accepting houses, largely as it exists today, was gradually built up – Schroder, Rothschild, Brandt, Gibbs, Huth, Brown Shipley, Behrens, Frühling and Goschen, Kleinwort, Hambro, and Samuel form the oldest group in that order. Some have since been absorbed; most of them retain the names under which they first traded.

Although their operations covered short-term credits in the form of acceptances, medium-term bonds, and long-term loans for accounts of foreign clients, they tended to specialize in the areas and merchandise where they could give their guarantee with greatest confidence. Not only the Rothschilds brought powerful clients from the Continent. Hambros had been the bankers of the Danish Royal House whose later Norwegian and Greek offshoots also became their clients. Hope & Co. and Baring Brothers seemed to remain indentified with one political stream, for in addition to being bankers to the United States Government they floated France's national reconstruction loan after Waterloo while Rothschilds continued to help the Central European princely houses to get on their feet after the destruction of war. When the *risorgimento* seemed to have fizzled out in military defeat and Papal intrigue, Hambros at Cavour's request undertook in 1851 the restoration of the fortunes of the House of Savoy by raising a loan of £3,600,000. This was one of the biggest so far made by London to a foreign government and brought its reward when Hambros and Barings joined forces to issue the bonds of a united Italy after it adopted the gold standard.

Financing World Trade

But it was still the opening up of the West which provided the main stimulus to the greatest development of British merchant banking in the second half of the nineteenth century. By 1848, with the rise of the clamour for popular government, the era of the power and influence of the Rothschild family was drawing to its close, even if they figured in such coups as the purchase of the Khedive's Suez Canal holdings for the British Government. There had already been mutterings in 1827 about their alleged behind-the-scenes influence when the British Parliamentary Opposition, supported by *The Times* – ever ready to buy cheap applause by joining in the latest popular chorus of cant and denunciation – objected to the appointment of John Herries as

Chancellor of Exchequer because of his connections with the banking family. However, by the time the Third Republic had obtained a tenuous hold on French loyalties and the British franchise had been extended by successive Reform Acts, the Rothschilds were respectably ensconced in the social élite of the countries where they mainly operated. They had laurels enough on which to rest.

The new merchant banking houses set up in London by the families who had crossed and recrossed the Atlantic within a generation were naturally those most prominently identified with New World financing. The most famous banking hierarchy of the Western world Morgans, was first established in London. In 1838, George Peabody, an American merchant who shipped rails for American railroad construction, set up a London office which was to grow into J.S. Morgan and Co. and father the renowned New York banking house; in Britain it became in 1910 Morgan Grenfell & Co. The Alsatian trading family of Lazards, after opening warehouses in Louisiana and following the 'forty-niners' (to whom they sold picks and shovels) round to the Californian goldfields, were back in Europe again as the century advanced. The great service all these houses could offer was to arrange for American bills to be traded at the same price in Liverpool and London as in New Orleans, Baltimore, Philadelphia, New York, and Boston. And when in 1866 the first transatlantic cable was opened, the whole picture of merchant banking in the New World, particularly where the cotton trade was concerned, changed radically. British manufacturers could now make their own selection from samples and make offers by telegraph: one after another the merchant bankers moved out of commodity dealing and concentrated on providing authorities and guarantees against shipments. This meant a shift of their main activities away from Liverpool to London and at the same time made the latter even more of a magnet to the international trader.*

The merchant bank whose origins and evolution perhaps best typify the whole interplay of the factors which created the financial institutions of London and which at the same time played its part in adapting them to the fresh requirements of each successive economic

---

* Sir Robert Kindersley, as he then was, said in evidence to the Macmillan Committee on Banking in 1931: 'It was largely through the channel of these merchant banks that England was enabled to take such a leading part in the building of railways and other developments abroad, to the great advantage of our export trade and also that London became the market and distributing centre for such a large number of raw materials and other commodities.'

development, is Brown, Shipley & Co. When Alexander Brown, a Belfast merchant, set off in 1798 to Baltimore, he could hardly have foreseen that he would found a banking dynasty which would establish two realms, one in the New World and the other in the Old. But his affairs so prospered not only from the importation of Belfast linen, but also from exporting cotton and tobacco to Britain, that in 1810 his son William Brown was sent back to Liverpool to look after the British end. As business continued to expand, in 1825 a Delaware Quaker, Joseph Shipley, was brought in to help him, and later became a partner. The Continental Blockade had stopped the supply of flax and potash for the Irish linen manufacture, but stimulated such a demand for cane sugar that the risks of blockade-running were well worth taking. The same sugar trade made the substantial fortune of an English trader in Cuba, Drake by name, and passed on to the German manager, Alexander Kleinwort, who married the daughter of his London agent.

Alexander Brown & Sons in the meantime moved into the profitable new field of railroad finance. 'We send you by the conveyance,' wrote Alexander Brown to William in 1827, 'two copies of the proceedings to make a railway from this City to the Ohio River. If this is accomplished it will resuscitate Baltimore.'* Since the only steam railway in the world at that time was the Stockton to Darlington line, this was certainly pioneering.

The use of bills as collateral – with all the attendant hazards – was now spreading. When an outflow of gold from Britain in 1836 precipitated a major, crisis in the following year, the Bank of England raised its discount rate and refused Anglo-American merchant bankers' bills as loan collateral. Many of the best-known merchant banking firms of the time went bankrupt so that only the industrious researcher in City archives can rediscover names which were once household words. But the credit of W. and J. Brown was so good that the Bank of England was ready to advance them £1,950,000 so that they could honour their cheques – the only Liverpool merchant bank to enjoy this privilege while the crisis lasted. Shipley himself, who had handled the negotiations with the Bank of England, received his partnership as a reward and the house went on to establish one of the first United States steamship lines. The New World branch of the Brown family on their side bequeathed to American financial life the

---

* *Heir of Adventure: The Story of Brown Shipley & Co.* by Ayton Ellis (Circulated Privately), p. 33.

house now known as Brown Brothers Harriman, one which today enjoys a particularly sympathetic international reputation.

The social rise of the merchant bankers paralleled their financial progress. William Brown was knighted, helped to found the Bank of Liverpool, in 1824 became a freeman of Liverpool and was elected to Parliament in 1847, appointed Deputy Lieutenant of the County in 1856, High Sheriff in 1863, eventually commanded one of the local volunteer battalions, and inevitably was a leading member of the local hunt. There has remained a certain tradition in Brown Shipley of producing from its trainees what are now referred to as 'top people', who in latter days have included Lord Norman (Montagu Norman), Lord Chandos, and, most recently, Mr Edward Heath.

In the eastern hemisphere, those who caught fortune's golden smile by the poet's prescription to gather gear by every guile justified by honour enjoyed even more legendary rises to wealth and eminence, while at the same time adding to the material resources of mankind. Such was the story of the descendants of a Jewish immigrant from the Netherlands, Samuel Ben Amschel, who in 1758 settled in London's East End and whose son Marcus built up a business in ornamental caskets, frames, and needle cases decorated with sea shells bought from sailors. From there Marcus extended to general merchandising between the Far East and Europe. The opening of the Suez Canal meant shorter voyages and the telegraph brought speedy intelligence about prices and shortages. When in 1868 the silk crops in France and Italy failed, Marcus imported Japanese silk at a good profit; as telecommunication also meant that knowledge of shipping movements could be centralized at any one moment, his son, young Marcus, who had sailed to the Far East in 1872, chartered bottoms to transfer surplus rice from Siam to India where famine was raging.

By linking Far East trade to shipping possibilities, the Samuels built up their great fortunes, became bankers and preserved the humble shell which had furnished the livelihood of the original East End family, as the symbol of the 'Shell' oil empire. For by becoming European merchants in Japan, the Samuels had been selling, *inter alia,* lamp oil to Japanese fishermen in exchange for rare shells. The possibilities of marketing oil in the Far East were becoming daily more obvious and young Marcus saw that the basic problem to be solved was the transport of bulk oil from the Black Sea to refineries and storage tanks on the Asiatic coasts. This meant undercutting the American companies, notably Standard Oil, by finding fresh sources of crude. After long negotiations the Samuels obtained them, designed their own tankers, and sent a nephew out to the Far East to set up shore installations. In 1892 the first 'Shell' tanker – *Murex* – took on its first cargo at Baku and set sail for Bangkok through the Suez Canal. By the end of the century there was a tanker fleet of eleven and in 1914 Shell Transport and Trading Co. – fifty years later the bluest of 'blue chips' on the London Stock Exchange – was moving ninety per cent of the oil passing through Suez. The Shell red can had become a world symbol.

The financial and trading mechanism which the merchant banks had been largely instrumental in creating brought its own problems and risks, and as the nineteenth century progressed these began to show signs of being too large for the merchant banks to solve by themselves. The changed emphasis is well illustrated by the South American economic crises of 1825 and 1890. In the former the Duke of Wellington brought in Nathan Rothschild to advise Lord Liverpool's government on how to cope with the general fall in securities which had followed the collapse of unwise British investment in South American mining ventures. In the latter it was the Bank of England which had to step in to support Barings. There were many of these 'panics' – in 1826, 1836, 1846, and in 1893, while the century finished in 1899 with a 'Boer War Panic'. The notion of a Victorian era of calm security in contrast to the economic turmoil of our own times is not borne out by the facts.

Nor were the merchant bankers quite the adventurous takers of risks that the present-day legends would have us believe. They had perhaps a head start over other entrepreneurs for getting on to a good thing but they were always sensitive to the first mutterings of rumour about reputation or solvency and preferred to get out too soon rather than too late. As a general rule in acceptance business, the amount of credit given to any one firm was limited, no matter how good might be its reputation, and since the documents which were the title to the goods remained under the control of the merchant banks until the consignment reached its destination, and even then were only delivered to the local merchant to an amount warranted by his credit, the security was first class – provided the accepting house knew its shippers and its correspondents. Getting out a little early did not prevent a well-established accepting house from recouping later on since the field of reward was enormous. In the decades after the repeal of the Corn Laws, the hey-day of Victorian liberal free trade, Britain's own exports increased from £47 millions annually to £200 millions, to which must be added the proceeds of an expanding and profitable re-export and entrepôt trade.

This meant that fluctuations in world trade had their immediate reaction on the credit of City firms who depended basically on bill finance for their operations. Baring Bros indeed dealt only with firms with established credit, no matter how promising a newcomer might appear. They could afford to play it safe. Even in 1834 George Brown had written to his brother William when some cloud had appeared on the business horizon, 'I am aware that some risk must be run in any business but as our dear father used to say, that as we have now made our independent fortunes, they will increase rapidly with the accumulation of interest.'

Perils of Ascendancy

The merchant bankers themselves were undergoing a metamorphosis into something strange as well as rich – membership of the English 'Establishment'. '. . . & Sons' were not the same men as dear father, whether he had been a Frankfurt Jew still conscious of the humiliations imposed by South German princes on his community before the enlightened rule of Prussia brought emancipation and assured legal status, or a New Englander who would scorn to receive a knighthood from a descendant of George III. But men desire the regard of their fellows as much as they do life itself; for most men riches are only a means to this, not an end in themselves. In 1847 Lionel Rothschild became the first Jew to enter Parliament. In 1897 the first Marcus Samuel was elected an alderman of the City, next year he was knighted, in 1902 he became Lord Mayor, and for his Great War services and his support of the Navy's plans for conversion to oil, he was made the first Lord Bearsted. Today the roll-call of the boards of the accepting houses numbers a platoon from Debrett.

The heads of families have in some cases stepped out from a banking role leaving perhaps a cadet branch still active, like the Goschens, or eventually, as with Sir Gerard d'Erlanger, have withdrawn from a scene which was no longer theirs. One or two have preferred to anglicize their names although most have remained proud of the evidence of their origins in the historic trading cities of Europe.

17

The Schroder family, who possessed their patent of nobility before they settled in London, only reluctantly gave up their German nationality in 1914. Amalgamations have brought into the merchant banking world still older names of financial history such as the Mocattas who were already bullion merchants and smelters when the Bank of England was founded, and at once became its silver brokers. When Mocatta and Goldsmid were taken over by Hambros in 1957, Mr Edward Mocatta, the eighth generation since the firm was established in London, moved on to the board of the merchant bank. The final arrival of the merchant banks at the pinnacle of the British banking system was attested by their representation on the Court of the Bank of England – in 1935 seven members out of the twenty-four. They had become an institution.

Straightaway they were exposed to the rigidities, as well as enjoying the privileges, of being institutionalized. For though the capacity to call on a million pounds was a powerful asset in the first half of the nineteenth century, the chief assets of the merchant banks, as their history amply illustrates, were the men who ran them, their flexible outlook, and their capacity for sizing up the potentialities of a new situation. The various town and country banks had at first an only tenuous hold on existence with fewer resources at their disposal than the Browns, Kleinworts, and Rothschilds. In the panic of 1825 the famous bank of Sir Peter Pole & Co., although agent for some forty-four banks, had had to close its doors. But between 1835 and 1935 there were progressive amalgamations and mergers into the big clearing banks of today, while the City itself gradually ceased to be an exclusive affair of groups of top-hatted directors and messengers exchanging information and hand-written notes within a privileged field, where personal contact was synonymous with professional skill.

The London money market had developed its own institutionalized mechanism presided over by the Bank of England which kept a watchful eye on the world-wide deployment of short term funds whether of domestic or foreign origin. Sampling the bill portfolios by buying parcels for discount itself, the Bank maintained its own control over the acceptance business and dropped its unmistakable hints from time to time if their composition seemed to be stretching the notion of a bill of exchange too far. Its 'suggestions' for the rates the Bank would like to see for the next tender of Treasury bills had become the all-important indicator in guiding the money market towards a rise or fall.

The depression of 1931 put the final curb on the ability of merchant banks to play the role of major financiers to foreign governments. In the 'twenties the bills of the latter were still being offered in London and other main centres on the lines of British treasury bills – Hambros had Greek, Finnish, and Norwegian bills on offer, Barings Argentinian, Rothschilds Chilean, Schroder on behalf of the German cities, and of the merchant bank acceptances totalling £145 millions in 1931, £45 millions were German and frozen under the moratorium. Although they were gradually repaid and Latin America in practice caused greater losses and worse headaches than Central Europe, the merchant bankers after 1931 found themselves part of a system where freedom of action and automatic adjustment had been replaced by deliberate management.

When the crisis broke, the accepting houses with some £60 millions of capital resources, had £105 millions deposits, nearly all foreign, while £50 millions of their acceptances were for countries where moratoria had been declared. Their deposits fell by forty per cent and Schroders, Kleinworts, Hambros, Lazards, Barings, and Rothschilds, who in that order held the majority of acceptances, had to take them off the market and hold them. Contingent liabilities became actual. The Bank of England intervened through the discount market and gave special facilities to houses which needed them, to permit bills to continue to be financed. By the end of 1932 acceptances had been reduced to £80 millions and deposits were stable. Team spirit and good organization had prevented any failures. But the crisis afforded clear proof that family resources were not enough. The Rothschild millions could no longer sway the destiny of nations. The day had been won by the community consciousness of the City presided over by a central bank which at that time had no power of ordinance or sanction.

There was a further factor inhibiting any pioneering spirit in the accepting houses. Institutions suffer from inertia unless their purpose is continually reassessed within some wider framework of human goals and they are then adapted and reformed to assist in attaining them. There is a natural tendency for those who form an ascendancy to think that in arranging matters to suit each other's convenience, they are advancing the public interest. And since the welfare of the nation and the prosperity of the City had historically been so interwoven, the temptation for financial leaders to succumb was doubly strong. The family-like atmosphere of the whole British

19

ascendancy up to 1930 misled its members too often into thinking that the public good was at stake when they were only organizing their own comfort. This was perhaps the real 'Great Illusion' of the 'twenties and affected not merely Bloomsbury literary cliques believing that they were promoting the cause of literature by praising each other's works. Even Lord Brand, perhaps the most distinguished merchant banking personality between the wars and who served Lazards for some fifty years, seems, in spite of the sage counsel he is reputed to have given government and City in two great conflicts and their aftermath, to have shared the illusion. In *War and National Finance,* compiled from his essays and papers, he had written in 1920 that financial leaders in all countries 'are the only people who understand what is happening to the world and the necessity, if our civilization is not to disappear, of co-operation by all to save it.'

The continual purring of a well-oiled machine such as the City, operated by men who know each other well enough to affect a disarming casualness, does tend with time to lull the operators into a belief in a permanent order of reasonableness. The absence of the daily needs which press on those who are less well blessed with worldly goods helps to heighten the illusion. Though a certain cunning is permissible, convention sets bounds to the ways in which it may be practised and privilege in any case limits the practice to closed groups. The temptation for a self-conscious man to behave like the institution of which he believes himself part, becomes irresistible. The imperatives require him to own racehorses, dabble in art collecting, attend bridge parties and indulge in the ritual slaughter of God's creatures according to the seasons of the sporting calendar. Finally he finds himself living up to the newspaper profiles about himself and diverting so much artificial heartiness into the cultivation of his stereotype that his view of changing reality becomes blurred and distorted. At that point an ascendancy needs a rude shock from outside or a major intrusion by those who apply the skill according to a different set of rules.

The Creative Factor

The essence of merchant banking was creation for profit, not mere function or adaptation. Those who came to London from East and West profited from the fact that the City was the centre of two inter-locking financial systems, one that of the United Kingdom itself and the other extending through and from it to cover most of the world. In applying his skills to make the most of these two spheres of activity, the merchant banker became himself a creator of credit and in so doing he became a creative element in the whole process of manufacture and trade.

During most of the nineteenth century it was the wealth of Britain which was put at the service of the world: by the end of the century it was the created wealth of the world which was being put at Britain's disposal. But whatever the source and direction of the funds, by their passage through London they were transmuted into something new. Nothing illustrates this so well as London's transformation of the age-old skill of money-changing, as practised in the arcades of markets and temples and in medieval jewellers' booths, into the international money market of today. Although New York, Zurich, and Amsterdam – all strategically placed at the nerve centres of the great system of telecommunications which crosses and criss-crosses the globe – have at various periods enjoyed advantages of political security, 'safe' currencies, absence of governmental restrictions on the movement of funds, none of them have been able to produce or duplicate anything akin to the London money market. The creation was not in the skill since, in fact, the chief dealers of many of the leading London institutions which deal in foreign exchange and arrange credits came themselves from Switzerland, the Low Countries, and Germany.

It was the manner in which London reconceived the technique which made it creative. It is the European capacity to form new concepts which makes creations more than the sum of the objects from which they are fashioned and by realizing them through institutions has laid the basis for the growth of Western power, whether political, economic, financial, military or scientific. Since the Port of London handled goods from all the world, its traders had to deal in bills made out in the currencies of the whole globe. Though the Swiss may have grasped the mechanics of currency dealing, they never had to practise it in a context of world trade: if the Dutch understood the world of trade as no one else, they had never had to cope with London's volume and variety of transactions. Even if the Americans had to handle as great a volume of trade through their ports, they lacked London's sensitivity for the human diversity involved in the whole process.

21

Those who were both merchants and bankers thus had a head start and even now half the business of the London foreign exchange market is handled by the merchant banks. Indeed the ritual article on merchant banking in the annual banking reviews of the leading British dailies usually depicts the foreign exchange dealing room with its switchboard prominently centred and its dealers carefully posed with phones at the ready. Until the First World War the 'market' itself consisted of the accepting houses, whose representatives, with a few foreign bill brokers, held regular meetings on the floor of the Royal Exchange. The present London Foreign Exchange Market, which means all the institutions authorized by the Treasury to deal in foreign exchange, comprises 120 London banking houses (British, Commonwealth, and foreign), all represented on the Foreign Exchange Committee. Dealings now take place by telephone, telex, or cable with the other financial centres of the world, while dealers and brokers have their own direct telephone lines. No longer is there a physical meeting place and the day-to-day functions are delegated to a special subcommittee which liaises with the Bank of England, whose representative in turn attends the meetings.

In this business the hundred years' start of the merchant banks and their close and long-standing relationship with banking houses abroad enabled them to be more flexible in their offers and requests than some of the later arrivals: this has until recent years been their main counter to the advantages of bigness. For the use of mobile spare cash of the international trading and financial community – which is in essence what the so-called Euro-currencies consist of – is not in itself a new feature. But the ability of merchant bankers to transfer it in its original form to any country with a reliable currency and banking system and by means of swap conversion to make it available to local borrowers in their own currency, has made London the most important market for 'Eurodollars', i.e. loans denoted in US dollars made through the European money markets. They are usually, though not always, funds belonging to non-US residents. By this means foreign funds have been made available to assist in meeting short-term financial requirements in the United Kingdom while otherwise unemployed British funds have been employed to the best advantage abroad.

This type of transaction has been frequently attacked as in some way jeopardizing the 'stability' of the exchange rates, of introducing 'hot money', of being the heresy of borrowing short and lending long. This is discussed later. Suffice it to say here that the merchant banker as the man who straddles the two worlds, the domestic and foreign, keeps a close watch on the inward and outward flow of funds, and with the benefit of his direct access to the Bank of England, his key role in the London money market, and his daily rearrangement of trade finance for both British and foreign clients, is himself an important balancing factor. In striking his own balance he is doing so also for the two interlocking systems. The fact that the surplus from their identifiable foreign exchange and short-term earnings enables merchant banks to produce the benefit of an invisible export is proof enough that the balance is struck in Britain's favour.

Even in the age-old trade of handling gold – still the ultimate clearing medium for world trade – the accepting houses remain the main agents. They are all authorized dealers in bullion. All of them can handle it for customers, while the London Gold Market itself, through which the principal dealings in the world's gold are still carried out, consists of Montagus, Rothschilds, Mocattas, Sharps Pixley, and Johnson Matthey, which, apart from the last, are either accepting houses or owned by accepting houses. A representative of Rothschilds is the chairman of the daily 'Gold Fixing' at which the price of gold is fixed. If more than eighty per cent of all gold produced outside the Soviet bloc is marketed in London this is basically because it comes from territories which were once part of the Empire and the capital which developed the mines and smelters was provided almost entirely by the City.

Subsidiary gold markets exist in other capitals, but if tons rather than ounces are involved, London is still the only place where sales can be arranged. The gold, mainly from South Africa, is supplied to the London Gold Market by the Bank of England, which though not formally a member of the body is naturally consulted by the 'Gold Fixing' group. Even though silver is now primarily of industrial interest and United States Treasury sales are the main means of meeting demand over and above current production, it is to the London market in turn that other sellers of silver usually come, for in London they find the most active bidders and the best prices.

A Brave Front

Merchant banking has not therefore been merely a function, even a highly adaptable one, of finance, commerce, and industry. It has been

23

one of the main factors in the process by which London grew to be a world financial centre and from this has hitherto derived its main interest as a profession. And in its outward aspect it bears all the hallmarks of its historical establishment. This does not mean simply the panelled parlours and boardrooms, the portraits of eighteenth and nineteenth century founders, the framed charters and documents with historic signatures. These are to be found in all manner of City boardrooms and counting houses.

It is rather in the manner in which the whole bank functions that its history is revealed. As the top-hatted representatives of the discount houses and bill brokers arrive at a gentlemanly forenoon hour, the manager in charge of the cash department and his assistants, either suavely solid or young and presentable, are ready with their statement of the anticipated movement of funds for the day both in and out, and – allowing for safety margins – are well aware of what balance is available to the callers as they doff their hats. The rate is either fixed on the spot with no query, or left open until next day. The three-inch news item on the financial page of next day's papers may mention briefly that conditions were easy or that money was tight with some additional phrase suggesting difficulties: but in practice all the latter meant for the merchant bank and its money clients was an afternoon round of telephone calls based on hints made during the forenoon. An apparently casual morning remark from the cash department to the foreign exchange department had released massive funds from three or four centres in Europe or from New York and no one appeared either tight or easy.

The main banking hall of any accepting house presents outwardly much the same picture as that of a clearing bank. The underlying atmosphere is by comparison unhurried. The bill department is apparently conducting a slow but steady check of their piles of documents. The regional desks which take up most floor space do not seem to be trying to beat any deadline and only overheard telephone conversations in foreign languages reveal the wide-ranging nature of their activities, while those sitting apart in obviously more super-visory roles appear deep in study. But after midday the finished products come steadily forward as packets of bills ready for collection, and the cheques, usually in five figures and sometimes in six, are gathered for signing over lunch by a director or other 'full signatory'. The afternoon stream of callers go straight to the counters where they know their packets are waiting. There is something of a rite about it all – one which is none the less impressive by being carried out with the informal elegance which comes naturally to the English and evokes the muttered admiration of the foreign visitor as he is conducted upstairs to lunch in the boardroom.

This is hardly the picture with which the public is fed by the popular press – the 'tough bargainers', the 'astute financiers', the 'takeover battlers'. Is the façade of tradition merely maintained to lull the suspicions of the unwary while other matters are cooked up in the privacy of the parlours? Or is all the tough talk merely a publicity line of the hired hacks who specialize in 'image making'? In themselves toughness, astuteness, and ingenuity are not bad qualities, and are semantically reconcilable with confidence, trust, and a good name. Building the Baltimore and Ohio railroad required all six attributes and the go-ahead though small merchant banking house of Close Brothers, which began in 1792 as calico merchants and nowadays is largely an issue house and investment group, proudly describes how in its early activities in the Klondike, it survived by spreading layers of sovereigns over the tops of sacks of meal to convince the clients that the bank was able to meet its commitments.

Do the toughness and astuteness merely boil down to rather more versatility and some fresh gimmicks inside the privileged circle? Or are they being applied to new problems in a way which will both widen the scope of merchant banking and enable the accepting houses to take on fresh outside challengers? The 1931 crisis showed that while the bankers were clever enough at their old skills, some of these had ceased to be relevant in the face of new realities. This can be one of the unfortunate consequences of believing legends, of which one of the most dangerous is that merchant bankers have had better inform-ation than anyone else, even their governments. The nineteenth century records show in practice that on European and American affairs they were no better informed nor wiser than serious newspaper readers of the time. The rulers of the day were receiving good factual intelligence from their own sources and like a present-day Minister or civil servant coping with importunate visitors, they were often merely being polite in thanking M. de Rothschild or any other caller for his valuable information and suggestions.* In a closed circle information

* Talleyrand's saying is often quoted: 'The English Ministry is always informed of everything by Rothschild ten to twelve hours before Lord Stuart's dispatches arrive.' However, Jas. Rothschild's letter on such an occasion as the Belgian revolt against the Dutch throne in 1830 states briefly: 'My dear Brothers. The news that the

is liable to be graded according to the standing of the source rather than by factual content and when privilege is under assault there can be grave misjudgements as to the power of the attackers.

The challengers are already there in force. In the 'twenties the clearing banks had already moved into the acceptance business: now they are looking for ways and means of entering into competition for foreign deposits, and by creating new subsidiaries are trying to solve the problem of having to pay attractive rates. The foreign banks in London who have even fewer restraints of this nature, are poaching openly in the preserves of the accepting houses: they appear to have no respect at all for any British sporting calendar. The influx of American banks in the 'sixties was the largest any City generation has seen: they were only following the precedent of the Browns, Morgans, Lazards and others. The French and Japanese are open for business in Lombard Street like any British commercial bank; under cover of 'representative offices' the Italians – who after all gave the street its name – scout round judiciously for business. Current and deposit accounts with members of the Accepting Houses Committee rose from £844 millions at year-end 1963 to £2,446 millions at year-end 1969. In the same period current and deposit accounts at overseas banks in the United Kingdom rose more than proportionately from £2,890 millions to £16,690 millions.*

Direct intrusions into the circle of privilege have continued. Singer and Friedlander, formally recreated in 1920 as a bank, had their origins in a stockbroking firm, founded in 1907, and forced to close down in World War I because of the German nationality of its chief partner. The addition of two brothers from the famous Viennese banking family of Hock, brought to London up-to-date personal knowledge of the inter-war financial problems, notably in arbitrage, of Central Europe. In 1933 the partnership was converted into a limited company and thirty years later with total assets of £35 millions, Singer & Friedlander could satisfy the Board of Trade that it should be treated as a banking company under the provisions of the

Belgians have dethroned the Orange dynasty has shocked everyone deeply. *Rentes* fell to 60.25 but closed at 61.19 and the five per cents at 91.15 while ducats were 65.4.' At the July Revolution, his letter – very much to the point but nothing more – was: '*Rentes* remain at 58.20 and from today all the *Gardes Nationaux* must wear uniform, so that you see nothing but soldiers.'

* Appendices Two and Three contain the general banking statistics and acceptance totals for the seventeen Accepting Houses as far as these were available on 1 December 1970.

Companies Act, 1948. Hitler may have sent others unwillingly to London but once here the exiles have stayed. In 1947 Mr Siegmund Warburg set up his City bank, and when the post-war period of restrictions was over in 1958, he rapidly moved to the forefront in every sphere of merchant banking. Within existing houses there were internal changes of ownership as 'new men' infiltrated with ambitions of their own.

How have the older accepting houses reacted? Are they moving out to weave some new creative thread in the contemporary world? Their annual statements – like those of all chairmen – pay lip service to a changing world scene: their assets and profits grow from year to year so that outwardly they do not appear to be missing chances. They can point to their own banking subsidiaries in New York, Johannesburg and Sydney. Samuels, not long before its merger with Philip Hill, Higginson, Erlangers Ltd, had appropriately enough, in view of its own origins, sold a stake of 600,000 shares to one of the successful Jewish entrepreneurs of the post-war world, Mr Charles Clore, who brought in his own tanker company, British Oil, as well as his issuing house, Investment Registry, one of the main instruments by which his £100 millions Sears empire was built up. Even such phenomena as mass tourism find a need for merchant banking services. The pre-war practice of each bank obtaining foreign notes directly for its customers could never cope with today's tourist flood: and as a 'wholesaler' for the supply of notes to other banks, to tourist and airfreight agencies, Brown Shipley deals in vast quantities of notes which never touch the United Kingdom. More intriguing still, a Hambro associated company was mentioned in connection with the promotion of Wimpy bars on the Continent.

These ventures alone, however, hardly point to a chapter as glorious as the era of great state loans, the growth of the London bill as the chief financing medium of world trade, or the period from 1870 to 1914 when no less than forty per cent of the £3,600 millions lent by Britain to overseas countries was provided through the intermediary of merchant banks. Is it that when Britain's role in the world is shrinking, the merchant bankers' tasks are shrinking too? Lord Brand had his first taste of responsibility as a member of Milner's kindergarten when the frontiers of Empire were still expanding, when the replacement of savagery by law and welfare was thought proper, and pride in being British was not held to be immoral. Even in the crises and depression of the 'thirties, Sir Robert Kindersley spoke out on the

27

side of courage and initiative in the councils of the City. Although a Baring served the Bank of England as Governor from 1961 to 1966, and became British Ambassador in Washington in 1971, the public responsibilities demanded of the merchant bankers in their more personal capacities require more conformist roles nowadays and, while all public-spirited men, they may well be inhibited by the prevailing philosophy of 'not rocking the boat'. The Chairman of Schroder Wagg, Mr Gordon Richardson, was enrolled to preside over one of these many government inquiries which seem to invite the answer 'No'. Sir Giles Guthrie gave up the chairmanship of Brown Shipley to cope with one of the Augean stables resulting from political cowardice and bureaucratic ineptitude. Others again are invited to sit on the various councils and committees by which Westminster and Whitehall create the illusion that great plans are afoot, and which after some years of impotence are quietly superseded or disbanded. On the boards of the merchant banks themselves appears that slightly intriguing figure of establishment respectability, the retired ambassador, *si symbolique de je ne sais quoi*.

As 'dear father' said, the family fortunes will go on increasing even if merely put out to usury. But does this offer a career of promise to a new generation of Britons? And is there not some new concept of national life trying to get through and in the formulation of which the merchant banks should be playing a leading part? Unless they play a major role in the main creative stream of economic life it is hard to see how they can maintain an independent existence for many more decades. Can they attract lively minds and give them the stimulus of responsibility? These are also questions for the country as a whole. The answers are most likely to be found by recognizing, under the debris of legend, what were the truths of the past and trying to relate them to the potentialities of the future. The merchant banks must justify their survival by maintaining the creative impulse of their origins; indeed this is the only justification for anyone's survival.

CHAPTER TWO

The London Bill and the Crisis Years

Acceptance Credits

The history of the bill on London illustrates most vividly how the survival of the merchant banks depends on their ability to create and recreate. After half a century of growing ascendancy and another of unchallenged supremacy, the bill seemed threatened with eclipse; but in the unlikely post-war world of 1945 it made a remarkable comeback. A form of finance which has stood the tests of time, two world wars, and inflation, shows by its very persistence that it must have some irreplaceable function. Its usefulness may at times have been challenged both by domestic developments in British banking and by the course of world events. The challenge was always met. The accepting houses never failed to adapt their bills to meet new needs even when changes in banking might have appeared to rob them of their very *raison d'être*.

When the merchant bankers established themselves in Fenchurch Street and in the back courts and lanes of the City at the beginning of the nineteenth century, the other banks in Britain – apart from the Bank of England itself – were local and family affairs subject to crisis and failure whenever comparatively minor local business setbacks or bankruptcies occurred. By the 'thirties, however, the 'Big Five' clearing banks, products of an internal process of amalgamation and rationalization, controlled eight per cent of the banking deposits within the country and were themselves moving into the foreign field and actively discounting bills for their clients. Yet, if their expansion impinged on the activities of the accepting houses, it did not displace them. The main threat to the established merchant banks came from

29

the unforeseen consequences of the two World Wars, which were to have as far reaching political and economic consequences as the Wars of Revolution, the opening up of America, and the British imperial expansion east of Suez.

For despite every precaution, the merchant banker is still a man who shoulders a risk. The trials of the hero in the Victorian novel underline the perils of putting one's name on other people's pieces of paper. If the Victorian heroine risked the fate worse than death by having a champagne supper in a private room at Maxim's, Trollope's curates and Disraeli's pushing young politicians were liable to find that their occupation had gone as a result of endorsing the bills of the plausible black sheep they had met at the episcopal or ducal palace. And even dukes in their time had been led astray over acceptances: the ledger of one of Italy's oldest banks shows clearly that a ruler of Siena, by putting his signature to what seem to have been usance bills, had been inadvertently financing the duchess's lover.

As well as having to underwrite the reputation of those whom he accepted as clients after they had been introduced into his - strictly non-arachnoidal - parlour, the merchant banker took an additional time and space risk. For his signature on a bill enabled exporters to obtain cash as soon as their goods had been dispatched, and permitted the buyers or importers to defer payment until the goods were in safe hands or even until they had in turn resold them or reconverted them. Thus, at an agreed price the bank or accepting house, by adding its name, takes the burden off other shoulders.

Yet the bill, for all its venerable ancestry, remains in itself a simple instrument. It is *any* piece of paper, provided it is given a bill stamp, on which a person (*the drawer*) writes an unconditional order to another (*the drawee*) requiring him to pay on demand or at some determinable date, a sum to the order of a person (*the payee*) or to a bearer. A London bill is one addressed to a drawee resident in the United Kingdom and payable in sterling in London. If the person to whom the bill is addressed, or indeed any other person, signs the bill he becomes the *acceptor* and the bill is then known as an *acceptance*. By signing the bill the acceptor takes the responsibility of payment at maturity, in normal practice after a period of up to six months. But the drawer still remains responsible on the bill and, should it be dishonoured, he will compensate the holder or any other endorser who has paid it in the meantime. Under an acceptance credit on which the credit taker draws on the merchant bank, it remains the responsibility of the *drawer* to put the *acceptor* in *funds* in time to meet the acceptance at maturity.

But if it is so simple why is the great panoply of the City – the accepting houses, the bill brokers, the discount houses, and the powers and responsibilities of the Bank of England – brought into the matter? Why do bills change hands so many times and why do clearing banks on the one hand refer their customers to accepting houses for some of their bill facilities and then a month or two later buy the bills at a discount and put them in their safes? Why are so many men apparently taking a rake-off in the form of fractional discounts?* Could not Mr Bloggs the Merchant fix it all up with his local bank manager in the first place? On the surface it looks like another of these carefully preserved conspiracies of privilege which the English are so artful at maintaining and which only needs a rough, honest outsider to turn up and expose it for the sham it really is.

The answer is that, in an ideal world, Mr Bloggs and his branch manager could arrange it all. But the attainment of such a world would require a society with a stable population and a fixed demand for a limited number of goods. Since, however, men's needs everywhere vary, the means of satisfying them will for ever be in unstable equilibrium; this includes the needs of the merchant for credit. 'Credere' means 'to believe' and tomorrow's belief will never match up with today's credit supply. So the clearing banks dare not tie up all their resources for ninety days; some other houses must discount the bills to furnish the merchants with credit, and the discount market in turn must ensure that the bills are readily on offer to those who have funds available for short periods, until they have to meet some other demand for them. Credit, therefore, derives from movement and the instability of movement creates ever fresh needs. The acceptor's good name is the pivot around which the system develops its dynamism; at the same time it can prevent a centrifugal breakdown.

As the creator of acceptance credit the merchant banker deals in a wide variety of bills. The original bill drawn to cover a movement of goods, which had attached to it the documentary proof of the transaction such as a bill of lading, a consular attestation, or an insurance policy, etc., is the *documentary bill* and can be negotiated without delay by the seller of the goods or the exporter. The *finance*

---

* *Discount:* The amount of deduction, calculated on a basis of per cent per annum which is allowed for the immediate payment of a time bill which has still a period to run before maturity.

bill, drawn to finance the holding or processing of materials or the purchase on credit of components for assembly, or to give customers some form of instalment terms, often, on the other hand, requires fresh drawings allowing credit for periods of up to eighteen months. Thus it is linked not so much to any one specific underlying transaction but rather to the successful outcome of a series of transactions. Consequently it depends even more on the good names of drawer and acceptor.

But whether the merchant banker takes the documents as security or gives an 'unsecured credit' based on his examination of the firm's financial situation, the drawer's credit facility is still extended to him on the basis that he will provide cover in time for his bills to be honoured. The actual operation of an acceptance credit consists of the merchant bank accepting the bills, discounting them in the money market, and placing the funds at the client's disposal either by crediting them to an account he keeps with it, paying them over to his local bank, or sending him an order. If arrangements are made for the credit to be given over a period during which maturing bills are paid off and replaced by fresh ones, it is known as a *revolving credit*. For giant international companies such credits run into several million pounds, covering, for example in the case of oil concerns, the movement of crude oil to refineries and the distribution and sale through retail outlets of the refined petroleum products. The great mass of bills received by the merchant bank as a result of these transactions have to be sorted out, discounted, dealt with at maturity, and the company's creditors satisfied without hitches or delays in payments or notifications. The procedure has to be followed in all the same detail whether it is for an international giant or for a small trader shipping one consignment abroad.

Even where manufacturers or traders draw bills of exchange directly on those who buy from them (the so-called *trade bills*) they can still secure an acceptance credit by depositing the bills as collateral with a merchant bank. And it has been, and still is, the strength of London that foreign firms trading with each other, whose goods never touch these islands, can frequently have their bills accepted at better rates and with fewer complications than in their own countries. If the London merchant banks possess something which is 'unique' it·is their ability to offer this service as a result of their world-wide reputation and high standing within London. The enjoyment of this service marks out a firm as being of high international standing and for Britain itself it has meant more than just a useful invisible export, important though this may be for our balance of payments, but also the adherence of foreign friends and allies who have stood by her in times of need, even in wartime at the risk of life and limb.

At home the finance bill (generally for amounts of not less than £25,000) has by extension increasingly provided short-term working finance for industry by furnishing credit from the date when a manufacturer or entrepreneur signs a contract to that on which his goods have left his factory gate and he has been repaid. The bill business gives the true merchant bank, as against those who have appropriated the title, the status which comes from power. 'Two good names on a bill give quality to the bill. They also lend lustre to each other. Nothing adds so much to the standing of even the greatest firms as to be seen to enjoy the confidence in each other which is implied by the association of their two names on a bill.'*

The 'lustre' is also the bread and butter of a merchant bank. In return for having his bills accepted, the customer has to pay an acceptance commission over and above the discount rate and this represents the foundation of the bank's earnings.† If, as happens in a proportion of cases, the bills have to be drawn in foreign currency, the merchant bank works out the appropriate rates, 'current' or 'forward' according to the date on which payment is due and – nowadays where exchange regulations permit – arranges a 'swap' into other currencies. From these foreign exchange dealings has grown up a great mass of expertise in the world's currencies and a profitable second source of earnings.

The Limits of Bill Finance

But whether domestic or foreign bills are involved, the principle is that acceptance credits are only granted for the financing of current trade and not for capital purposes, and that the transactions are self-liquidating. By buying parcels of bills in the discount market, the Bank of England conducts a continual sampling operation which enables it to form a tentative opinion on whether the spirit and letter

* *The Bill on London,* published by Chapman and Hall for the Gillett Brothers Discount Co. Ltd (Second Revised Edition, 1959).

† Appendix Four contains a short list of definitions of the main categories of bills.

of the acceptance system are being observed, and it will not hesitate to raise queries with the acceptors or discount houses if it finds some apparent distortion of the pattern. There is nothing wrong about the extension of the concept of finance bills and indeed the Macmillan Committee in 1931, noting that the use of domestic bills of exchange had fallen into comparative disuse in the early part of the century, recorded the opinion that all concerned would benefit by their increased employment in home business.

The Bank of England's authority in this respect rests on the privilege enjoyed by members of the Accepting Houses Committee of having their bills discounted by it and thus be called 'Bank of England bills'. Their 'finest rates' depend on this privilege since the Bank thereby expresses its satisfaction as to their standard of means, liquidity, and standing. The practical implication of membership of the Accepting Houses Committee is that in return for observing the duties and responsibilities of clearing banks, the members enjoy the same privileges of the latter vis-à-vis the Bank of England.

The commission charged by a merchant bank varies according to the standing of the customer and the terms of the credit arrangement.*
It is mainly a risk premium: as the accepting house's undertaking to pay the bills at maturity is unconditional, it assumes the risk of the customer failing or delaying to pay his debts. But it also includes remuneration for the occasionally not inconsiderable work done in scrutinizing documents, thus enabling the customer to concern himself mainly with these aspects of bill finance which affect his own internal bookkeeping.

The professional experience required of a merchant banker consists basically of the knowledge and understanding which will enable him to suggest in discussion with any trader or manufacturer how his commercial efforts can best be advanced by the use of acceptance credits and other facilities, how to use his bill finance sparingly but effectively, and when in funds how to get the best return for them within the terms of his company statutes. In addition to the procedure and conditions for issuing letters of credit and drawing and accepting bills, this requires a knowledge of patterns of trade and manufacture, and of how the main varieties of bill can be adapted to each situation. This in turn involves an understanding of how the money market works, when money is seasonally tight, when it is plentiful, and what is likely to happen at the financial Hogmanay when balance sheets are

---

* Appendix Five contains an (imaginary) specimen of a Letter of Credit.

being dressed up, funds are being called in, and a fine accounting display is put on.

The discount market is not a particular place or building but consists of eleven 'discount companies' and other houses which specialize in dealing in money, short-dated bills of exchange and bonds, and Treasury bills. When they resell the bills at a slightly lower percentage, this is known as rediscounting. The 'Bank Rate' is the advertised minimum rate at which the Bank of England will discount eligible bills and is normally fixed by the directors at their weekly meeting each Thursday.

Since the First World War, however, the general preference of commerce and industry for overdrafts as against bills has meant that the clearing banks' ratio of advances and investments to deposits has borne virtually no causal relationship to the discount rate although this continues to be the gospel taught by most academic economists up and down the country. The advances are stimulated or discouraged by other types of advice or pressure from the Bank of England and 'decided by the clearing banks themselves on the basis of their appreciation of the general economic situation. Since the clearing banks rarely sell bills discounted for clients or purchased in the open market, it is the merchant, overseas, and foreign banks in the City who create the supply of bills and influence the rates. But because the clearers satisfy their need for money by sales of Treasury bills or by calling in money lent 'on call' or at short notice, the strain falls on the discount houses and bill brokers who, if they need help, as a last resort, obtain it in the form of rediscounts or advances from the Bank of England. One of the special features of the London money market is that the British banks make their adjustments without direct recourse to the central bank so that the marginal importance of accepting and discount houses extends far beyond what is indicated by their published balance sheet assets.

Because, for all practical purposes, there is a regular supply of bills close to maturity, they are available for liquid funds and, since they bring in a fair return, foreign banks too are ready to keep funds in London so long as they have confidence in Britain's ability to manage its financial affairs competently. Indeed foreign banks of good standing count on being able to open acceptance lines with British banks available by the drawings of their clients on terms similar to those given to British customers. The volume of bills, the supply of call money and of foreign funds, and the state of the discount market are all closely related and overlap unlike New York, where call money is in great part linked to the needs and operations of the stock exchange. The modern British banking system has grown up round a 'money market' of world interest, of which the most sensitive part has been the requirement of the bill market.

But as a market which treated money as another commodity to be bought and sold at the most competitive rates, London houses ran risks as well as offering an attraction to competitors. By August 1914 the merchant banks were accepting bills for an amount equivalent to three or four times their own capital. As private partnerships in which the liability was that of the individual partners, this was a risky situation; Barings had already experienced this when confronted by the South American crisis in 1890 and had thereafter proceeded to adopt the form of limited company. After World War One, Lazards and Hambros led the movement to the further creation of merchant banks as limited companies. It was indeed a remarkable gesture of self-confidence that so many continued as private partnerships until well after World War Two.

The Cheap Money Era

Like the rest of Europe in the post-Versailles era, the merchant banks tried – gamely but vainly – to rebuild the pre-1914 world. Their error was pardonable for it was shared by all the British Establishment. Even at the hungriest level, the unemployed at the street corners could only look back to the 'good old days'. There was nothing to look forward to: the mirage of the land fit for heroes to live in faded as soon as the phrase ceased to be of value in serving political ambition. Domestically the merchant banks did not face any immediate challenge in 1918; after their Edwardian hey-day they had perhaps become rather Olympian and expected customers to call rather than sally out themselves. In becoming more like bankers and less like merchants, they had lost some of their former close contact with commercial houses.

After World War One many of them, understandably enough in view of the upset conditions in Europe, insisted on the guarantee of foreign banks before granting credits to foreign firms, the so-called *reimbursement credits,* and the foreign bank naturally took a commission off their own client, so reducing the merchant bank's share.

The result was that the clearing banks and foreign and overseas banks based on London, moved in as competitors in this business and brought down the rates for reimbursement credits. The great mass of foreign acceptances held are probably now of this nature.

In spite of this competition and the 1931 crisis and subsequent currency restrictions, the merchant banks were up to 1939 gradually recovering their old volume of acceptances. But the statistics by themselves are misleading, for the bill on London had suffered some bad setbacks. The number of foreign credits had dwindled both relatively and absolutely, while the new demand for acceptance credits was coming from domestic industry and commerce profiting from the long period of cheap money which ran, except for a brief period on the outbreak of the war against Hitler, from June 1932 until November 1951.

During this era bank rate was two per cent and over a large part of it the discount rate was about nine-sixteenths per cent. This permitted the merchant banks to claim a generous acceptance commission and at the same time keep their credits at an attractive rate compared to bank overdrafts of five per cent per annum. The result was the reversal of the trend at the beginning of the century when inland bills had tended to go out of favour. As a result of the cheap money years many British concerns who had never thought of drawing bills, learned to know the flexibility and rapidity of this method of obtaining finance, provided they had been able to secure the services of one of the leading accepting houses. There is now a fairly widespread custom by which many British firms use both kind of facilities, clearing bank overdraft and acceptance credit, depending on which is cheaper or most appropriate to the transaction.

On the other hand, the clearing banks were finding new points at which to penetrate into the preserves of the merchant bankers. Their foreign exchange dealing rooms, profiting from the general introduction of the telephone after World War One, steadily extended their operations to the point where they could at short notice provide foreign importers of British goods with credit lines through their banking correspondents. This had the effect of reducing the amounts normally kept by foreign banks in current accounts with accepting houses, who had provided services to their overseas associates similar to those of the foreign departments of the clearing and Scottish banks.

On the whole the 'thirties were a period when the merchant banks, thankful to have come relatively unscathed through the debt standstill crisis, were taking no great initiatives in the foreign credit and banking fields, and were content with profitable domestic acceptance business. Here the longevity of the leading merchant banking families was probably no small factor. Not only did they set store by the older, more leisurely, and admittedly more gracious ways, but were naturally far from anxious to risk the family assets in an uncertain world. The cheap money era meant that the accepting houses could more or less fix the acceptance commission to suit their own notion of a fair profit margin. This may have meant that fresh opportunities were missed or that they counted too comfortably on the perpetuation of some types of business which later proved to have only a limited span. But given the upsets of economic crisis, civil strife, and ominous signs of war, the gain seemed on that side of wisdom represented by continuity. After all, the presence of the same person with views culled from the sapience of a lifetime is a source of strength for an institution. Even in 1964 the late Mr Alfred Wagg, at the age of eighty-seven, appeared once a week in Schroder Wagg, and flags were flown on his birthday – a remarkable tribute to a contemporary of the first Lord Bicester of Morgan Grenfell and of the first Lord Kindersley of Lazards.

The shrinkage of world trade in the early 'thirties also hit those accepting houses who still fulfilled – either directly or through subsidiaries – some of their original functions as merchants. Brandt's timber trading was sufficiently extensive to be maintained as an active sector of their operations as was the cocoa and tropical produce business of Kleinworts, conducted faithfully from Liverpool as the historical port of entry from the Western and African worlds. But in the depression years it was hardly worth maintaining separate produce departments, particularly when autarchic trading policies were followed by the main European states, and bilateral trade arrangements – some of them thinly disguised barter deals – were having sad consequences for the Port of London with its apparatus of commodity markets, brokerage houses, warehousing and reshipment facilities.

Some accepting houses, reluctant to jettison a century of trading experience, made not unsuccessful endeavours to maintain their confirming house service, i.e., they assumed vis-à-vis British manufacturers the responsibility for accepting delivery or making payment for goods ordered from them by overseas buyers. The confirming house sends the manufacturer a *confirmatory order sheet* and the order can then be regarded by him as having been placed on account of the confirming house and not that of the overseas buyer. The confirming house usually has its own shipping and insurance departments so that it can provide a complete service to handle the exports of firms too small to set up their own export departments. This service, which is much used by small machinery manufacturers, remains well suited to coping with exports to Africa, Asia, and Latin America where documentary and payment arrangements tend to be complicated. After the Export Credits Guarantee Department had been established as an autonomous department in 1932, the confirming houses arranged for a general insurance against the risks of the overseas buyers – in any deals they handled – not fulfilling their contracts. And, although various types of services for exporters have made a much-publicized and usually short-lived appearance in latter years, this old-established arrangement by merchant houses probably still remains the most efficient and dependable scheme of its nature.

One aspect of merchant banking which acquired increased significance in the 'thirties was their share issue function. This was often undertaken to meet the need of a new company for a share register to be run for it by a house of good repute, which could qualify for the status of trustee for their debenture issues. Not that it was anything new for banks to take part in the issue of shares for companies. London houses had helped to launch the issues of some of the great American corporations, as for example Kleinworts, in association with Lehman Brothers, in the cases of Goodrich, Woolworth, and Sears' Roebuck. After World War One the scale of company reconstruction and expansion was such that family enterprises, even with the relatively light taxation burdens of 1920, could no longer cope from their own resources. The first public issues were mainly fixed-interest with what, by present-day standards, appears to be an extraordinary discount rate for first-class firms. The underwriters presumably made excellent profits from their own holdings, while such was the excitement in 1922 when Helbert Wagg issued £1,500,000 six and a half per cent First Debenture Marconi Wireless Stock – with valuable concession rights – that police had to be called out to control the crowds. And, as the public began to grow interested, the late 'twenties experienced a spate of investment trusts founded and managed by issuing groups.

The situation was not always edifying. The 'twenties also saw the emergence of numerous 'bucket shops' whose share prospectuses were masterpieces of concealment rather than of information.* Gullible members of the public got their fingers badly burnt. Although the London share-issuing mechanism is still, and rightly, under fire for its deficiencies, it seems a model of perfection today compared to the state of affairs in the 'twenties. Even reliable firms suffered from the improvised *ad hoc* arrangements. The first Marks and Spencer issues, a Mortgage Debenture and Preference underwritten by the Prudential, were a complete flop. In retrospect the stockbrokers seem to have based their trading on the most outrageous tips and gossip, with little organized effort at seeking and supplying factual information, and were generally only prepared to assist in launching an issue when the Stock Exchange was in such a state of general buoyancy that anything went. The crash of Clarence Hatry with debts of £19 millions revealed the extent of the danger as well as the ignorance – at times culpable – of the City itself.

The Macmillan report in 1931 consequently recommended that issuing institutions should vouch to the investor for the intrinsic soundness of the issues made. Arrangements were made for a number of leading firms to consult with the Stock Exchange authorities and advise on the price of issues and themselves act as underwriters. This was an important beginning although merchant banks who were also issuing houses could hardly have foreseen what it would mean for them in the 'fifties. Some of them even appeared uncertain whether this was a proper role for them to undertake. Their attempts to rebuild the pre-1914 world had been rather more along the lines of the British world-wide trading tradition. In this they certainly deserved well of their country. Governments as well as the League of Nations had encouraged international lending as a matter of policy (*en passant* it may be recorded that none of the League's own loans have been repaid since 1939), and if in 1938 Britain still covered twenty-five per cent of her imports from the income of her overseas investments, this was largely thanks to the example set by the merchant bankers almost a century before. The total of British long-term investment on the eve of World War Two was £4,500 millions, a war chest which was to prove vital in our struggle for existence.

---

* 'Bucket shop' is defined by the *Shorter Oxford English Dictionary* as: 'An unauthorized office used orig. for smaller gambling transactions in grain, and subseq. extended to offices for other descriptions of gambling and betting on the stocks etc.' (US 1882).

That perspicacious French observer of the British banking scene, R. J. Truptil, in 1936 had seen the accepting houses as 'a sort of outward radiation of the power of the British banking system'.* Commenting on what he saw, he continued: 'A banking system cannot properly be explained by a series of tables and graphs, it remains an organization whereby one set of men endeavour to facilitate the conservation and the circulation of riches which have been created by other men. All banking problems have a moral and a social side – a human aspect.'† In this context, it is worth while recalling that the relative calm with which the City coped with the 1931 crisis had its sure foundation in the confidence of men who trusted one another, who were acting according to a code; in an authority which maintained itself not because it could invoke penalties but because of the general belief that it was being exercised in the national interest. It is something which newcomers to London have to learn. It might seem easy to pull off a fast one in the face of tradition and privilege but the sapping of community consciousness which would result from widespread sharp practice could bring the whole structure down, crushing the sapper as well.

War and Readjustments

In the event the structure did come under the threat of bombardment as well as the strains of siege. The conflict of 1939–45 offered no great banking drama like that of 1914 when Morgan Grenfell had stepped in to supply the machinery and contacts required for the prosecution of the war by the British Treasury, the Bank of England, and the French Government. In 1939 it had ceased to be that sort of world nor was it any longer that sort of war. The maintenance of orderly trade, as far as this was possible under conditions of a conflict which eventually affected the whole of human consciousness, was the first essential. The professional contacts and networks of the merchant banks were not neglected although it was mainly in the sideshows, rather than in the main theatres, that they were put to use. The high-level relationships of Hambros in the Scandinavian countries provided the framework of an organization for pre-emptive buying to counter German attempts to obtain strategic materials and for setting

* *British Banks and the London Money Market* (Jonathan Cape, 1936), p. 166.
† *Ibid*, p. 18.

up safe shore bases for daring sallies to ship key machinery for our own factories. In the Iberian peninsula, Kleinworts' connections with leading Spaniards and Portuguese were put at the disposal of the men who ran escape and evasion lines under the noses of Abwehr and Gestapo.

It was, however, primarily as individuals that the merchant bankers served the country into whose establishments they had become assimilated. For a time, as head of Special Operations Executive, the late Sir Charles Hambro brought political finesse as well as a profound knowledge of European financial personalities to a delicate task where his fiercest opponents were to be found among those on the Allied side who had different notions on how to win both war and peace. Others, as advisers in wartime Whitehall or on Washington missions, lived to experience that strange milieu where a Secretary of State's marginal approval on a well-turned minute induces the euphoria that the lot of mankind has somehow been advanced. Most of the merchant bankers fanned out into a dozen theatres of war where parachute descents behind enemy lines, prisoner-of-war endurance, and decorations for valour proved that their pre-war Territorial Army service had meant more than the decorative mess-kits dangling with chain mail which had so often been the main attraction of the older militia. When it was all over, unmilitary figures in Military Government uniforms, some with decidedly exotic accents, were the first outward indication that the British merchant banking houses had begun – at times literally – to pick up the bits.

At that particular moment, all the merchant bankers could say, as they surveyed the war-ravaged scene of 1945, was that the bits would have to be picked up. But into what pattern they would be assembled, neither they nor anyone else could have forecast. And whether the private banker would have any say at all in the method of assembly of the broken pieces was even more of a question mark. On paper there were still Rothschild millions. But even if they could have been speedily mobilized, as after the Napoleonic Wars, they would have been a drop in the bucket compared to the reconstruction needs of any one country, much less of Europe. Nor were the families or partners the same single-minded groups devoted to one notion of money-making. Their first task was to salvage their own assets for their various family purposes. Some famous merchant banking dynasties debated whether the best course was not to assemble the family resources into trusts, close down for ever the guichets at which the messengers had doffed their toppers, and settle down in Barset-shire or find a place in the sun in the Caribbean.

But for the majority withdrawal was not so easy. Letters began to come in from Paris, Brussels, Amsterdam, Hamburg, Frankfurt, Genoa, Milan and Vienna and other centres, typed on distinctly *ersatz* paper in such premises as were available after wartime bombardment and meeting the generous office and accommodation requirements of Allied military governments. 'Dear Sirs. We write to advise you that we have recommenced business at the above address and trust we may have the pleasure of renewing our hundred-years-old connection with your goodselves. You will appreciate that our records are somewhat . . .' Apart from the challenge these old relationships offered, there were banking assets to be recovered, bills of 1939 to be settled, and a maze of claims to be cleared up; before long the mechanism was beginning to function.

There was a difference. In 1918 all had believed that a simple return to 1914 was possible. This time there was no such illusion. Probably 1931 had been the true watershed for the City and it knew that the future would be different.

For one thing it was impossible to determine whether sterling could hope to stand on its own feet until the peacetime pattern of manufacture and trade had been re-established. In 1945 some £3,567 millions was held in London in the form of balances owed to both members of the sterling area and to foreign non-sterling countries. In the 'thirties, when a sterling area was first delimited and the mechanism to operate the currency arrangements was created, the figure was between £400 millions and £800 millions, depending on the normal swings of trade. But this had been swollen by wartime needs; non-sterling area countries together held £1,240 millions while the overseas sterling area held the remainder. The liabilities to the former were the consequence of the abnormal trading relationships of the war years and in themselves a testimony to the world's belief in final British victory. For the latter they were the first-line external reserves: indeed India, Pakistan, Ceylon, and Egypt had between them accumulated holdings which were considerably greater than the gold and foreign currency reserves of Britain itself. Canada had meantime hived off into a dollar area linked to the United States.

There could thus be no question of 'setting sterling free'. The pent-up wartime demands of the sterling holders could not have been met by our productivity. An ill-advised attempt under American pressure to run a form of semi-convertibility came to nought after our first post-war dollar loan had been dissipated. Under the circumstances there could be no basic trust in sterling and no one would hold it if they could find a stronger currency. Nor was there much hope that agreements could be negotiated to fund the balances; the sterling area countries in particular wished to use their accumulations to finance their own reconstruction and future development. Eventually special agreements had to be made which created a category of blocked accounts into which these balances were placed and from which they could be withdrawn only gradually.

Since no other country was carrying such a burden of short-term indebtedness, sterling became doubly sensitive to every unfavourable development in internal British economic affairs. Our main hope was to make the economy grow fast enough to ensure a satisfactory balance of payments' position in the belief that with time sterling might once again become a reserve and trading currency medium. Under these conditions there seemed little immediate prospect of restoring the bill on London to its pre-1931 pre-eminence. There were other obstacles. Bulk-buying under government arrangements was the order of the day during the Labour governments, and perpetuated long after the need for it had passed; it had become a vested interest of Whitehall bureaucrats mainly concerned to keep in being the V-Day government departments and their own civil service grades. Their arguments of self-interest fitted in only too well with the Labour concept of *étatisme*.

So as sea-borne trade picked up in both importing and exporting countries, it was largely financed by the clearing and deposit banks, not only because their capacity for doing so had greatly increased over the period but also because their nation-wide organization gave them an advantage in a Europe where communications were still disrupted, while they lent themselves more easily to the mechanism of central control. The central banks naturally preferred as few transferable sterling accounts as possible and the merchant banks found that one correspondent after another had to close down his account with them. The Commonwealth deposit banks, notably the Australians, were quick to profit by this and moved in to take over the profitable financing of the wool trade, once a great stand-by of the London accepting houses.

A new phenomenon had changed the international money scene as a result of the war – the appearance of Switzerland as a centre of world banking business. Her well-protected neutrality had made her a haven for refugee money; her unscathed economy, her high standard of banking probity, her stable political system, as well as that unique feature in the chaotic world of 1945, a freely convertible currency – all these combined to make Zurich, Geneva, and Basel into attractive safe havens for funds. The Swiss banks had not sought this position. They had grown up to meet the needs of cantons and of local industries; their officials possessed the limitations as well as the shrewdness of peasant and *spiessbürger*. But as far as the techniques of currency arbitrage went, they were as skilled as any bankers in the world and were quite prepared to carry out large-scale operations of a speculative nature for their clients, provided their banks ran no risks and stood a fair chance of making a profit on the margins. And, in a world where there was so much sterling that nobody could use, their operations did represent a continuing marginal pressure against the pound.

Such is the perversity of human nature that those who had imposed restrictions began to find abhorrent every notion or suggestion of freedom. British Treasury officials tried to evolve new ingenious ways of preventing the use of sterling by those who might have acquired it perfectly legitimately or impeding its acquisition by those who wished to exchange it against perfectly sound assets. As the regulations became more byzantine in character and complexity, the profits for those not subject to them became even greater. Inevitably the 'sinister but influential men in Zurich' – who by themselves were not particularly influential and not at all sinister – acquired ever fresh clients, and the 'sterling leak' assumed by 1947 astronomical dimensions – at least in the imaginations of Dr Hugh Dalton and Sir Stafford Cripps.

The merchant banks found themselves as severely rationed as the British housewife or the British tourist counting his foreign currency allowance in Continental hotel lounges. The Bank of England could only allot them a fixed ceiling for their transactions, whether in sterling or any other currency. In the field of trade they could meet only a fraction of the credit requirements of British and foreign clients and saw them gradually turning to the clearers who remained the preferred instruments of central authority for handling authorized transfers of sterling. There was no possibility of a resumption of their pre-war short-term loan activity, much less of arranging long-term international bond issues.

Even if they had been free the accepting houses would have been unable to play their old role overseas. In France the doors were firmly closed. The controls imposed by government on the creation and use of credit by French commerce and industry, the regulations – usually futile – to maintain the purchasing power and standing of the franc, the needs of a succession of national plans, left no opportunity for independent operations by foreign banks on behalf of French clients. A few faithful French customers still used London bills for their purchases in the sterling area but the French banks could also offer the services of their London branches and at most passed on modest quantities of documentary collections to City houses and spread their short-term deposits over a number of them to keep up connections in case they might be useful. Germany was still slowly rebuilding its banking system and until the economic miracle had fully developed by the early 'fifties, offered few opportunities for the short-term business traditionally favoured there by British merchant banks.

Mussolini's banking heirs, the Italian parastatal credit banks and medium-term finance houses grouped together under the state holding company IRI (*Istituto per la Ricostruzione Industriale*) were admirably adapted to the tasks of financing internal economic reconstruction, handling Marshall Aid counter-part funds, and conducting export and import finance under the highly professional but strict directives of the Italian central bank. The Italians, who had introduced the craft to Lombard Street, showed that once freed of their political incubus they had lost none of their cunning. The Iron Curtain descended to cut off the contacts which had been tentatively re-established with Prague and Budapest in 1945 and 1946. In any case the Central European defaults of the 'thirties, their outstanding interest and redemption payments, the chaos of war and the post-war Communist expropriation of foreign assets hardly made the area an attractive one for banking operations. The once-proud Viennese private banking houses, which had done battle with the Rothschilds for *k. und k.* financial business, were reduced to small-time black market money deals. Latin America remained in its normal state of permanent revolution and reaction, restrictionism, and currency chaos.

Although some old foreign contacts and lines of overseas business had been renewed, it was obvious that these would never be the mainstay of the merchant banks. Valiant efforts were made by them directly to encourage the export drive which was held necessary if Britain was to earn its keep. Some merchant bankers went even further, trying to resuscitate their commodity and merchandise departments or subsidiaries, and, as part of the dollar export endeavour, set up trading corporations in the United States to promote sales of British goods in both North and South American Continents. The good intention hardly deserved the outcome. The general purpose merchant house fits somewhat uneasily into the United States of today compared to the early years of last century in Boston, Baltimore and New Orleans. The best known of the post-war enterprises of this nature, Hambro Automative Corporation of New York, was nevertheless outstandingly successful in promoting and organizing the sale of British motor vehicles,* while Kleinwort's Drake-America Corporation Inc. was developed into an agency exporting United States goods to Europe, Latin America, and the Middle East.

London's Comeback

But it seemed as if the 1931 prognostications would be fulfilled, and that the merchant banks would be mainly concerned with what happened at home. There was no shortage of tasks in the domestic field. Even if the great bulk of the acceptances were handled by the clearing banks, post-war British industry desperately needed finance for every aspect of its manufacturing and trading operations and the clearing banks were in no position to meet them all. 'The pattern of interest rates in Britain and in other countries is encrusted with rigidities based on tradition, institutional behaviour, and guidance from the authorities and these rigidities have offered opportunities to less inhibited traders in money.'† Not that merchant bankers are particularly uninhibited persons nor are the clearing banks conscious of being bowed down beneath a load of sin. It is rather that each group operates within a different conceptual framework. The relationship between some interest rates is firm, as for example between Bank Rate and those allowed by the clearers. Some are absolute and were apparently determined by a contingency either long forgotten or now assumed to have been an emanation of divine will; such appears to have been the basis for the $2\frac{1}{2}$ per cent per annum Post Office Savings Bank rate which remained unchanged for more than a century before

* The assets were transferred in 1963 to a new company described as British Motor Corporation-Hambro Inc.

† J. E. Wadsworth, Economic Adviser, Midland Bank. Lecture to the Faculty of Actuaries, Edinburgh, 18 November 1963.

the Labour Government introduced a modification in 1965. Other institutions follow their own ellipses in interest rates, although still in some relationship to the Bank Rate curve, as in the case of insurance companies and building societies. And the varying speeds of circulation of categories of credit-worthy paper continue to act as a diversifying factor in determining the cost of new credit facilities.

So, in spite of Dr Dalton's cheap money policy, not all post-war demands for credit could be met at the same rate at the same moment. New types of facilities emerged to meet the needs of new borrowers. Local authorities needed money. Hire purchase finance companies needed money. Manufacturers hit their overdraft ceilings or the clearers' own liquidity requirements prevented them increasing their facilities, even though new orders received by their clients could only be met if they found additional credit for expansion. By the end of the 'fifties there was a significant change in the City. Money was actually flowing *into* London again while the merchant banks, in addition to playing an important marginal role within the British economy, had already started looking outward. What had happened? Was there still some special skill which London alone seemed capable of exploiting to the full and had the City embarked on a new process of creation?

So it seemed. The men of Zurich may have been extremely clever at sensing when to squeeze out an additional fractional rate on the safe-haven funds as they moved back and forward through their hands, like medieval money-changers contriving to remove an almost invisible shaving from the gold ducats they handled. But it was quite a different matter within Switzerland, when it became a question of putting the funds to work. The Swiss authorities tried to discourage the influx of money, and even put obstacles to the use of the Swiss franc as an international currency either for the purpose of holding official reserves or as a unit for international loan transactions. Deposit rates were repeatedly lowered and bank charges increased. While queues of first-class borrowers were lining up in Zurich, Geneva, and Basel, those who had deposited their money in Switzerland were reluctant to lend it long, and there was no large Swiss money market to encourage a rapid turn-over of short-term funds.

Although the US dollar was also freely convertible, the American money market, geared to serve the New York Stock Exchange and, through it, American home industry, could not offer London's money market services. The American banking system, regulated since President Jackson's day as an organization to meet the credit and savings requirements of local communities and controlled by three separate and often disputing Federal agencies* was not geared to any procedure which facilitated the rapid mobilization of spare resources for external employment. While American banks had operated overseas for many years, this was primarily to offer a service to their home clients. The most internationally-minded had naturally enough been those concerned with immigrants' remittances, such as the Bank of America, or the Eastern seaboard banking and finance houses which owed their origins to Anglo-American merchant banking families. In the 'sixties, this began to change, but for the first post-war decade the United States did not so much miss a chance as not realize that it had a chance at all.

Other overseas countries which had escaped unscathed from the war had not only to concentrate their resources for domestic development but were even looking to London as the traditional source of financial support and investment. Their banking systems were even less geared to a world role; Canada's, for example, is a strange mixture of restrictive near-monopoly by her larger banks, and inadequate supervision under a mass of contradictory regulations over other borrowing and lending activities.† In the post-war period the Canadian economy should not have been a net user of foreign funds if its banking system had been at once open and competitive, and at the same time had allowed for timely federal inspection and direction. But, as the Canadian authorities themselves admitted, much of the capital inflow from 1958 to 1961 was the result of inappropriate domestic policies. Australia's chief credit concern was to finance her exports and she viewed with suspicion any moves by British accepting and discount houses which could be interpreted as attempts to operate within the Commonwealth itself. It was not until 1964, when the Australian trading banks began to find that their snug little world was being disturbed by a lively but erratic unofficial money market, that the Reserve Bank of Australia seriously faced the need to create a mechanism for a sound and effective internal bill market. This was in strong contrast to the South Africans who had also a large internal expansion to finance, but not only loyally supported British efforts to keep the Sterling Area solvent and continued to sell their growing

*Comptroller of Currency; Federal Reserve Board; Federal Deposit Insurance Corporation.

†This was still the conclusion in April 1964 of the Canadian Royal Commission on Banking and Finance.

output of gold through the Bank of England, but gave the warmest welcome to the operations of the London accepting houses.

Neither did Germany, as her economy revived, possess the institutional arrangements for moving into the international money sphere, or for arranging longer-term marketable paper for foreign borrowers. Although her big banks are of the mixed type and engage in underwriting and investment, these activities had not been developed to any great extent outside Germany's frontiers. This was not solely the consequence of wars and post-war capital shortage. The traditional German industrial reliance on the banks for loan capital inevitably throws a heavy responsibility on the latter, makes them sensitive to any suggestion of instability in the economy, and at the same time reluctant to undertake the type of venture familiar to the City of London. Even at the end of the 'fifties, when the German export surplus as well as the country's growing prosperity caused a continuing inflow of foreign funds, the authorities thought in terms of stemming this rather than of devising ways of putting the money to use internationally. Revaluation upwards, tried in 1961, seemed the easy way out. Since the big three German banks (Deutsche, Commerz and Dresdner) hold majority interests in fifty-eight of the country's biggest joint stock companies, blocking minorities in a further 138, and are represented on the supervisory boards of directors of 318 German joint stock companies (including 150 chairmen), their main concern is consequently to maintain and strengthen this domestic ascendancy. In spite of the considerable resources at their disposal and an extensive range of first-class international connections, the German private bankers, apart from the pushing and adventurous Rudolf Münemann who created for some years what was virtually a one-man internal money market, preferred to make their profits from portfolio investment operations, rather than from credit or true underwriting operations. Some indeed are less 'private' than they appear, since their capital often contains a major participation by one of the big banks or their nominees.

In France and Italy, as countries severely hit by inflation and currency depreciation, the post-war industrial structure was characterized by heavy company indebtedness, with extensive undervaluation of assets and 'hidden reserves'. The French and Italian systems were thus geared to maintain the supply of long-term *debt* money to industry, while there was on the latter's part a reluctance to raise new equity for fear of endangering share prices. The need for periodic braking action on debt increase by the use of straight credit squeezes meant that Paris and Rome were deterred from playing any international role analogous to the City in its financial hey-day, at least so long as the French and Italian economies were conducted on a purely national basis.

So, as Europe revived, a gap appeared and the London merchant banks moved in to try and fill it. The advantage to British banking of possessing a truly competitive money market told against the Continental systems which had been developed as instruments of direction either by the State itself or by dominant interests within the State. The Continental systems are undoubtedly more rational and aim at bringing under institutional control factors of credit creation which in Britain are stimulated by the forces of the market. Institutions can bring about purposeful growth provided those who direct them have themselves creative positive minds. Unfortunately the complexities of the institutions themselves may in turn militate against initiative and creation, so that the outcome is too often control for control's sake. Amsterdam, alone among the Continental financial centres, shares something of the City's approach to the business of money and credit creation. But the disruption of war, reconstruction priorities at home and in Dutch overseas territories, the even more difficult task of economic redeployment when the Indies were lost as a result of the Anglo-American stab in the back, gave the bankers of Amsterdam and Rotterdam more pressing pre-occupations. The London merchant bankers had a fresh chance. How did they take it?

CHAPTER THREE

Ventures in Ideas

Revival of the Bill

In retrospect the openings offered to merchant banks in the post-war world seem less a matter of chance than the natural consequence of their history. This had placed them at the seat of custom between the City with its inherited good name and a still disorganized outside world groping uncertainly towards a new identity. And, in spite of the restrictive measures of governments, merchant banks had still a certain room for manoeuvre. From 1945 until 1958 the clearing banks had been subject to 'directive' controls over their lending, and the capital market was 'encouraged' by the authorities to keep down new issues. Bill finance gained new popularity, not only because of the cheap money factor but as a means of increasing working capital, particularly in the case of large companies, in the form of acceptance lines often totalling several millions and shared out amongst each other by syndicates of accepting houses. Since the increase in credit was directly related to manufacturing and trading activities, the Bank of England took a tolerant view. And by spreading the credits among other accepting houses, the leaders of the syndicates ensured that the risks, such as they were, were well spread and that the task of selling and discounting the bills would be eased by giving some variety to their individual parcels of bills.

Even though some of the merchant bankers themselves had accepted with resignation that the twilight of the London bill had set in, the weekly returns of their own bill departments contradicted their pessimism. Admittedly between 1958 and 1960 acceptances issued by the members of the Accepting Houses Committee on foreign accounts amounted to between twenty-five and thirty-one per cent of their total as compared with some eighty-eight per cent between 1928 and 1930. But the figures of the largest merchant banks, although struggling against the handicap of the two-tier Bank Rate which raised the cost of discounting prime bank bills, bear witness to the recovery. Acceptances by members of the Accepting Houses Committee had risen to £355 millions by end-September 1970.

If the bill on London may never again enjoy its former supremacy as an instrument of world trade, the more enterprising accepting houses, usually as a result of the efforts of younger managers less infected by their elders' nostalgia for the days beyond recall, showed that the London market could still facilitate bill transactions between two 'third' countries. Credit restrictions in Continental countries, coupled with high local bank rates, made it possible for London houses to compete in the financing of such trade, by paying the supplier in the appropriate currency and debiting the buyer with US dollars, Deutschmarks, or other equivalent advances at rates based, according to the status of the parties, on the New York prime loan rate. The Bank of England must of necessity scrutinize closely a process where drafts in foreign currencies between foreign countries are accepted for the actual amount due. But so long as the merchant banks bring sound judgement to bear in working out from forward currency rates at what cost finance can be made available, and provided they deal only with clients of undoubted standing, reimbursement after 120 days in the appropriate medium offers a useful procedure for earning foreign exchange. The telex permits a client anywhere in the world to be given the rate at which London will pay his suppliers and convert his invoiced currencies into the currency in which he is prepared to make the reimbursement. The method lends itself particularly to imports from the Common Market into 'third' countries at lower rates than those offered directly by European suppliers.

Meanwhile, since companies using acceptance lines were mainly active in the international field, the routine business of discounting and collecting was in itself an important factor in restarting the world-wide machinery of trade credit, as the money market in turn needed short-term funds to deal in bills. The merchant banks started to reach out to the spare funds of Zurich and New York, swapping them into sterling and putting them to work. As world trade began to revive, such funds increasingly comprised not merely 'funk' money from Swiss numbered accounts, but also the proceeds of legitimate trade, left on deposit until their owners were ready to use them, either to purchase raw materials at a favourable moment in the annual trade cycle, or to finance some new manufacturing venture – often in the sterling area – or until they could be distributed as dividends. Gradually the proceeds of trade have grown to be the predominant element in the Euro-currency market while the speculative sallies of the 'gnomes of Zurich', so beloved of political demonologists, play an increasingly subordinate role. Indeed by the time 'hot money' had been discovered to be the root of Britain's exchange troubles, it had ceased to be a significant factor. The merchant banker takes his deposits for agreed periods from reputable international clients known to him, generally some great corporation whose operations follow an annual rhythm, and he in turn looks for takers on similar terms who require the money for trade, for security, or for some short-term book-keeping purpose. Since most of European-owned funds of this nature were expressed in dollars and deposited with New York banks to ensure free convertibility, 'Euro-dollar' became the inevitable expression in popular parlance.

The Euro-dollar Market

Many of the firms and houses who possessed the dollars had been the clients of the accepting houses in the days when the London bill was king, and if it was now the dollar which was 'as good as gold', it was still the good name of a London merchant bank which came readiest to mind when, in the era of telephone and telex, the financial director or comptroller of a firm had to make a decision in a matter of minutes. Very often the outcome is that several million dollars are moved a few hundred metres along a Düsseldorf street although the transaction itself is conducted through London.

Within Britain itself there were borrowers enough, notably local authorities who had to assume ever-increasing burdens in the 'forties and 'fifties as a consequence of the welfare society, the growth of public housing, and the need to rebuild our cities to meet the requirements of the twentieth century. The use of foreign short-term funds to help in the long-term reconstruction of war-ravaged British cities has been questioned as a possible breach of the sound banking canon of never borrowing short to lend long. Naturally, the merchant banks themselves matched the maturities of their own borrowing and lending. The local authorities' requests, channelled either directly to the London banks or through brokers who specialize in this field, are carefully balanced by the lenders against the availability of funds. The merchant banks made short-term funds available to bridge a temporary gap until city chamberlains and borough treasurers had sorted out their long-term borrowing needs and sold bonds with maturities to match the amortisation lives of their recently acquired assets.* The sympathetic study of how to meet local authority requirements has been a major factor in the impressive growth of Singer and Friedlander's extensive operations in the North of England.

The clearing banks, whose major responsibilities include keeping domestic rates as stable as possible, took little part in the Euro-dollar business. Since they would in some cases have had to pay twice as much for Euro-dollars as they were paying on domestic deposits plus, in the event of switching, the added cost of forward cover, this would have left them with no margin after conversion into sterling for the money market. In addition, investment in local authority loans would not have qualified vis-à-vis the Bank of England as liquid assets.

Some of the criticism directed against the growth of the Euro-dollar markets of London and Amsterdam has, of course, not been disinterested even though made in the name of economic orthodoxy. Of the $3,000 millions deposited in London at the end of 1963, only twenty per cent actually came directly from North America, while Western Europe was probably the source of more than half. In turn about $1,200 millions of the total was lent to Western Europe. Since some of the main suppliers and takers have been great German firms with world-famous names in engineering, metallurgy, and chemicals, the German bankers have at times been extravagant in their denunciations of the Euro-dollar traffic, at times resorting to warnings to German firms not to count on London, and to London to beware of the doubtful financial position of German industry. These can hardly be considered suitable tactics for a profession which exists by the creation and maintenance of confidence.† Something perhaps of the

* This is discussed in an article 'Local Authorities and the Capital and Money Markets' in the December 1966 issue of the *Quarterly Bulletin of the Bank of England*.

† Germany's central bank, the Bundesbank, which since its postwar establishment has been outstanding in the field of monetary co-operation, appears to take a more relaxed view, judging from an address given on 27 June 1964 to the European convention of Chemical Engineering by its President, Dr Karl Blessing, who said: 'As

mercantilist spirit of eighteenth-century German principalities survives in its country's bankers, even if German industry is without peer in the development of new techniques, modern administration, and the training and welfare of staff and workers. Besides, no challenging group of private banks exists to oblige the main German credit banks to develop new and flexible ideas.

The best estimates show that about ten per cent of the total Euro-dollar loans made by London go abroad directly to non-banks and, as the Bank of England said in its Quarterly Bulletin of June 1964: 'The market has helped to stimulate banking competition and reduce interest rates in the main borrowing countries, and has probably added to the total funds available for the finance of international business.' The main central banks, including the Bank of England, appear to have accepted that the short-term money market has now developed its own balancing mechanism which can operate independently of the overall economic situation. As they improved their own arrangements for collaboration through the Bank for International Settlements, the International Monetary Fund, and by means of bilateral swaps, their policy was for some years to set wide bands within which short-term operations were conducted, trusting on the expertise and maturity of the operators. However agitation for close control continues.

long as the volume [of the Euro-dollar market] is kept roughly at the present level, as long as the classical banking rule that maturities should be congruent is maintained in its essentials, as long as one does not turn "long" into "short", and as long as the funds are not lent to borrowers whose financial standing is not of the best order, there is not very much to be said against this market which in a certain sense exercises a levelling effect on interest rates. While it is true that certain infringements of the said classical banking rule have been recorded and that the financial standing of the. borrowers has not always been unimpeachable, I do not share the opinion of those who profess to see in this market something similar to the short-term indebtedness of 1931.'

The Bank for International Settlements estimated that the net volume of Euro-currencies in use in September 1963 was $7,000 millions of which $5,000 millions were in US dollars and, according to the Bank of England Quarterly Bulletin (June 1964), of the latter $3,000 millions were on deposit in London. In spite of President Johnson's measures in February 1965 to reduce American lending abroad, the BIS estimated that at the end of March 1965 the net size of the Euro-currency market was about $9,000 millions, somewhat more than $7,000 millions of which was in US dollars.

More recently the BIS estimated that, after rising from $17,500 millions in 1967 to $25,000 millions in 1968, net Euro-dollar credit outstanding through the reporting banks went up further to $37,500 millions in 1969. On the sources' side, about $2,200 millions of this $12,500 millions growth seemed to have been supplied by North America, $6,200 millions by Western Europe and $4,100 millions by the rest of the world.

For a risk undoubtedly exists. Any profitable line of business soon breeds its own middlemen, and the Euro-dollar and other short-term traffic has brought into being a number of highly skilled brokers in Paris, Zurich, Frankfurt, Hamburg and elsewhere, who maintain contact with the financial departments of large companies, with banks and finance houses, and the European offices of New York brokerage firms, and pass out their requests for money to the main centres of supply. This service is important, and indeed has become essential, but it represents a danger. It is tempting for the credit manager or chief dealer to sit back in London in the sure belief that this Europe-wide network will offer him business. And so it will, and its practitioners have developed a good nose for those who are takers as well as for those who can be givers, but they are no substitute for the executives of the merchant banks themselves getting out and around, learning first hand in New York, Chicago, Paris, Amsterdam, Frankfurt, Stuttgart, Essen and elsewhere what is the state of manufacture and trade and how the individual firms are faring. Equally important is to know when experienced personnel in any important enterprise are being replaced by new men, and when old fogies have been finally retired to make way for new blood.

Lack of this first-hand knowledge was the major factor in the losses incurred by finance houses throughout Europe and North America in the various ramifications of the 1963 American vegetable oil affair. It was also a reason why European banks (not British ones) had badly burnt fingers in some of the much publicized German bankruptcies of the 'sixties. The close and detailed intelligence available to the London market has been as important as its financial skill. The merchant banker dare not abandon his oldest professional qualification – of possessing a thorough knowledge of the men with whom he does business. It is at his peril that he remains bound to his desk.

London as a Loan-raiser

Per contra from the first-hand contacts and knowledge acquired in the development of the Euro-dollar market came the revival of London as a centre for raising long-term international loans in spite of the ban on the use of sterling for such operations. In playing a leading part in the short-term international field the merchant banks had gradually built up the intelligence which enabled them to plan longer-term placings and bond issues. They had learned where dollars were available to take up paper with a good yield, which – thanks to the reputation of the sponsors – would be readily negotiable and offer redemption terms fairly thought out and planned with foresight. So when the Swiss authorities found that they had to put a brake on the use of safehaven funds and on the level of borrowing rates, and the price of borrowing raised for foreigners in New York by the added cost of Washington's 'interest equalization tax' imposed from July 1963, the City was back in the market with both the required technique and the ability to summon up the necessary resources. The borrowers were foreign, the bonds were denominated in currencies other than sterling and were placed outside the United Kingdom among non-UK residents. It was the London skill which was being bought. Already in 1964 $252 millions worth of long-term bonds were thus placed through the City.

The method of arranging such loans is still a matter for sharp international controversy, reflecting less genuine conceptual differences than national attitudes and underlying jealousies, where the gap between French and German professions of faith as good Europeans and the human urge to have and to hold is the most obvious discrepancy. The British merchant bankers have themselves taken up sides in the debate partly out of loyalty to their main Continental associates, partly because of the deference due to the prejudices of potential borrowers, and partly from sincerely-held beliefs as to the future evolution of the international organism of trade and finance. The sharpness of the debate at least shows that competition characterizes banking as much as does combination, and that borrowers have therefore a genuine choice.

A certain nostalgia for the days of sterling ascendancy still lingers on. Mr Jocelyn Hambro, Chairman of his bank, has been most vocal in urging a relaxation of the Bank of England's attitude towards sterling loans as against dollar ones. Even though Scandinavia, the traditional Hambro foreign field, has in principle had access to the London capital markets under both UNISCAN and EFTA agreements, few sterling loans have in fact been raised for the Nordic countries, partly because of the higher sterling rates as compared to dollar, but mainly because under the Exchange Control Act 1947, British issuing houses have not even been allowed to make sterling-denominated issues in Paris.

Consequently Hambros itself had to turn to the dollar denomination in arranging its Scandinavian loans, which were almost entirely taken up on the Continent as the loans yielded less to UK residents who were not allowed to sell their interest coupons in the investment dollar market. London's role was that of providing not the capital itself but a speedy, flexible and relatively informal mechanism and, in a world where states with advanced industrialized economies are becoming increasingly woven into an interdependent financial system, this has been no mean contribution. The international bond-issuing syndicates themselves reflect by their groupings and differing outlooks the complicated relationships of such a world.

Not that the Continental bankers were blind to the opportunities. The Belgian Banque Lambert, as much by active publicity on its own part and on the part of its international associates as by the realities of placing power, pushed itself into the limelight as a syndicate leader in dollar loans, bringing in M. Samuel & Co., and Philip Hill, Higginson, Erlangers (later Hill Samuel) as occasional British partners. In July 1964 the Banque Lambert sponsored a $25 millions bond issue for Finsider, the Italian state steel combine, a novel aspect of which was a ten-year warrant entitling bond holders to buy ordinary shares at advantageous rates in the future. However, the slow absorption of these bonds by the international market, even allowing for the political uncertainties of the Italian political scene, indicated that advance planning of the placing and an attractive coupon remain more important success factors than novelty.

Another method of arranging large loans which has been tried out was the 'parallel loans' concept much publicized by Dr Herman J. Abs, Chairman of the Supervisory Board of the Deutsche Bank, Germany's biggest credit bank.* Dr Abs's idea is in fact neither

---

* The concept as defined by Abs in an article in *The Times* of 11 March 1964 is: 'I would define a European Parallel Loan as the simultaneous floating of several loans of one issuer in Europe with each participating country raising one loan in its own currency, the terms and conditions of all the loans being uniform as far as possible and only differing where absolutely necessary. Such a parallel action would accumulate the available resources of the European capital markets involved. As each issue would be made out in the currency of the country concerned the loan would be acceptable to all groups of investors.

'A further point to be discussed arises from the different interest levels in the various countries. In this respect, the aim should be to provide all the national loans of a European parallel transaction with the same coupon: the various interest levels could then be balanced to a certain extent by a difference in issue prices.

'With respect to the terms and conditions of the national loans I do not think there should be any essential difficulty in achieving a standardization of the most important elements – maturity, interest payments, redemptions, etc. Furthermore each indi-

C

original nor new. The simultaneous flotation of loan tranches in several financial centres, denominated in the local currency with as uniform conditions of issue as markets allow, had already been tried out by Helbert Wagg in 1922, thanks to the perspicacity and hard preparatory work of Messrs Max Bonn and Albert Palache. This method might become of considerable importance one day if we ever arrive in an era in which *each* of the denominated currencies is capable of holding its value. However, under present conditions,* British merchant banks who have paid it enthusiastic lip service still fall back on dollar denominations or currency 'conversion options' which can hardly be said to be true options at all.

Thus, the City of Turin loan, floated in November 1964 under a group of banks led by S. G. Warburg, who had taken over the task from the small but old-established London merchant bank of Da Ponte, and which was heralded as being quoted in sterling, was in fact a Deutschmark loan with a fixed exchange rate for sterling. Since for British investors this meant the same conditions as any non-sterling security, it was neither 'parallel' nor 'sterling', and the 'after market' probably required more discreet support than usual until the rates had stabilized. A Danish loan denominated in Swiss currency and arranged by a syndicate led by Morgan Grenfell brought resentful reactions from the Swiss bankers themselves although their whole prosperous position rested basically on the use of Switzerland as a secure centre for flouting other people's currency regulations. The first 'parallel loan' announced as such, the 1965–80 bond issue for the equivalent of $215 millions by ENEL, the Italian state electricity authority, in July 1965 was characterized by the absence of 'parallelism' since the underwriting banks competed against each other both nationally and internationally in their offers to potential investors and placing groups. The differences in issue prices, ninety-six per cent in Italy itself which took two-thirds, ninety-five per cent in Germany, Holland and Luxembourg, and $95\frac{1}{2}$ per cent in France were thus largely meaningless and, not surprisingly, the separate tranches for each country suffered varying fortunes and were not fully subscribed in at least three countries. It was an expensive loan (with a six per cent

vidual loan should be introduced to the stock exchange of the country concerned so that all tranches of a European Parallel Loan will be dealt in and officially quoted in Europe.'

* Under present conditions there are considerable differences in yields of government securities (let alone company securities) in their respective currencies – as may be seen from the graph in Appendix Eight.

coupon) for the borrower and was perhaps launched when the international bond market was not at its best. From the defects in the mechanism, however, lessons can be drawn for future ventures.

The loan-raising medium which reflects a genuine endeavour to work towards a broad European capital market is that of the 'unit of account' denomination, a creation of Professor Fernand Collin, President of the Kredietbank of Brussels, the leading Flemish bank. Loans of this type have been the work of a syndicate headed by the Kredietbank itself and of which Kleinwort, Benson was the first British member. The system, which offers a protection against exchange risks so far not procurable through any national currency, consists of fixing a parity for a unit – the present gold parity of the US dollar was chosen for convenience – against which its value can be reckoned in terms of the leading seventeen currencies of the world at existing rates. The bonds can be purchased at these rates in any one of the currencies and must similarly be repaid at this rate in any one of them. Only if all the currencies were devalued (at which point the exchange risk factor would have ceased to be relevant) would the unit of account itself be affected. The investor has thus even protection against revaluation of his own currency, which is presumably the basic objection to it by some national monetary authorities and central banks!

Clearing and reference units must sooner or later form the basis of integration of the national economies of Europe, and already the High Authority of the European Steel and Coal Community presents its annual accounts and balance sheet in units of account. The legal rules – at present the chief complication to the wider use of the unit of account system – will with the advance of integration cease to come up against national obstacles and may even find favour under EEC's own legal charters as a basic protection of the investors' interests vis-à-vis arbitrary acts of executive authorities. In the meantime some twenty-three international unit of account loans with an aggregate nominal value of some UA $234 millions had been sold to investors by September 1970.

How Far Should Freedom Go?

Not all the anxieties and objections of central authorities towards British merchant banking initiatives in creating an international bond market have been without foundation. The proportion of the great pool of Euro-currencies which can be regarded as reliable long-term money seeking genuine investment and a regular return is unknown. And some ordering principles are necessary to assess the comparative merits of borrowers or groups of borrowers. For one major default or moratorium by an over-strained debtor could precipitate a market crisis with financial and social repercussions on national economies – perhaps not of the order of 1931 but serious enough to spell the end of the comparative freedom enjoyed by the selling groups vis-à-vis national banking authorities.

Even granted the virtue of the free mechanism of the market, the somewhat lemming-like habits of City institutions have their dangers. The rush by merchant banks to be sponsors of prestige loans will not necessarily serve the longer-term investment priorities of European governments. If the participants in the process do not correct the shortcomings, some outside deleterious factor will begin to operate or some external authority will step in and take over. The over-eager sponsorship of Danish loans in 1964 resulted by the summer in signs of saturation which set back the chances of equally worthy borrowers. But no sooner was the summer period of digestion over than Hambros began again with a $10 millions $5\frac{3}{4}$ per cent twenty-year-loan for the Jutland-Funen Electricity corporation. Although the Danes enjoy a Nordic reputation for honesty and for meeting their obligations, their economy is small and specialized and the problems arising from inevitable moments of economic deceleration will double in complexity under too heavy an external debt burden.

The flood of Japanese bond issues, totalling $103 millions in 1963 and early 1964, began to worry even the Tokio Finance Ministry and the Bank of Japan so that by July 1964 they were temporarily putting the brakes on Japanese borrowing abroad. The first Japanese commercial straight bond offer abroad, the fifteen-year $12 millions loan in December 1964 for Sumitomo Chemical Company Ltd., although sponsored by an American house, White Weld & Co., and bringing in no less than seven of the City's merchant banks as well as some eight Continental houses, had to be scaled down from the intended $15 millions and the price reduced to be certain of success. But altogether the Japanese sold bonds to the tune of US $357 millions, Dm.1450 millions, £5 millions and Sw. Fr. 110 millions in Europe in the sixties; fifteen of the thirty-nine issues were made on behalf of the central government, local governments, or the development bank, while thirteen issues of convertible bonds and eleven issues of straight bonds were made for companies. Coupons ranged from a low of 5.5 per cent in Swiss francs in 1964 and 1968 to a high of 7.75 per cent. in US dollars in 1968. The German authorities and bankers have since 1964 agreed on a periodical braking procedure over Dm bond issues for non-residents whenever they felt the market needed a rest, since an overload can develop quickly even in a time of prosperity and expansion.

Political events which seem trivial or irritating in a London banking parlour may in the local capital be important in maintaining stability and internal tranquillity. The negotiations for a loan for Austrian nationalized industries in the spring of 1964 brought N.M. Rothschild and S. G. Warburg unwittingly into the hazardous maze of Viennese politics. The coalition principle of 'proporz', by which the two main political parties, People's Party and Socialists, share in the spoils of office and keep controversy muted in a land which less than two decades ago was torn by armed strife, has its mysterious projections on the Austrian banking world, resulting in the two accepting houses being left in a somewhat humiliating state of suspension which better political intelligence would have helped them to avoid.

Nevertheless, the British merchant banking initiatives with European syndicates have unquestionably been a major factor in mobilizing the experience and resources of the main financial centres and reducing Europe's demands on United States capital. Syndicates which could underwrite the European Coal and Steel Community's $25 millions $5\frac{1}{4}$ per cent loan in November 1964, and whose British members were Hambros, Rothschild, and Warburgs, rightly felt some irritation when one of the first big loans of the European Investment Bank was entrusted to New York houses to the exclusion of European banks and timed for a period when year end demands for cash reach a seasonal peak. The strength and capacity of the Europe of tomorrow will only develop if its institutions begin by showing confidence in their own Continent.

For the individual member of a merchant bank the task of helping to organize such loans and bond issues is probably the most rewarding in fresh experience and in the satisfactions of responsibility. Often to his own surprise a young debutant on the international scene finds himself guide and friend to the chamberlain of one of Europe's historic cities, to a senior official of a Ministry of Finance, or even the financial director of a great enterprise, instructing him on the methods of international underwriting and placing, what are acceptable forms of guarantees, and what are the essential data for a prospectus which will satisfy the investing institutions of London, New York, Amsterdam, and Frankfurt. From these encounters he in turn can acquire the knowledge and the understanding which are basic to his skills as a banker. Whatever institutionalized forms Europe's future capital market may take, they will still be built on the essential foundations of human communication and confidence.

If credit must go to any one individual for the post-war re-emergence of London as an active centre for international issues, it is to Mr (now Sir) Siegmund Warburg. His own initiatives ensured that the merchant banking fraternity would not be allowed to amble along leisurely paths and, by challenging his competitors, forced them to re-examine not only their functions but perhaps their whole *raison d'être*. The other banks had been well enough aware of the possibilities, were ready enough to act as members of selling groups, or had attached themselves more or less formally to various international underwriting syndicates. On a narrow view membership of a selling group is a satisfactory enough role, with a useful commission to be collected in return for offering clients advantageous paper, and the first reaction of many accepting houses to the early loans sponsored by S. G. Warburg may well have been that this was all much more trouble than it was worth. But the maintenance of placing power depends in no small part on being in a position to dispense profitable underwriting opportunities and on keeping one's name to the fore whenever others have first-class loan projects in store. It tends to be a slightly traumatic experience for a merchant banker to open his morning paper and repeatedly find the name of one of his rivals heading the statutory full-page announcement of a new bond issue for the Ruritanian Telephone Coy. If his name *never* appears, he begins to be worried in case he will also be overlooked when the selling group for some particularly attractive issue is being assembled. The Warburg challenges looked particularly formidable since they were linked to the massive placing power of the old-established New York investment house of Kuhn, Loeb & Co.; their joint ventures had also included repatriation of a large parcel of AEI shares and the sale of Bush House. In 1956 Siegmund Warburg became himself a partner in the New York house.

The pattern of international lending is obviously not set firm and over a long enough period, its evolution will be determined by the bargains it will offer to lenders. Some of the large private borrowers of recent years may have to start turning their attention to the need to make substantial retentions from their profits if they are to maintain a reasonable poise with their financiers: credit is not a complete substitute for net assets. Governments, who hope to have reliable access to foreign capital markets, will have to demonstrate that they can also attract their domestic savers by raising loans at home and that they can maintain a favourable business environment. Political uncertainties will therefore intrude and conditions in regions such as Latin America will remain such that the risks must be undertaken by the Inter-American Development Bank with its United States backing, even though the Bank of London and South America* has kept the door to Latin America open by discounting trade bills and putting its good name to long-term loans for a number of viable-looking investment projects.

Finance for Capital Goods Exports

However, the demand for capital goods continues in Latin America and elsewhere, and so does the need for British firms to sell them in export markets. By creating a mechanism for raising medium-term finance for such exports the merchant bankers were able to offer a solution. It was a field of activity which most accepting houses entered rather reluctantly, feeling themselves not too well qualified for the task. But the general industrialization of the world and the growth of consumer goods manufacture in the former European overseas

* The Bank of London and South America (BOLSA) did not have a sizeable number of bills open with Europe when the Accepting Houses Committee was formed on 5 August 1914 to cope with the problem of the outbreak of a widespread war in Europe. Although BOLSA is not a member of the Accepting Houses Committee, it nevertheless carries out all the functions of a merchant bank and acceptances were shown in its 31 December 1969 balance sheet at £15,082,000. With subsidiary and associated companies in Latin America, the Caribbean, and France, in addition to UK interest and other branches in New York, Tokyo, Zurich, Spain and Portugal, BOLSA's 1969 balance sheet total amounted to £799 millions with net assets of £33 millions or so. In September 1970 it was announced that an agreement in principle had been reached for BOLSA to absorb Lloyds Bank Europe to form a new company, Lloyds and Bolsa International Bank, with a share capital of £39.8 millions of which Lloyds Bank will hold 51.2 per cent. and Mellon Bank International 12.6 per cent.

65

territories have steadily increased the proportion of equipment and machinery in Britain's foreign trade. The Export Credits Guarantee Department, originally part of the Board of Trade, greatly expanded after the Second World War to assist the export drive, had long provided insurance cover for such exports, but the lack of the actual credit itself too frequently proved a barrier in the way of British firms securing contracts for overseas installations. In the first decade after the war the main obstacle was fear of the potential strain on our balance of payments if exports were to be paid for only gradually over a number of years. When the Treasury and Bank of England eventually permitted ECGD to give insurance cover up to ten years, the next problem facing the British capital goods industry was to find someone to arrange the credits.

Bankers, after all, derive their funds from their depositors and have liquidity ratios to maintain. They cannot themselves be providers of long-term finance and both clearing and merchant banks have on occasion been unjustly blamed for not fulfilling their responsibilities to export trade. It is true that a brave effort was made soon after the war by a group of three merchant banks to finance the export of aircraft and aero-engines on deferred terms and this facilitated some £63 millions worth of exports before it was finally wound up. Some accepting houses had been rather half-heartedly lobbying with the central authorities for solutions such as the creation of medium-term export finance institutions which would issue negotiable paper or bonds to be discounted or held as security. This system functions successfully in some European countries, notably Austria. One obvious source of funds was the insurance companies, but no orderly procedure existed by which they could combine and study the problem. At most, exporters, provided they were large firms of first-class standing, could make *ad hoc* arrangements with individual insurance companies or pension funds, but they could not count on future credits nor was there any method of finding out which insurance companies were prepared to co-operate.

Once again it was the initiative of one individual which overcame the obstacles and created a new credit instrument. As a result of the persistence of the late J. V. O. Macartney-Filgate, a managing director of Lazards, regular machinery was established for this type of finance, first for ship and tanker construction and then for hydro-power installations; eventually a pattern was set for every type of engineering product. Once the trail had been blazed there was a rush to follow and Macartney-Filgate's scheme was formalized by the creation of the Insurance Export Finance Company (INEFCO) into which insurance companies could channel funds for export finance and which by 1964 had underwritten exports totalling over £100 millions.*

The established procedure is that the British firm concerned with an export contract calls in the services of a merchant bank, which first examines the proposed terms of the contract to ensure that it will meet the requirements of those providing the finance and also that the credit terms offered and requested are reasonable in the light of prevailing interest rates at home and abroad. At the least the verbal *nihil obstat* of ECGD has to be obtained and an approach made first to banks who can provide short-term and medium-term facilities. Then follows the drafting of a series of agreements and letters, beginning with the merchant banks, representing the consortium of the credit providers, signing a financial guarantee first with ECGD and then with the foreign buyers or importers – usually a public or semi-public body in the case of heavy equipment – outlining the terms under which repayment would be made over a number of years. The British firm remains responsible for its contract regarding prices, supply and deliveries.

Rightly, the most publicized examples of such medium-term export credits have been the series of agreements for financing the supply of chemical plants to the Soviet Bloc, the general framework of which was first worked out in the spring of 1964 by ECGD and Russian officials. A consortium organized by Lazard Brothers and the Midland Bank thereafter undertook to advance credits which may rise to £100 millions over a period of fifteen years, beginning with one for a £30 millions polyester fibre plant. During the same period Lazards conducted negotiations for a £4,000,000 credit to the Czech import agency. STROJIMPORT, for the purchase of a fertilizer plant. The credit syndicate for this consisted of Barclays, Lloyds, Martins and National Provincial as well as INEFCO. Then followed under

* Until January 1965 when the Labour Government announced a fixed interest export credit scheme to be operated by the clearing banks, this remained the chief medium-term facility at the disposal of British exporters. On 31 March INEFCO's Chairman, Mr J. A. Pollen, announced that new plans for refinancing its business were being abandoned. While INEFCO remained responsible for firm commitments already entered into, it ceased to add to them. Under the new scheme merchant banks may still be, and have been, conveniently nominated by their clients to co-ordinate the arrangements where more than one clearer is involved.

Lazards' auspices, a £4,000,000 credit for a polythene plant for Bulgaria, in which Lloyds Bank was the main participant, while talks between Lazards and the National Bank of Hungary were initiated for a £15 millions 'shopping list' credit for the purchase of British equipment. Including credit arrangements for the supply of a £4,500,000 polythene plant to China, Lazards probably arranged about £450 millions of medium- and long-term finance between 1962 and 1970 to facilitate the export of British capital goods.

Such agreements have not been confined to the Communist countries. The £25 millions contract secured by a British construction group to build a 500-mile pipeline in Algeria depended in the last analysis on the satisfactory completion of financial arrangements by Kleinwort, Benson both for the £18 millions covered by ECGD and provided by National Provincial, Barclays, Lloyds, and INEFCO, and also for a £7,000,000 credit from the Kuwait Fund for Arab Economic Development. In Latin America Kleinwort, Benson also arranged, on behalf of the Midland Bank and INEFCO, a ten-year credit covering most of the £2,500,000 contract for the supply of railcars to the Mexican State Railways. In 1964 the technique was extended to cover a combination of syndicate credit and sterling bond issue to finance the construction of a Finnish steel mill by British companies, where Lazards with the appropriate clearing bank and INEFCO support arranged some £6,500,000 of finance to be repaid in half-yearly instalments after the completion in 1968; at the same time Lazards, in association with Schroder Wagg and Hambros, placed £1,450,000 worth of sterling bonds for the Finnish company to pay for other auxiliary British equipment.

In this twentieth-century development of merchant banking, as before, knowledge is only acquired by experience. Working out the average rate of the cost of finance raised from so many sources over so many different periods is the least difficult aspect of the problem. Each lender has different legal and other conditions to which he may have to conform by statute. The foreign parties bring utterly different notions and nomenclature. The situations in which the ECGD guarantee might theoretically have to be invoked begin to multiply, and the Department itself begins to find fresh snags while the insurance companies' security considerations must be reconciled with commercial risks; this last reconciliation is only possible if ECGD is satisfied at every turn. As the crucial stage approaches, a merchant bank may find that over a dozen of its key personnel are being committed to full-time work on the project. In such operations political complications seem unavoidable and several Whitehall departments have to be consulted and their ambiguous utterances twisted into some form of derived meaning. There are excitements and there are moments of deep depression before the newspaper reader's eye half takes in the photograph of a signing ceremony and then passes over to the next item.

Yet, having lost an Empire and become again an island workshop, this service is one of the main strands of Britain's lifeline. Political anxiety over the possible inadequacy of our export credit arrangements is understandable, although most of the complaints have been ill-founded. Ultimately the credit-worthiness of potential buyers must be the deciding factor, and there is no economic benefit to the country if this is lightheartedly set aside. Where British exporters study the possibilities and limits of credit facilities with their bankers before they start tendering they find that the City possesses a flexible and adequate mechanism to service them. On occasion American or German competitors may offer easier 'deferred terms' within the framework of political or 'aid' considerations, but those who advocate Britain's following this example may find in the end that they themselves will be paying the price from their own pockets in the forms of additional taxation. In fact no other European capital can mobilize so rapidly the same quantity of long-term commercial funds as London; no country has with such lighthearted casuistry as Britain found ways round the Berne Convention on the limits of export credits.

Even after the details of the original medium-term financing agreement have been completed, the task of the merchant banker does not end. The foreign buyer's promissory notes may have to be placed, arrangements made to cover their payment at maturity, and the supply of finance managed as economically as possible in relation to a range of sub-contracts allotted over a number of years. The venture should thus represent a continuing profitable return: the merchant bank takes its initial fee and can look to an annual management charge while the collection of funds and placing of paper at periodic intervals are precisely the types of operation which enable a financial house to extend its contacts and maintain and increase its standing in the world's money centres.

In a world of large-scale construction and development schemes where the participants may come from many countries, the planning of such financing arrangements will grow. As the Soviet Bloc turns more and more to Western Europe for assistance in remedying its technical deficiencies, and orders whole complexes of factories, such as an Imperial Chemical Industries £50 millions chemical plant and a Fiat $600 millions car plant the demands on long-term export credit-raising facilities will be intensified. There will always be scope for flexible and competitive services and, if British merchant banks find a way back to lands where their forebears, such as the Brandts, once traded in timber and furs, it will be because they have been ahead of others in maintaining these.

Attempts at Overseas Expansion

The ventures of merchant bankers encounter obstacles enough even in overseas areas of European settlement. In South Africa the leading merchant banks have their own subsidiaries or affiliates, and the Hambro family possess extensive holdings in the mining finance corporations. But in Australia, although the admission of City skills and the creation of a bill market with a backing of discount houses would be the most effective counter to the unofficial Australian money market created by a growing volume of funds, estimated at £A190 millions, which nullify the open market operations of the Reserve Bank, the central authorities still fend off non-Australian intrusions. From time to time the lights seem to go amber and in 1964 Schroder's Chairman could point in his annual report to a significant increase in the use of acceptances through New York of their Australian affiliate, Darling & Co., Ltd, while in June of the same year, the Common-wealth Treasurer, Mr Harold Holt, disclosed that over the past year the Reserve Bank had been studying the conditions for the estab-lishment of a sound and effective bill market.

However, when in February 1965 the Commonwealth Treasury finally approved a plan, it became clear that the official section of the market was to be limited to nine accredited short-term money market companies already operating in Australia. The trading banks would be the only official accepting houses and the lender-of-last-resort facilities of the Reserve Bank would be available only to the official market, whose bill portfolios were to be limited to some five per cent of their total holding of paper. This would hold them down to between £A9,000,000 and £A10,000,000, clearly no solution to the problem.

Nevertheless, Antony Gibbs & Sons and Kleinwort, Benson made arrangements with a group of Australian interests to incorporate a merchant banking company, Merchant Bills Corporation, in the hope that London skills could at least operate at the unofficial end of the market; here they will have to compete with Australian United Corporation, a creation of Morgan Grenfell and Lazards, while Development Finance Corporation, with links to Philip Hill, will operate in both official and unofficial markets.

In Canada the realization of the dream of turning the potential energy of the Labrador plateau watershed – some 1,500 feet above sea level – into electricity appeared to be obstructed for a time by Quebec politics. The original conception of the Churchill Falls hydro-electric project arose out of conversations between Sir Eric Bowater and Joseph R. Smallwood – the Premier of Newfoundland and Labrador – on developing the iron ore deposits, the forests and the hydro-electric potential of Labrador. In August 1952 Anthony and Edmund de Rothschild were eventually entrusted with the long task of joining up the basic outline of the Bowater-Smallwood ideas with the multiple details which would turn it into reality. The British Newfoundland Corporation was incorporated on 17 April 1953 by N. M. Rothschild & Sons, Anglo-American Corporation of South Africa, Anglo-Newfoundland Development Company, Bowater Paper Corporation, English Electric Company, Frobisher and Rio Tinto. A definitive agreement was signed by the Lieutenant-Governor of Canada, Sir Leonard Outerbridge, on 21 May 1953, conceding to the Corporation (usually referred to as 'Brinco') the right to choose 50,000 out of 70,000 square miles in Labrador and 10,000 out of 20,000 square miles in Newfoundland on which the mineral rights would be granted. In addition the company received all the un-alienated water rights of the Province. A 1,500 square mile timber concession on the shores of Lake Melville was also granted.

In 1955 Brinco assigned its mineral rights to a wholly owned subsidiary, British Newfoundland Exploration, usually referred to as Brinex. In 1958, Brinco transferred all its rights, options and assets relating to the water potential of the Upper Churchill River and watershed to Churchill Falls (Labrador) Corporation, a subsidiary 57 per cent owned by Brinco, 34 per cent by Shawinigan Water and Power and 9 per cent by the Province of Newfoundland and Labrador. The Churchill Falls (Labrador) Corporation sub-leased the right to develop the power potential of the Unknown River, a

71

tributary of the Churchill River, to the Twin Falls Power Corporation – an associated company incorporated in 1960 in which Churchill Falls (Labrador) had two thirds of the votes and one third of the equity while Wabush Iron and the Iron Ore Company of Canada had one third of the equity each. When in October 1966 Premier Johnson announced his government's approval of the letter of intent for the sale of power to Hydro-Quebec, the main Churchill Falls project was able to go ahead. There were forty miles of dykes to be built to make up total reservoir areas of some 2,567 square miles. In May 1969 the definitive Agreement with Hydro-Quebec was signed for the sale of all the power and the monies finally raised which totalled $1,073 millions. When completed in 1976 the project will produce about 34,500 million kilowatt hours a year out of an estimated total Churchill River potential of some 50,000 million kilowatt hours a year.

In the face of slow progress in Australia and Canada in 1964 and 1965 and of the disproportionate risks of Africa and Asia, merchant banking eyes turned increasingly to Europe, either seeking new forms of association with European banks or establishing a foothold of their own. The 'economic miracles' of the 'fifties and the relatively rapid business expansion of the Common Market countries had already prompted fresh portfolio investment interest in the Continent by more sophisticated investors; since British clearing banks are barred from undertaking activities in this field which are normal with their Continental opposite numbers, a merchant bank usually emerged as the British member of the various investment groups blazoned with their EURO-prefixes, and perhaps presenting a somewhat misleading picture of banking solidarity. A more accurate indicator has been the acquisition of or participation in continental banking and finance houses. Rothschilds and Lazards, although operating independently of the French houses bearing the family name, had naturally retained particularly friendly links with them. But the example set by Samuel Montagu & Co. Ltd in participating in the Guyerzeller Zurmont Bank A. G. in Zurich has been followed by others. During 1964 S. G. Warburg acquired a controlling interest in the Frankfurt bank of Hans W. Petersen, from which after a series of transactions eventually emerged the Effectenbank Warburg (Frankfurt), while Rea Brothers combined with Conrad Donner of Hamburg to take a fifty per cent interest in the Amsterdam Crediet Maatschappij. Relying on their own good name, Kleinwort, Benson have registered an embryo subsidiary in Brussels as Kleinwort, Benson (Europe), SA, with an eye to the long-term development of EEC and its credit institutions.

Hambros has probably the widest spread of such participations, as befits a bank which in 1961 had already, by an investment in the New York house of Laidlaw & Co., begun to develop in the United States the type of all-round services offered by a merchant bank. This grew into Hambro-American Bank and Trust Company established in New York on 1 November, 1968, and now a highly successful bank in its own right. Hambros has a holding in the Paris Union Européenne and in 1964 moved on beyond the Alps with a substantial minority holding in the Milanese private bank, Banca Privata Finanziaria, hitherto solely owned by one of Italy's new men, Signor Michele Sindona, who, from successful real estate and property deals, has built up a holding company with sufficient blocks of shares in leading Italian enterprises for him to be invited to join their boards. Profiting by the Spanish government's acceptances of World Bank and OECD reports on the need for new Spanish commercial credit and investment banks, Hambros has joined with a group of European institutions in the creation of Banco Europeo de Negocios, to finance new enterprises in Spain. The moving spirit behind this was Banca Popular Español, the fastest growing commercial bank in Spain. In 1965 a similar Hambros' participation was taken in the capital increase of the main Greek development bank.

There sometimes seems to be a similar process working in the opposite direction. The Banque de Paris et des Pays Bas S.A. combined with S. G. Warburg, Lehman Brothers of New York and a number of British financial institutions and insurance companies to set up the Banque de Paris et des Pays Bas Limited in 1964 under the chairmanship of the late W. Lionel Fraser. The London office became a fully owned branch of the French parent company in December 1969. The importance of entering into joint ventures should not be exaggerated. Kleinwort, Benson have for some years had a link with the Banque Nationale pour le Commerce et l'Industrie in the London British and French Bank without there necessarily being any great burgeoning of common Anglo-French banking ventures. The acquisition of a profitable participation does not imply some new policy objective. And where there may be one, the hopes of the partners may prove unrealizable in the different framework of each other's countries. 'European Enterprise Finance', created early in 1964 by Samuel Montagu & Co., fourteen Continental and four American banks, to develop new technical projects, is unlikely to parallel exactly the progress of the American promoters, the American Research and Development Corporation, a $34 millions venture capital company which finances its customers through convertible bonds. The permutations and combinations of Continental and British merchant banks who have set up joint subsidiaries in independent African territories may well find after the first fine rapture of 'development' that the ambitions and fantasies of black dictators begin to take precedence over the canons of sound finance.

Nevertheless, what is new is the extent of this formal interweaving of European banking allegiances; with Europe as a whole going through an expansive phase and individual countries such as Spain on the verge of new economic chapters, there will be a place for the services of a great network of modern credit institutions. Pan-European ventures will require corresponding financial arrangements, and it may be some consolation for Britain's long exclusion from the Common Market that her banks still played a part in it. The bill on London may have lost some of its international standing, for the present at least, but its creators seem to have retained theirs. If a Channel Tunnel is finally built, London merchant banks will doubtless be called upon to assist in raising the £160 millions or so required; Mr Leo d'Erlanger, grandson of the founder of the first tunnel project, is chairman of the Channel Tunnel Company, and Lord Harcourt of Morgan Grenfell is a British member of the Study Group.

What Benefit to Britain?

How far can all these activities be said to bring benefit to our balance of payments, as against profit to the merchant bankers themselves? Operations conducted abroad, such as acceptances on foreign account or overseas advances financed by foreign funds, produce identifiable earnings in foreign currency. Less easy to tie down in terms of advantage is the function of the merchant bank in providing a connecting link between the domestic and foreign economies. Although an exporter may earn money in foreign currency, and an importer none, both are still essential links with the outer world. So in its money business the merchant bank in turn will be either an importer or exporter of funds and its direct foreign currency earnings vary accordingly.

The total foreign earnings of merchant banking activity have never been accurately estimated but must annually be a comfortable seven-figure amount. However, much of the foreign earnings for which it is responsible will not appear in its own books. The additional wealth from a well-managed foreign portfolio will accrue to the owner; the merchant bank responsible for the management may well receive its remuneration in domestic sterling.

The London merchant banks should therefore be considered not merely as separate entities but also as part of a larger body. Aesop's fable about the dispute between the organs of the body as to their relative importance is equally applicable to the British economy and the merchant banks are only one of the groups enabling it to function at home and develop its overseas extensions. The large inflow of foreign exchange from 'invisibles' – consisting of interest, profits and dividends, services and transfers – more than doubled between 1959 and 1969. Gross private 'invisible' receipts rose from £2,019 millions to £4,005 millions while gross payments rose in a lesser proportion from £1,404 millions to £2,644 millions, the net result being an increase in the foreign exchange inflow from £615 millions in 1959 to £1,361 millions in 1969. The large foreign exchange earnings by 'invisible' services over the years have substantially mitigated the adverse consequences of the UK burden of government transactions – costing £789 millions in 1969 – which might otherwise have necessitated some cutback in imports. Prior to the crisis of confidence which developed at the end of 1964, foreign exchange dealers had rarely recorded undue selling of sterling during recent periods of so-called 'pressure on the pound', while visible trading deficits seemed to bear no identifiable statistical relationship to the calls on Sterling Area reserves; this indicates that some powerful buoyant factor had remained at work. Whatever the contribution of the merchant banks to invisible earnings may be in statistical terms, it has certainly been on the side of buoyancy rather than acting as a depressive.* But at home, outside the bill business, what special expertise can the merchant banks still offer? If the Aesop analogy is pursued, are they an essential organ or are they beginning to atrophy, becoming at least removable like the appendix or the tonsils at the cost of only temporary discomfort?

* The United Kingdom Balance of Payments 1970 Pink Book shows that there has been no simple statistical relationship between total currency flows and the balance of trade visible and invisible at the dockside. Some of the unexplained flows have been quite large and raise the question whether short-term speculative activity in long-term gilt-edged stocks may have had a disturbing influence on the total currency flows met by the Bank of England.

Their operations in the foreign field have not been without some value to domestic financial arrangements. For example, the supply of funds available from short-term Euro-borrowings enabled them to produce new solutions to local authorities' borrowing needs, such as the scheme of short-dated bonds for Manchester Corporation initiated by S. G. Warburg, rapidly followed by the others. Inevitably there was a prompt reaction by the Bank of England which let it be known that it would not accept such paper as security for its own loans, thereby warning the discount market not to load itself with the bonds. If under the regulations at present permitting local authorities to issue negotiable bonds the market were to be flooded with paper of one to five years and acceptable to clearing banks as security for loans to discount houses, they could inflate bank lending. Local authority rates have already become a major factor influencing the movement of overseas funds in or out of London and certainly meriting as much attention as Treasury Bill comparisons. The total temporary debt of local authorities at the end of 1964 exceeded £1,700 millions, of which just over £1,100 millions was for periods of up to seven days, while £680 millions was from banks and other financial institutions. Any attempt to bring order into this must in the end be for the benefit of the country's credit structure.

However, by moving into the one- and two-year municipal bond field, the merchant banks put themselves at a sensitive tactical point in the market and their decisions as to where they steer the short-term foreign and domestic funds deposited with them inevitably attract even closer attention by the central authorities, particularly in view of the expanded volume of commercial bills which followed the 1963 rise on Bank Rate.* A local authority increase in demand – estimated as much as £300 millions if the bonds were to replace mortgage borrowing – could have sharp reactions on London and foreign rates. Soon enough a queue of local authorities – keen to issue yearling bonds – formed up at the Bank of England and, in spite of certain theoretical complications over selling them at pre-maturity dates, institutions proved ready enough to take them up. The funds thus provided were considerably cheaper than the longer-term funds which might have been more suitable to finance the building and holding of council houses and some councils were tempted to hold back from selling longer-term bonds in the hope that longer-term yields might

* One of the major discount houses estimated the increase in the bill turnover in 1963 at nine per cent.

fall. They might well have come to no harm if the United Kingdom's management of her economic affairs had proved more conducive to the re-emergence of reasonable internal price stability; but prices did not stabilise and bond yields rose substantially, completely upsetting the original costings on which much local council capital expenditure had been incurred. In view of this, the Bank of England control is likely to be reinforced by maintaining the principle that renewal of maturing bonds should be given broad priority over new issues.

The Bank of England warning in this case once again illustrates the continuing responsibility which attends the status and privileges of an accepting house; the letters from the Governor circulated to them through the Accepting Houses Committee carry the weight of a directive, if not of a direct order, however diplomatically the wording may be phrased as 'suggestions'. When accusations of lack of initiative were made against the accepting houses in the immediate post-war years, they were in many cases only conforming to the great mass of official restrictions, suggestions, and 'hints'. It was not until 1958, when the British economy had its first major post-war monetary boost, that the banks – clearing as well as merchant – were freed from 'directive' controls over their lending. This touched off a huge upsurge in bank advances and an equally unprecedented boom in hire purchase trading in which the clearing banks assisted mainly by direct participation in the principal finance companies, and the merchant banks by loans to the latter.

Credit in a High-Consumption Society

Here is a field of credit which has not only come to stay but will continually extend its scope. Britain's hire purchase debt doubled in six years to reach about £1,000 millions in June 1964 and stayed around that level until 1970. Credit may always have been necessary to oil the wheels of trade, but domestic credit on such a scale is in itself a major factor of social change and brings its own problems. If the American example is any precedent the growth of hire purchase debt will be a central feature of all industrial societies with a rising standard of living, and the estimate of the British total in 1984 is £3,000 millions. The dangers are obvious. When restraints were removed in 1958, the rapid extension of hire-purchase credit brought in its train a disproportionate rise in bad debts and up to 1962 the finance houses lost some millions of pounds. Although as a general principle the leading accepting houses had directed their main lending to the larger and older-established houses, some of them had their fingers burnt. The organization of medium-sized hire purchase finance houses, known as the Industrial Bankers' Association, suffered a sharp blow to its prestige when one of its members, G. and C. Finance of Brighton, had to impose a stop on withdrawals of deposits, and again when Theo. Garvin had to announce a voluntary liquidation. In advertising for deposits from the public a code of conduct in the employment of resources is a first essential. If, by their association with the hire purchase finance world, merchant banks bring an influence to bear in developing sound guidelines for a category of credit operation destined to assume such massive proportions in our century, they will deserve well of the community. 'Check-trading' for example, is believed to have an annual turnover of some £40 millions.

Since the boundary between genuine consumer credit and compulsive instalment buying remains blurred, some of the variants, at times shading into gimmickry, may expose the depositor to a wider range of risks than he believes he is accepting. Abuse inevitably brings central control and restrictions, with all the rigidities and insensitivity to timing which are the corollaries of public intervention. There is therefore benefit to both sides in any form of association between these newer forms of finance and the older traditions of responsibility, putting experience gained from one activity at the service of another, as in the case of Sir Mark Turner, the Chairman of Mercantile Credit, who is also a member of the board of Kleinwort, Benson. One of the biggest independent hire purchase finance houses, Lombard Banking, has on occasion made arrangements to draw on S. G. Warburg for financial advice.

The American pattern of a high consumption society emerges also in the rapid growth of plant leasing and the financial methods appropriate to it. Begun in the United States in 1950, leasing operations within ten years had risen to $400 millions annually and since then it is estimated they have topped the $2,000 millions mark. Under this system a firm hires or leases equipment from the manufacturer via a finance house, which acts as the formal supplier, over a set number of years at a fixed rental per month or quarter, or an agreed portion of a year. Towards the end of the leasing period the hiring charges fall steadily until the monthly charge is often the equivalent of the annual charge. It was first introduced to Britain in

1961 when leasing firms were set up with United States know-how. By 1964 the three major firms involved were arranging over £10 millions worth of leasing annually. The rates are high, and the system can make progress only if there are offsetting advantages such as tax exemption claims. But since 1962, a thirty per cent rate of investment allowance has made it cheaper for British enterprises to make straight borrowings for new plant, while on the Continent of Europe one established feature in companies' annual accounts is the ample depreciation allowance coupled with tax exemption and medium-term credit – usually state-sponsored – for equipment purposes.

Among the merchant banks Hambros has been a leader in the development of leasing and is now one of the biggest operators in this field. It has its own international leasing department and a $28\frac{3}{4}$ per cent interest in Equipment Leasing Company Ltd; its partners are Chase Manhattan Bank and Standard Bank. Through Hambro International N.V. it has interests in Elcon of Norway, Leaseplan Nederland N.V., Nordania of Denmark and Skaba of Sweden. It is also in partnership with the Schlesinger Organisation and the First National City Bank of New York in the First Consolidated Leasing Corporation (Pty) of South Africa. Leasing has also been applied to containerization and Hambros is a shareholder in Container Finance (Bermuda) Ltd which was formed primarily to lease containers to a large shipping company. The Cayman Islands Leasing Company has also been formed to give a similar container service. In 1969 Kleinwort, Benson were prime movers in the formation of Airlease International, a partnership of eleven members, including four clearing banks and four accepting houses, to increase the scale of financial participation in the leasing of large jet aircraft.

Even under the canons of orthodox audit the concept of 'assets' can be stretched quite far, but the difficulty of representing machinery and equipment as banking assets for institutions which are basically short-term lenders is not so easily overcome. The renewed popularity of factoring in Europe mainly as a result of American influence and example, presents another aspect of the problem, and one which the interested merchant banks have tried to solve by assisting in the formation of separate factoring companies for which, under appropriate safeguards, financial facilities can be arranged.*

* The main factoring groups are International Factors (Tozer Kemsley and Milbourn, Hill Samuel, First National Bank of Boston), Shield Factors (Rothschilds, Kleinworts, ICFC, Anglo-American Shipping, C. T. Bowring), Portland Factors (J.

To the profane, all this may be evidence either of versatility or simply of fear of being left out. But the experiments have to be made. Along the streets of the business quarter in every British city and large town proliferate the offices of hire purchase finance companies, building societies, mortgage companies, loan societies, and 'banks' of one kind or another. The bidding for institutional, company, and private liquid funds and savings at rates above those of the London money market becomes fiercer and at times the main emphasis of credit seems to be shifting from producer to consumer. As takers of money at 'flexible' rates and as givers in situations where 'special' rates can be asked, the merchant banks must compete or fall behind. If the best way of studying the workings of the new varieties of credit and of assessing the risks of particular situations is by participating in the process, the accepting houses are right to do so. At times, the canons of taste may seem outraged where promotion methods designed to catch the eye appear to take precedence over the more venerable tradition of trusting on solid reputation or respectable backing. 'Money Without Borrowing', said a half-page advertisement in the leading papers when a finance company, offered credit facilities based on yet another variation of the arrangement by which the financier goes through the contractual form of buying goods directly from a manufacturer or seller, reimbursing him, and then appointing him agent for the delivery of the goods and the collection of payment. Where, however, the new consumer credit houses are extending their own operations internationally, the limelight may be a major factor in success. The European group of hire purchase finance houses known as the Amstel Club (of which United Dominions Trust is the British member) made the decision in October 1964 to offer an international factoring service covering all the countries of Western Europe, and merchant banks cannot risk remaining behind in plumbing the possibilities of mutual credit business.

But if it is historically within the merchant banks' charter to devise

Gerber, Alex Lawrie), H. and H. Factors (Hambros, Keep Brothers, Credit Consultants, Walter E. Heller of USA, and Continental Illinois National Bank and Trust). However, individual merchant banks continue to run their factoring services and Wm. Brandt's Sons has for some years made a point of advertising its experience and facilities in this field. The essence of the system is that the factor buys debts that are owed to a company as they arise and collects them himself. The company concentrates on negotiating the contract and delivering the goods. The main psychological obstacle to the system is the fear that the buyer may resent an arrangement which appears to make him the object of a 'debt collection'.

new means of financing the exchange of goods, their motives for participating in the numerous international property development financial groups registered over the past few years throughout Europe appear somewhat obscure. At home the merchant banks have played a key role in the supply of 'bridging finance' to British property development companies, particularly in cases where they also acted as issuing houses, and could consequently work out advantageous combinations of short- and long-term borrowing for their clients. The extensive and traditional property ramifications of the Samuel family give them a fund of experience from which their merchant bank can profit to offer customers such as the Shell Contributory Pension Fund, opportunities both for loan finance and share options. But other banks hitched their good names rather too rapidly to some of the new stars of the post-war property world and found that the expectations of 1960 were not matched by the dividends of 1964, and their investment managers were in consequence having to advise clients that they should regard their property holdings as good 'recovery stocks'.

If the City thus landed itself with one or two North American white elephants in the property field, this underlines the moral that the skills of property development financing depend largely for their success on local factors which cannot always be controlled from banking parlours in London. On the Continent of Europe there may still be numerous cities calling for reconstruction and planned development, but these will take place in accordance with national needs – political, cultural and emotional, as well as financial. The rigidities of the prefectural tradition of bureaucracy, the unending procedures of permits, the scratching of steel pen points charged with purple ink on *papier timbré,* these are features with which local finance houses are best fitted to cope, just as British property developers are best equipped to fathom the motivations and reactions of English and Scottish municipal authorities. Not surprisingly Australia, where British-type laws and conditions apply, has been the most successful overseas property development field for merchant banks, notably Guinness Mahon, Schroder Wagg, and Hambros.

Mobility or Size?

The hazards of financing property development on an international basis do illustrate, however, that merchant banking – if it is to maintain a distinctive character – lies in maximum mobility of the resources it affects to control. Any financial rigidity is liable to prove fatal, if not to solvency, at least to independence. And the new structural framework into which merchant banking is now trying to put itself, appears to be part of an attempt to achieve the seemingly impossible, namely to combine mobility and consolidation. If the post-First War world saw a change from private partnerships with unlimited liabilities into limited companies, one of the main developments since 1945 has been a regrouping of the associated interests and activities of medium-sized and smaller merchant banks into holding companies with the banking house itself and its own assets appearing formally as a group subsidiary. The motive may in some cases have been to facilitate the transfer or disposal of family holdings, in others it may have been to improve their own capital-raising power, and to extend participation by the investment public. An immediate tactical objective has always been to separate banking and non-banking assets.

Among recent moves of this nature was the renaming in 1963 of Viking International Corporation, acquired through a reverse bid by the merchant bank of Guinness Mahon & Co., as Guinness Mahon Holdings. It then took over the bank as its subsidiary and a year later increased its capital to £2,500,000 by a one-for-three scrip issue. Montagu Trust, whose five shilling shares were offered in 1963 at thirty shillings, included in its formation not only the merchant banking and bullion broking house of Samuel Montagu, but an old-established Lloyd's and general insurance broking firm as well as several investment trusts, giving the group total assets in 1969 of over £293 millions.

In December 1964 Keyser Ullmann, whose main assets had been the Keyser and Ullman banking companies, sold the latter to the Hocroft Trust in which it already held a 42·76 per cent stake. This meant that Keyser Ullmann's principal holding became a seventy-eight per cent share of Hocroft. In 1968 Keyser Ullmann bought up the remaining shares in Hocroft and in 1969 sold David Harris, White & Carter (Councils), and Endura Electrical Industries to raise capital for the banking side of the business. S. Japhet & Co., renamed Charterhouse Japhet & Thomasson, continues to grow within the framework of the Charterhouse Group.

But because the process can rarely be undone, senior partners are liable to finish up as juniors, and would-be controllers as the controlled, and it needs to be entered into with circumspection. Inevitably strong personalities clash in the early days, and tentative associations often end in agreement to separate. For a number of years new acquisitions of the £20 millions holding company, Minerals Separation (such as that of Hecht, Levis and Kahn), were handled in collaboration with S. G. Warburg. But in 1964 Mr S. G. Warburg resigned from the board of Minerals Separation, while the latter in turn sold its holdings of Mercury Securities, the parent company of S. G. Warburg & Co., and by the end of the year was reported as holding discussions with the Bentworth Trust, controlled by Hambros, for new joint ventures. Meanwhile Mercury Securities itself has gone on building up its own group of companies with a range which includes insurance broking, Social Surveys (Gallup Poll), Brandeis Goldschmidt & Co. – a profitable metal broking concern – Elkington Copper Refiners, as well as Metropolitan Pensions Association. The stated policy of Mercury Securities is in fact to invest its funds by purchasing not less than fifty per cent of the outstanding equity of financial and commercial undertakings; in March 1969 the total declared assets were over £202 millions. In spite of the size and spread of the controlling Cowdray interests, Lazard Brothers in 1963 joined with the Standard Industrial Group to form Industrial Selection Trust, and a year later were exchanging directors with the ritual assurance that no closer integration was contemplated beyond direct representation for each company on the other's board. As a result of a bid made in December 1969 for the balance of the shares, Standard Industrial Group became a wholly-owned subsidiary of S. Pearson & Son. Nearly four-fifths of Lazard Brothers share capital is held by S. Pearson while the Lazard Frères et Cie. Group still hold one-fifth.

The advantage of having banking facilities under their control has not escaped the notice of more thrusting personalities and groups. The acquisition first of Higginson & Co., and then subsequently of Erlangers, gave the Philip Hill Investment Trust a valuable adjunct for banking purposes, and an entrée into the issuing and take-over world, which was reinforced under the conditions of its bank's merger with M. Samuel. Sir Isaac Wolfson, having acquired Ralli Brothers through his General Guarantee with the apparent intention of developing it as an investment holding company, sold out to Slater Walker. Slater Walker Securities acquired Drages – which owned half the share capital of Ralli Brothers – in 1968 and the remaining shares in 1969, Ralli Brothers being renamed Slater Walker Limited (incorporating Ralli Brothers (Bankers) Limited) in 1970. Mr Maxwell Joseph acquired control of Robert Fraser and Partners through Giltspur Investments and its subsidiary company Montrose Trust which now owns some 20 per cent of Robert Fraser & Partners (Holdings). The West Country financier, Mr Julian S. Hodge, having reorganized the widespread interests of his group, in which Standard and Chartered Bank now hold 22 per cent of the share capital, set up his own merchant bank with its first branch in Birmingham. Lesser-known business groups appropriate the label by setting up subsidiaries to arrange issues and placings, or to borrow and make advances against holdings of securities.

At this point the question of 'What is a merchant bank?' ceases to be purely semantic and becomes relevant to the future nature of the profession. A *konzernbank,* however well it may be managed and however strong financially the controlling interests, cannot hope to be accepted as possessing the same freedom as the accepting houses. The *konzernbank* may be a form of consolidation but does not offer mobility, and stands in a completely different relationship to its parent group. So, although fresh competition may be highly desirable, the stretching of the concept of 'merchant bank' to group finance subsidiaries probably is not. Admittedly the management of a family fortune in an age where the value of money falls annually at about three per cent compound interest does raise its own problems, and association with a holding group offers a partial solution. In some cases the merchant banks may be strong enough to enter into such alliances *au pied d'égalité* as in the case of the acquisition of fourteen per cent of M. Samuel's equity by Mr Charles Clore, the transfer to the bank's management of his own investment portfolio estimated at £50 millions, and the cession of Investment Registry with its issuing and company registration facilities. The further series of transactions leading up to the merger with Philip Hill represents a very considerable strengthening of the Samuel family's financial position.

But when bigness has to be buttressed by more bigness there is always the risk of public attention and control if suspicion begins to grow that some sectional, commercial or financial interest is making an undue claim to privilege. Once the clamour starts, as it will whenever there is some form of misfortune or scandal, no belated profession of public interest will be sufficient protection. All who claim the title of 'merchant bank' will suffer accordingly. Here the merchant bankers themselves bear the main responsibility. More than most professions they are given to arguing what is their own legitimacy and, in a changing financial world, there is everything to be said for such reassessments of their special role and how to make the best use of their resources. But, in yielding to the demand for publicity about their activities, some of them have created an impression of uncertainty and of striking about in all directions in the hope of hitting any random target, or at least putting up a chance plump bird. Some of their sallies may indeed reflect a certain dilettantism, doubtless inevitable in families where over several generations there has been an absence of those daily drudgeries which discipline the mind and for which school codes or boy scouting can never be a substitute. But if the older merchant banks start playing the role of jack-of-all-trades, it becomes too easy for status seekers to abuse the label.

In practice most of the initial merchant banking participations announced at the time of the formation of a new company or consortium are very small, often purely nominal, for there are limits to the assets which can be tied up in outside ventures. Their intention as promoters is usually to see that the company is floated publicly as soon as possible and then recoup their investment. But the ethos of the merchant bank itself is inevitably affected by a spread of minor responsibilities into a miscellany of domestic British undertakings. There is naturally no virtue in going into risky ventures in Ruritania when exactly similar ones in the Home Counties will bring a better return. But when the main emphasis of work and board discussion is on such tasks at home, there will undoubtedly be some narrowing of vision, and the looming presence of a powerful associated or parent group breeds a different type of executive mentality from that stimulated by the problems of negotiating with overseas authorities, assembling international syndicates, and remaining on the *qui vive* for the change in foreign breezes which may spell success or setback. Any enterprise where initiative and imagination are not encouraged will find itself playing an increasingly subordinate role in someone else's scheme of things. This need not be financially disadvantageous to the participants but will change the character and eventually the status of the profession.

The New Challengers

Remaining on the *qui vive* is a must for merchant bankers. The post-war course of events illustrates that when they are on to a good

85

thing others will rapidly follow. The scheme for medium- and long-term export credits in association with INEFCO soon whetted the appetites of the clearing banks for the joys and sorrows of international finance. The Midland Bank set up the Midland and International Banks Ltd, jointly with the Commercial Bank of Australia, the Standard Bank, and the Toronto-Dominion Bank. Initially the Midland and International seemed to be examining the possibilities of virtually every international field covered by merchant banking except the provision of permanent and risk capital.* The usual assurance that 'the new bank will not seek to undermine or supplant traditional banking relationships or the activities of existing banks' has not prevented it from taking and offering short-term funds on the same basis as the accepting houses. In five months of trading Midland and International built up £30 millions worth of deposits and led the British side of a $12,500,000 $6\frac{1}{2}$ per cent mortgage issue for Irish Base Metals, the Continental share being spread among mineral and finance groups some of which had hitherto figured as associates of London accepting houses. Subsequently the Midland bought a one-third stake in the share capital of Montagu Trust.

By forming a 'European Advisory Committee' with Deutsche Bank, the Amsterdamsche Bank, and the Société Générale of Bruxelles to extend special facilities to one another's customers and pool investment information, the Midland Bank also broke new ground for a clearing bank. In the domestic field, Forward Trust Finance Ltd, a subsidiary of the hire purchase firm, Forward Trust Ltd, set up by the Midland and the Clydesdale Banks, had already begun to engage in merchant banking matters, and in February 1965 it was nominated as the British member of Export Finance International, the others (all associated with the members of the European Advisory Committee) being Gesellschaft Für Absatzfinanzierung in Germany, Financierings Maatschappij Mahuko NV in Holland and Banque de la Société Générale de Belgique SA (together with its associate Eurolease) in Belgium. Through Exfinter, as the new group will be called for short, an exporter of capital goods in any of the four countries will be able, in case of need, to put his customer in touch with a source of credit finance in the importer's own country.

Not far behind follows the National Westminster Bank. Already in 1907, by taking over the foreign banking business of Burt & Co., the

---

* Article in *American Banker,* 25 May 1964.

Westminster had established its first Overseas Branch in Cornhill, and Westminster Foreign Bank, which grew from these beginnings, went on to set up its own offices in France and Belgium. In 1963 payments made by the Westminster under documentary credits for goods passing between third parties, exceeded those it arranged for British exports and imports. In 1964 it joined an international consortium to sponsor a £5,000,000 loan for Japan. In August 1964 Westminster significantly subscribed a further £1,920,000 to raise the issued capital of its foreign bank to £3,000,000, while the latter took a shareholding in Banco de Financion Industrial formed by the Banco de Vizcaya to provide medium- and long-term finance for Spanish industrial development.

Barclays has taken up similar dispositions by joining with American and European banks in an analogous Spanish development bank, and has set up an export finance company with an authorized capital of £5,000,000 to buy export debts without recourse, to give credit to foreign buyers, and to handle all types of trade documentation. North Central Finance, a hire purchase finance firm, wholly owned by National Westminster, has started taking an equity interest in customers who can supply rental agreements for discounting, while Lloyds and Scottish Finance Ltd, jointly owned by Lloyds Bank and the National and Commercial Banking Group is diversifying its business. Within the National and Commercial Banking Group, William & Glyn's Bank and The Royal Bank of Scotland are provided with merchant bank facilities by Williams, Glyn & Co, which competes for deposits and is a member of the Issuing Houses Association. The County Bank is being promoted as the Group merchant bank of National Westminster. So far from 'taking over a merchant bank or two', as has often been suggested, the clearing banks are building up their own agencies.

The proposals made in 1963 to the clearing banks by the Governor of the Bank of England that they should bid for deposits seemed at the time to be possible only if the Bank itself were prepared to face the disturbing consequences of doing this through normal machinery. But the clearers have taken up his suggestion in a form which presents an even greater challenge to established accepting houses. The threat to the merchant banks may not be immediate. Special departments will have to be created in the clearing banks or their new subsidiaries, staff will have to be recruited with a fresh outlook and different background, and progress will of necessity be slow. However, as the EEC implements its plans for the harmonization and gradual .ntegration of the European financial and monetary systems, the clearing banks too will profit from the increasing uniformity and the merchant banks will lose their advantage of being the flexible operators who know how to overcome national barriers and differences.

This may still lie some way ahead. Although integration and unification are the slogans in vogue among the EEC participants, their capital markets in 1963 tended in fact to become more separated rather than unified as Western Germany, Switzerland, and France in turn prohibited payment of interest on short-term foreign-owned deposits and, to put a brake on inflation, several countries restricted borrowing abroad. Swiss franc loans, although as much as two per cent less than London rates, could still only be handed out one at a time at regular widely-spaced intervals to the select few who were permitted even to join the queue, such as Imperial Chemical Industries and British Petroleum. The total issue value of publicly placed foreign loans in Switzerland fell from Sw. Frs. 588 millions in 1963 to Sw. Frs. 339 millions in 1965 before rising to Sw. Frs. 1,088 millions in 1968 and Sw. Frs. 1,015 millions in 1969. The accepting houses have still a breathing space before British clearers and European credit banks can operate in concert. And in the meantime all of them face even more formidable competitors.

Although New York could not replace the London money market in the 'forties, the United States banks are now moving into Europe with their own impressive battle array and also on to a terrain opened up for them by the massive penetration of direct American investment in European industry, particularly in Great Britain. The investment itself has increasingly taken the form of a net capital inflow as against the previous main source in undistributed subsidiary earnings. With this has come a marked growth in activity on the Continent and in the United Kingdom by the leading New York banks, beginning as a rule with offers of credit facilities to American firms in Europe and then to local enterprise, usually undercutting the overdraft rates of clearing banks and at the same time holding out the prospect of services in North America and elsewhere. The pace quickened in 1964 with Marine Midland Trust Co. opening in Threadneedle Street with all branch facilities, closely followed by First National Bank of Boston in Moorgate, and by September 1970 there were some 32 American banks in London.

The great surge of direct American investment between 1959 and

1962, which increased its stake in Europe to over $10,000 millions, may have slowed up, reaching $20,000 millions in 1970, but in spite of growing European resistance to American industrial acquisitions and the United States Government's own restrictions of February 1965 on foreign lending, fresh licensing and technical agreements and joint ventures between United States and European companies will keep adding to the total. The readiness of American and foreign banks to bid freely for money and also call on their domestic resources makes them sharp competitors in the Euro-dollar market. In the past the ability of merchant banks to arrange their own stand-by credits with New York banks against possible non-renewal of Euro-dollar deposits gave them a certain advantage in international short-term lending. This may cease to be of significance in the face of American banking competition, quite apart from the effect of closer US government control of such types of foreign lending.

Sorties at Home and Abroad

Merchant banks cannot of course complain. They have never been backward themselves in finding ways of outflanking the prepared positions of others. They have in fact been launching their own counter-sallies in the English provinces, Scotland, and Ireland in search of new business. Rothschilds, after a century reopened a branch in Manchester, followed by Henry Ansbacher & Co. Kleinwort, Benson have closed their Liverpool office and opened one in Sheffield. Singer and Friedlander added a Nottingham office to their Leeds and Birmingham branches, and by purchasing a twenty per cent holding in Leadenhall-Sterling Investments, Guinness Mahon acquire direct connections with a string of companies, mainly centred round the newer industrial estates of the Bristol–Bath and Southampton areas. Dawson and Forbes, an associated company of Arbuthnot Latham, has formed a new wholly-owned subsidiary, Dawson and Forbes (Northern), to provide a full range of merchant banking services in the Lancashire and Yorkshire area; the Northern company is designed to consolidate and expand the existing business which Dawson and Forbes carries on through its office in Leeds.

In Dublin, Hill Samuel has a wholly-owned banking subsidiary, Hill Samuel & Co. (Ireland), to develop the same range of services as in London. Hambros has a 21 per cent shareholding in the Allied Irish

Investment Bank and Schroders has a 20 per cent shareholding in the Investment Bank of Ireland. None of the accepting houses are in fact strangers to Ireland and have always had a well-established clientele, and the Irish banks, while keeping a watch on these developments, have been far from unfriendly, realizing that Eire's expansion plans require the development of every type of credit facility.

On the other hand, the Scottish banks, presiding over what for many years had been a relatively stagnant economy, have cast a somewhat leery eye on encroachments from South of the Border. Until its general reorganisation the National Commercial Bank had a joint venture in Edinburgh with Schroders. Samuel Montagu acquired a minority interest for a while in the British Bank of Commerce incorporated originally as a private company in England in 1936. By 1957 this bank had accumulated heavy losses and was trading on a restricted scale when the present chairman, Mr Alexander Stone, who believed that there was a need for a comprehensive banking service in Scotland, acquired a controlling interest. Under his guidance the bank was restored to profitability and, in 1963, the head office was transferred from London to Glasgow where a new management team was recruited. In 1965 the bank was converted into a public company, and in 1969 a quotation was obtained on both the London and the Scottish stock exchanges. By 1970, a network of authorised representatives in 28 of the principal towns of Scotland and 15 major centres elsewhere in the United Kingdom, including a city office, had been built up, and subsidiary banking companies formed in Jersey and the Bahamas. Acceptances were shown in the 31 March 1970 balance sheet at £835,000. The British Bank of Commerce has wholly-owned subsidiaries in metal dealing, commodities, property and insurance broking. The commercial and industrial division of the group has acquired the entire share capital of a number of smaller Scottish firms and may possibly be building them up for eventual resale. Besides its discounting, underwriting, bridging and mortgage finance, leasing and plant hire activities, the banking side includes a subsidiary, Capital for Industry, which was formed in 1966 for the purpose of providing venture capital to companies with experienced management and good growth prospects. Another merchant bank, Noble Grossart, was founded in 1969 and its capital increased in 1970. Besides Ian Noble and Angus Grossart, the board includes Sir Hugh Fraser, William Wilson who is also a director of several companies in the Stenhouse Group, and Walter Ballantyne, the chairman of Ailsa Investment

Trust. The principal shareholders also include American Trust Company, Scottish American Investment Company and Scottish Northern Investment Trust.

The range of ventures abroad in which the merchant banks participate as independent financiers and entrepreneurs – as against those carried out in the role of agents for British clients – is limited by the Exchange Control Act 1947. Where they have a well-established local house of their own, as in New York with the J. Henry Schroder Banking Corporation, the Schroder Trust Company, Schroder Rockefeller & Co., and the Hambro American Bank & Trust Co., more scope is available. The activities of Hambro American Bank & Trust include acceptance financing. The amount of bankers' acceptances outstanding in the United States reached a peak of over $1,500 millions in the late 1920s and declined to about $200 millions in the early 1940s before expanding again to reach some $5,500 millions at the end of 1969. The creation of dollar acceptances has tended to be concentrated among the largest and best known banks in the United States (and their Edge Act corporations), foreign banks, and United States agencies of foreign banks. About 170 institutions, mainly in New York City and San Francisco, currently report their activity to the Federal Reserve System. When created by this select group of banks, dollar acceptances are considered to be prime quality money market instruments; for example, they are eligible to be used as collateral by banks when borrowing from Federal Reserve banks and may be purchased by the Federal Reserve in the secondary market.

In Western Europe itself, which is now approaching the stage reached in North America almost four decades ago, the main profit of the erstwhile financiers to crowned heads may well be from the financing of consumer tastes and the provision of consumer credit. And as Spain – Europe's main underdeveloped area – begins a new chapter in her economic history by the creation of seven great industrial growth and promotion centres with an initial capital requirement of £138 millions, auxiliary industries and a vast expansion of consumer demand will follow. Kleinwort, Benson have moved ahead with French retail interests to make a substantial investment in the first Spanish company to operate chain stores. In Germany, where rising wealth creates ever fresh consumer demand, the first announced venture of Warburg's newly acquired banking house was a partnership in a new German company to design and build shopping centres. For those who feel that merchant bankers

91

should be first and foremost associated with the extractive and trading efforts characteristic of their early days, sufficient of them appear to be represented in companies formed to discover oil and gas under the North Sea; Kleinwort, Benson indeed is participating directly with the Ionian Bank in the combined prospecting group of Phillips Petroleum, Petrofina, and AGIP.

Over the past decade the merchant banks have not lacked resourcefulness, and for those who can continue to display it there will be no shortage of opportunities in a world which, for the rest of the century, will be more avid than ever for credit. At times the merchant banker may feel somewhat daunted. The breakdown of the traditional divisions between City financial institutions, the fierce competition, the complications of official controls and restrictions – all these may tempt him either to play for security along safe, established lines of business or give up *some* of his independent status in return for the protection of bigness. But there will be no half-way house. Either he will have to surrender his independence completely or strike out boldly on his own. No line of business can be regarded as 'safe'. The radiant Euro-dollar morn may pass away, either because the American banks mop up the supply at rates which can offer no margin of profit to British dealers or because of changes in the world's balances of payments. No preserve is safe from trespassers.

Even the haven of a *konzernbank,* within some larger industrial or commercial grouping, will prove only as secure as Britain itself. Some recurrent misdirection in the British economic effort tends to set limits to industrial expansion at critical moments and puts an end to reviving hopes that the City can once more play abroad the role of a major credit giver. The merchant banker, as much as the rest of British finance, industry, and commerce, must make his contribution to rectifying this deficiency if the country as a whole is not to relapse into insignificance. European history contains many reminders of the fate which can overtake imperial bankers when there is no longer an emperor.

Recognition for the Future

A number of acts of recognition are required from the accepting houses if they are to continue to have an independent role. First, that nostalgia for the past is no substitute for present decision. Further, that there is no sacrosanct margin of profit or fractional percentage which is theirs by right. Thirdly, that areas of the world which were once their happy hunting grounds will not for many generations, if ever again, be profitable fields for risk capital. And, fourthly, that given the precarious British balance of payments, sterling loans must remain tied to the supply of British goods.

Some of the changes may have serious consequences for Britain, and the merchant bankers are justified in regretting them. As Sir Cyril H. Kleinwort points out:

The tendency for Government to monopolize the discount market through the Treasury Bill is undoubtedly a serious threat to the basic principles of the London money market. It can only be hoped that the Treasury will advise Government that day-to-day money, which by its nature is the cheapest form of money available and being the shortest term is also safest for those servicing it, should have at least a proportion reserved for the financing of short-term industrial transactions. To monopolize these funds exclusively for Treasury purposes is both unsound and contrary to the interests of the economy which is still dependent on the efficiency of its productive facilities.*

Yet for the longer term it is even more important to recognize that the changed functions of City institutions are not passing phenomena, nor the temporary consequence of restrictions and regulations which will one day be removed, but that they reflect a new changed emphasis on consumer credit requiring fresh notions of credit worthiness and new roles for finance houses. The world's capital markets too may be entering a new era, particularly as the United States moves away from reliance on monetary instruments towards directive controls over the market, of which the Interest Equalization Tax was only a fresh stage in a process begun under Roosevelt in the 'thirties. If the United States continues to adhere to the policy of low interest rates as a means of obtaining some sort of economic growth, the outcome will be a further and decisive retreat to the point where 'domestic' economies are isolated from external and international capital influence and movements.

Such an occurance could end the type of academic economic thinking which for a century and a half has persisted in the superstition that there are economic laws which operate independently of normal human activity and motivation and to which indeed these latter act as a form of impure intrusion. The consequence of the academic economist's fallacy has been the proliferation of an esoteric

* Interview with author on 18 March 1965.

jargon on monetary matters primarily designed for intellectual self-flattery and which has plagued generations of politicians, administrators, and men of affairs with totally misleading analogies. The final acceptance by the leadership of the world's most powerful economy that fiscal measures and debt management are the appropriate instruments of credit policy, the emergence of Western Europe with one 'domestic' economy directed within an institutional framework specially created for the purpose, and the scrapping of the traditional vocabulary of economic analysis will represent the opening of a new phase in world economic affairs.

All this points to a world where those who can command resources of imagination and skill will face opportunities and will be able to create new forms of mastery. There will be even fiercer competition and bargaining in the task of marshalling and channelling capital gleaned from many countries and centres, and in devising new forms of international credit, whether for hamburgers or hydrocarbons. The very vigour of this competition will challenge not only the efficiency of the City institutions but the very survival of London as a financial centre. The factors which originally created and supported the London money market – British political, industrial, and commercial supremacy linked to a fully convertible currency and a substantial favourable balance of payments – no longer operate. Impressive and effective though the conduct of the British Exchange Equalization Account may be in the short term, it can at best provide a temporary support for a country which should have been seeking a new role. The London money market must now justify itself as an entrepôt by the efficiency, flexibility and competitiveness by which it can secure and allocate funds at low cost. Far from tying their hands by narrower associations, merchant bankers with confidence in their professional capacity and human judgement may even find it wiser to keep them as free as possible. And for those who have recognized the implications of the emphatic changes in the world, opportunities should appear limitless – provided they do not clash with other concepts of the public interest.

CHAPTER FOUR

The Role of Issuing Houses

The Basic Procedures

Whatever the prevailing concept of 'public interest', for the individual businessman 'survival' means profit. Reconciliation is possible but not always easy, and nowhere is this so apparent as in the merchant bank's function as an issuing house. The entrepreneur can pose a straightforward question: 'What will be the return on the capital put into my business?' The investor asks: 'What will be the return on the capital I put in?' Although giving credit to a client or raising long-term capital for him form basically a single continuous process, a merchant banker assumes in the latter case a fresh responsibility – towards the investing public. This is still a very ill-defined responsibility, particularly as there is no special regulation or code which requires that a firm raising capital by a share issue should bring in a house which specializes in this service. The only requirement is that the officers of the firm should not lay themselves open to any fraudulent practice and, if they wish to have their shares traded, that they can satisfy the Stock Exchange conditions. With the collaboration of his solicitor, his accountant, and a stockbroker, a businessman can arrange his own issues and many firms do so, particularly family enterprises 'going public' for the first time.

Because the issue of shares is such a routine, even drab, process and because no special professional qualification is required, the merchant banks and other issuing houses perhaps hardly realized that they were assuming a public responsibility when this field of activity expanded in the 'twenties. But the fact that the merchant banks form the main core of membership of the Issuing Houses Association is the consequence of the indivisible nature of the process of credit-giving and capital-raising. The banker who has been arranging short-term credits for an industrialist and accepting his bills is the industrialist's natural confidant when he starts to estimate long-term capital needs. If the merchant banker also manages a large portfolio of investments for individuals and institutions – and most of them do – he will have a shrewd idea of what will be the interest of the investing public in the proposed share issue and of the price the market will take. If the industrialist wants to expand his own business by taking over someone else's, and seeks an independent opinion, it may well be his merchant banker who will give him the best estimate of what he should pay for it, both in terms of the assets to be taken over and his own financial prospects.

There is consequently nothing fortuitous in the names of merchant banks heading the regulation full-page advertisements in the daily press announcing an issue of shares and, if in some of the more publicized 'take-over bids' of recent years they have also stepped forward as advisers to the principals, this has been a natural enough development, although some of the journalese descriptions of their role may have misled not only the lay public but, given the English love of play-acting, even the participants themselves; the need to live up to a created image of themselves as 'tough', 'smooth', 'saturnine' or 'dynamic' seems to have conditioned the faces pulled for the benefit of the press photographers.

The issuing procedure itself is no mystery. In its most elaborate form it can be an *issue by prospectus*: but there are at least five other methods with shading differences. These are *offers for sale* (where the entire issue is purchased by an issuing house and then sold), *placings* (privately arranged sales), *introductions* (listing on the Stock Exchange of an existing firm's securities without new capital being raised), *rights issues* (to existing shareholders), and *offers by tender* (when bids are accepted at or above a minimum price). Nearly all issues of marketable government or government-guaranteed bonds are made by way of public prospectuses, and so are many issues of debenture and preference stocks by established public companies which already have bonds or stocks quoted on British stock exchanges.

The first step is for the issuer, if he does not already have an issuing house, to consult his clearing banker or auditor as to which one to approach. The virtue of this, as against a 'do it yourself' with lawyer, accountant, and stockbroker, is that the issuing house provides an organization designed to deal with a large number of applications, to advise on the form of issue most likely to be successful under existing market conditions, and can assist in making the inevitable ancillary decisions which arise over terms of issue and would otherwise involve elaborate correspondence or frequent travel. The issuing house normally pays a visit to the company's plants, warehouses, or other physical assets and, if it is a large company making its first issue, usually arranges for an independent report by accountants, industrial consultants, and others. The report will deal with the history of the company, details of its business, factories and plant, management, labour, competitors, reasons for variation in profit margins, taxation, in addition to summarizing the accounts for the previous ten years. The benefit of outside accountants specializing in presentation of company affairs for issuing purposes is that they may bring out inconsistencies in methods of depreciation, stock valuations, categories of reserves, etc., often arising from past changes in management or financial methods. In short, answers must be ready for the most exacting investment manager of the most conservative Scottish investment trust.

On a basis of this the merchant bank can suggest the appropriate type of issue and its provisional terms. Once this is accepted, the prospectus and other documents, such as the share certificates themselves, will be drafted by the merchant bank with the assistance of lawyers acting for the company. The accountants will at the same time prepare another short report which will appear in the prospectus, as required by the Fourth Schedule to the Companies Act, 1948, covering the profits and dividends of previous years and the assets at the last balance sheet date. The Companies Act requires details of profits for five years, but the Stock Exchange has extended it to ten years. The Articles of Association will have to be re-examined and at the time of its first issue a wise company also considers what may be its future needs and longer-term capital structure.

Once the terms of the issue have been tentatively agreed, borrowers subject to capital issues control (which means all non-UK residents and United Kingdom local authorities) must theoretically apply to the Capital Issues Committee of the Treasury, directly in the case of the former, and in the latter through the Bank of England. Consent is required for any capital flotations which exceed £50,000 a year by borrowers subject to the control. For all borrowers raising £1,000,000 or over, the Bank of England has to approve the timing of the issue.

Approval of the Bank is required for the terms on which fixed interest issues are made by United Kingdom and Sterling Area authorities.*

The next step is likely to be a letter of application to the appropriate stock exchange, London, Scottish, or provincial, requesting a quotation for the security. Preliminary negotiations for this request are usually handled by the issuing house and the issuer's broker, and prior arrangements have to be made to secure the support of at least two jobbers who specialize in the particular category of share, while the stock exchange will require to be satisfied that the latter will be supplied with sufficient shares to create a free market. An advertisement containing all the information legally required in the prospectus must be published in two leading daily papers and circulated to the Exchange Telegraph and to Moody's Statistical Service. If there are no hitches, the time between a decision by a company to go ahead with an issue and the actual launching can be six to eight weeks.

The prospectus itself must contain the number, type, and price of the securities being offered, dates for the opening and closing of applications, and a summary of the issuer's business, history, and prospects. The object of the advertising is not only to attract subscriptions but serve as a formal statement that the requirements of the Companies Act and of the stock exchange have been met. In large issues it is common practice to arrange for an underwriter who will undertake for a commission to buy any securities left unsold. Should the underwriter be the merchant bank which is acting as issuing house, it will probably nominate a number of sub-underwriters, sometimes other merchant banks, but frequently investment trusts or insurance companies.

If the issue is oversubscribed, as any successful one should be, the issuing house makes the allotment of shares to the applicants. Preference is given to genuine investors in so far as they can be detected, and in the spirit of stock exchange rules for a free market, to applicants for a small number of securities. When a heavy subscription is expected for an issue, the issuing house may require the full price of the securities to be paid at the time of the application to discourage the notorious 'stags', i.e., speculators who apply for many times more shares than they require in the hope of reselling them at a profit once trading starts. This requires an issuing house to have a

---

* Appendix Seven is a short list of the legal and customary regulations and authorities to be observed in making an issue of shares.

department with a large experienced clerical staff to sort out the mass of – at times barely legible – requests and accompanying cheques. The fee payable to the receiving bank for dealing with tens of thousands of applications is one of the reasons for issue by prospectus being relatively expensive.

As far as the cost of the operation goes, for a public offer of £10 millions debenture stock, this might amount to 2·5 per cent or £250,000. The largest single item would be the commission paid to underwriters and this spread assumes a charge of 1·25 per cent or £125,000. Broker's commission and the fee of the issuing house would add another 0·75 per cent or £75,000. Additional costs include 0·10 per cent for stamp duty and one-eighth per cent to brokers and banks in respect of any stock they arrange to sell to their clients. Since it is customary for a proportion of a new issue to be sold without this help, brokerage is probably paid in most cases on about two-thirds of the issue. The London Stock Exchange quotation fee would cost £1,575 and the advertisements about £6,000. The balance of £25,000 covers printing costs (prospectus, application forms, letters of acceptance, trust deed, and share certificates), legal and accountancy fees, and payments to the receiving bankers. After these initial costs of flotation are met, the issuer could expect to pay about £3,000 annually to maintain the share register and £1,050 to the trustees; both these services can be conducted for him by his merchant bank.

However, without underwriting, in the case of a small company the total expenses would be about £10,000 as a floor and up to £20,000 or £30,000 for large companies. If the issuer chooses to raise capital by a private placing plus a quotation, the spread may amount to only 1·25 per cent of the funds raised. In such cases, seventy-five per cent of the shares offered are sold to clients of the merchant bank or broker, and the remaining twenty-five per cent are taken by the jobbers to the issue, for sale to members of the public who ask their own brokers to buy for them. No basis of allotment is published but, on the assumption that the minimum figure is met, the charges are sharply reduced as selling arrangements are limited to the portion of the issue made available to the market. Almost seventy per cent of the cost of the flotation would go to the issuing house as its fee for assisting the issuer. Although the cost of private placings is much less than those for underwritten issues, the advantage is to some extent offset by the reluctance of brokers to put their names down on a jobber's list and so commit themselves to buying shares before they have seen a company's balance sheet and financial record. The technique can be used only in connection with relatively small issues, under £3,000,000 for example.

Combinations are possible. The objections to private placings can be met by combining them with quotations. It has in the past been possible to combine a sale of shares by the main shareholders with the raising of new money, provided that the total number of shares offered is at least twenty-five per cent of the capital, therby taking the company out of the surtax net.* If shares are already held by persons outside the partners or family, the Stock Exchange may agree to a smaller number of shares being offered. It has usually been through such agreements that merchant banks have arranged for their associated trusts and holding companies, as well as their clients, to make profitable long-term acquisitions. After a company has gone public it can increase its issued capital by means of bonus shares and rights issues. The merchant bank can advise in the documentation and size of the bonus but a rights issue will probably be underwritten and the applications and the cash received by the merchant bank.

An introduction requires no legal prospectus: this applies when shares are widely held before quotation and no new shares are in fact offered for sale, although the sponsors may ensure that stock is available to meet any resulting increased demand. Before giving permission for the quotation, the Stock Exchange requires an advertisement giving full details of the company and containing all the information which would have been required for an offer for sale. Except in the case of large foreign companies whose shares are traded internationally, introductions are rare in London although the practice is more widespread in the Scottish Stock Exchange, the Northern Stock Exchange and the Midlands and Western Stock Exchange, as local companies reach a stage when a quotation becomes worthwhile.

---

* A private company is usually liable to a surtax direction under section 245 of the Income Tax Act, 1952, but exemption is obtained from this if 25 per cent of the shares are held by the public following a quotation. Although there are disadvantages in the uncertainty as to whether a direction might be made, there is not necessarily much saving in surtax by going public, as the dividend which would be expected by the public will normally take at least as high a proportion of profits as would be acceptable to the Special Commissioners.

The 1965 Finance Bill, as it emerged from debate, accepts that the definition of a 'close' company will not apply to any quoted company where at least 35 per cent of the voting power is held by the public. Shares not considered to be held by the public will be those in the hands of a director or his associates, or companies controlled by directors or their associates.

Some 2010 applications for quotation were granted by the Council of the London Stock Exchange* for a total nominal value of £5,719 millions in the year ended 31 March 1970. Of this total £1,850 millions related to British Government Stocks handled by the Bank of England, £441 millions related to local and county councils, public boards and foreign bonds, and £3,428 millions to company securities. The total nominal value of new quotations includes securities which may not necessarily have changed hands, securities which have been transferred from one set of owners to another set of owners, and securities issued in exchange for some other assets, as well as securities which have been issued to raise *new* money for undertakings. Although quotations in commercial and industrial securities were granted to the tune of £3,428 millions, the *new* money received therefrom by companies was only £456 millions and of this only £409 millions was received by companies registered and managed within the United Kingdom. Companies raised about £199 millions by the issue of share capital and £210 millions by the issue of loan capital.

The Midland Bank Economics Department compiles statistics for new money raised by the issue of securities with a stock exchange quotation in the United Kingdom as a whole (but excluding borrowings by the British Government.) New money raised in the calendar years 1919 to 1930 varied between £203 millions and £384 millions, from 1931 to 1939 between £66 millions and £217 millions, from 1940 to 1945 between £2 millions and £20 millions, from 1946 to 1951 between £130 millions and £312 millions, from 1952 to 1960 between £296 millions and £567 millions, and from 1962 to 1970 between £507 millions and £864 millions. In 1970 £539 millions of new money was raised, £157 millions for local councils and public boards, and £382 millions for companies. Of the £382 millions of new money for companies, £52 millions was raised as share capital and £330 millions as loan capital.

The apparatus at the disposal of the London issue market for this total of operations consists of fifty-five members of the Issuing Houses Association, together with certain large firms of stockbrokers specializing in issue work. Beyond this is a wide fringe of issuing groups, often describing themselves as 'merchant banks' or 'investment bankers', generally associated with specific stockbrokers or financial promoters or formed to handle the issue business of some particular

* From *Statistics Relating to Securities Quoted* published annually by the Stock Exchange, London, EC2.

101

holding company. Most of the members of the Issuing Houses Association act at the same time as company registrars, providing the massive records and clerical staff for the registration of share ownership, recording of transfers, and sales.* The secretariat of the Association itself is small and shares the personnel and offices of the Accepting Houses Committee, housed in the Kleinwort, Benson building; but it is highly experienced and has the task of ensuring that circulars and directives are drawn to the attention of all members and that formal liaison channels exist to the Stock Exchange, the Bank of England, the Board of Trade, and all professional bodies who in any way may be concerned with aspects of share issuing.

An issuing house carries the formal responsibility of ensuring that the vendors of private companies receive proper terms in a new flotation, and for the benefit of the investing public have sought to establish by all reasonable means that the issue price is justified by long-term prospects. The final decision over the method of marketing new shares lies, however, with the Quotations Department of the Stock Exchange, with whom the issuing house has to establish a time-table as well as acting as co-ordinator for the work of the lawyers, valuers, industrial consultants, and others. The proud boast of City leaders – by no means unanimously echoed by the investing public and less committed experts – is that the policing of the London capital market through customary co-operation of issuing houses and the Stock Exchange is achieved at less expense and with greater effectiveness than by vesting such functions in a statutory body similar to the United States Securities and Exchange Commission.

The formal constitution of the London issue market is comparatively recent. The post-war need for capital and the growth of issue work brought home to senior investment banks and investment houses the need to speak with one voice on all matters of principle. The one thing they all wished to avoid was the repetition of the 'bucket shop' scandals of the post-World War One era. After the Issuing Houses Association was formed in November 1945, the first Chairman was, appropriately enough, the late Mr Lionel Fraser of Helbert Wagg, a merchant bank which had in the 'twenties successfully handled some of the first major industrial issues and foreign reconstruction loans; between the wars Mr Alfred Wagg was the outstanding figure among share issue experts. The first Vice-Chairman was Lord Bicester of Morgan Grenfell. Although there

* Appendix Six contains the list of members.

were growing pains over the initial exclusion of what were called 'West End issuing houses', little by little the Association asserted its authority and standing, a process made easier during the late 'forties and 'fifties by the amalgamations among issuing houses aimed at reducing overheads and concentrating the somewhat sparse talent and experience.

The importance of gauging the issue price was apparent during the 'fifties. For an expanding successful company it can be crucial, as the market value of its shares in relation to other companies is a decisive factor in determining whether it can make fresh acquisitions by offering shares, on terms it can amalgamate or merge with other companies in the same or related fields of business. For example, the market value of Rank Organisation shares in 1962 was £27 millions, but two years later Ranks were able to bid £30 millions for the Mecca chain. This was only possible because of the rise of Rank 'A' shares from the equivalent of eleven shillings to thirty-seven shillings at the time of the bid, a price based on the market's assessment of the company's potential. By the same token the sharp drop in share values at the end of 1964 put paid for a time to company expansion by acquisitions and recapitalizations.

Mergers and Take-overs

The needs of companies and industries for guidance on and assessment of financial factors which are neither under their own direct control nor directly related to their daily functioning and efficiency have been responsible for merchant banks being called in to provide outside advice on capital reorganization and mergers. Not all of them welcomed the limelight in the luridly written-up 'take-over' bids of the late 'fifties and early 'sixties. They were merely carrying out their professional task of ensuring the proper conduct of transactions 'which have as their object the transfer of the control of a company out of the hands of its existing shareholders into new hands'.* They

* The quotation is from *Revised Notes on Company Amalgamations and Mergers*, a 1962 edition of a booklet first issued in 1959 at the suggestion of the Governor of the Bank of England by the Issuing Houses Association in cooperation with the Accepting Houses Committee, the Association of Investment Trusts, the British Insurance Association, the Committe of London Clearing Bankers, and the Stock Exchange. The original notes were intended as a general guide but since then the Board of Trade under the Prevention of Fraud (Investment) Act, 1958, has set out

had been given the responsibility on behalf of their clients of ascertaining that, if a formal offer was being made, the basic requirements set out in the Licensed Dealers (Conduct of Business) Rules, 1960, were satisfied.*

A Panel on Take-overs and Mergers was established in September 1967. The Take-over Panel makes itself available for consultation at any stage – even before a formal offer is made. Its Code contains both general principles and rules. The general principles are based upon a concept of equity between one shareholder and another and indicate at least some of the natural limitations of a company's freedom of action beyond which the board could all too easily attract the wrong sort of publicity. For instance the Code states as a general principle that shareholders shall have in their possession sufficient evidence, facts and opinions upon which an adequate judgement and decision can be reached, and shall have sufficient time to make an assessment and decision. No relevant information shall be withheld from them. As a general principle, any document or advertisement addressed to shareholders containing information, opinions or recommendations from the Board of an offeror or offeree company or its respective advisers shall be treated with the same standards of care as if it were a prospectus within the meaning of the Companies Act 1948. Especial care shall be taken over profit forecasts. Some of the rules are closely defined as for example Rule 2, which states that if the offer or an approach with a view to an offer being made is not made by the principal, the identity of the principal must be disclosed at the outset, or Rule 3 which states that a board so approached is entitled to be satisfied that the offeror company is or will be in a position to implement the offer in full. Other rules offer more general guidance, such as Rule 10 which states that directors whose shareholdings, together with those of their families and trusts, effectively control a company, or shareholders in that position who are represented on the Board of a company, and who contemplate transferring control, should not, other than in special circumstances, do so unless the buyer

---

further rules mentioned in this chapter. A Panel on Take-overs and Mergers was established in September 1967 on the proposal of the Governor of the Bank of England and the Panel's office is presently located at the Stock Exchange, London, EC2. The Panel supervises the *City Code on Take-overs and Mergers* which was prepared and issued by the City working party originally set up in 1959 and reconvened by the Governor in 1967. Copies of the *City Code* may be obtained from the Secretary, Issuing Houses Association, 20 Fenchurch Street, London, EC3.

* SI 1960, No. 1216.

undertakes to extend within a reasonable period of time a comparable offer to the holders of the remaining equity share capital, whether such capital carries voting rights or not. In such special circumstances the Panel must be consulted in advance and its consent obtained. One of the general principles of the Code is that a board which receives an offer or is approached with a view to an offer being made should normally in the interests of its shareholders seek competent outside advice, a point which had already been made by the Issuing Houses in their Notes.

For a 'take-over bid' is basically an offer to shareholders, who must in equity be able to make their decisions on an equal footing and with equal knowledge of the facts. The holders of different classes of share and loan capital of the companies involved in such transactions have their own legal rights which require equal consideration by the boards. A board of directors is obviously the best channel of approach and *should* be the best source of advice to the shareholders. The first rule of the City Code therefore states that the offer should be put forward in the first instance to the board of the offeree company or to its advisers.

The sound business reasons for making a bid come under five general headings. The purchasing company may have unused manufacturing capacity which it can put to use by taking over the production of its new acquisition: the latter's factory can be sold thereby reducing the net purchase price still further. On the other hand, the purchaser may himself be short of manufacturing space and, particularly in view of Board of Trade regulations as to where he may build or extend his existing plants, the quickest and easiest solution is to buy the shares of another company with a suitable factory. An important factor has often been the economies which can be achieved by bulk buying – as in the retail trade – or joint selling, particularly in sales promotion expenses, and this motive has generally prompted post-war horizontal mergers of enterprises in similar trades. The fourth reason for bidding is when a company establishes that either its supplier or its customer is making a comparatively large profit and acquires it so that the group as a whole can benefit from vertical integration. Finally, acquisitions are made to buy up or eliminate competitors.

There should, therefore, be no melodrama about take-over proceedings nor mysterious behind-the-scenes manipulations by either principals or advisers. The dramas to a great extent originated in the conditions of dividend restriction when shares were unduly cheap in relation to earnings, and certain financiers, of whom one of the more prominent was Mr Charles Clore, discovered companies where the assets were not fully employed and could be readily realized for cash, and in view of low market prices were able to buy control very cheaply. In addition, the Issuing Houses themselves have stressed the importance of maintaining secrecy during the period of preliminary talks and before a formal offer is made. This is to avoid disturbance in the normal price level of shares. Once it becomes likely that an offer will be forthcoming, however, an announcement should not be delayed and, if there are signs that normal market prices are being disturbed, a preliminary statement should be issued. Joint statements, even setting out the disagreements of the 'offerer' and offeree', are desirable and the Board of Trade in turn stresses that the bidder should not make a unilateral announcement before the other party has had time to decide its proper attitude. Normally the prior approval of the Board of Trade is required unless communications which might fall within the ambit of section 14 of the Prevention of Fraud (Investments) Act, 1958, are made through channels which would be regarded under law as 'authorized'.

Here the 'principles and practices' require that boards of both offerer and offeree ensure that their shareholders are in a position to judge freely for themselves whether their interests have been taken fully into consideration. 'A Board should consider whether, in the interests of shareholders, it should seek competent outside advice,' say the Issuing Houses' Notes. The importance of outside financial advice becomes readily apparent if a board is faced with more than one offer as happened in some of the major post-war competing bids as, for example, that involving Kemsley Press, Odhams, and Thomson. The merchant banks can on such occasions undertake the drafting of documents which may follow each other in rapid succession, and send out the actual offer, thereby avoiding the necessity to submit a mass of paper to the Board of Trade. The sooner the documents can be issued the better, as the shareholders have a right to know when a serious and responsible offer has been made, and boards should be ready to facilitate direct approaches to them so that they can hear the case themselves. However, the importance of impartiality and of outside advice needs no underlining.

The first step to be taken by any outside adviser is to determine whether the offer bears any valid relation to the 'real' value of the assets and, even if these are evaluated annually for balance sheet purposes, the task of the financial adviser is to re-examine them afresh within the framework of the offer. This covers such points as how inventories are drawn up, i.e., at cost or at valuation, and how sales values and depreciation scales are determined; land values, trade investments, realizability of securities and the dates of the next dividend coupons, impending payments and payments due, categories of debt, unissued shares, and the goodwill element in capital reserves – all these come into the appraisal. The basis of making up the companies' annual books may have been changed without the individual items having been re-examined and reassessed and, if the intangibles of business prospects are reconsidered, the whole outcome of an outside investigation may look very different from the picture presented at the last annual general meeting, not because of any motive of deception or concealment but because the circumstances of a bid are of a completely different order. The experience gained by a merchant bank preparing reports for share prospectuses becomes invaluable in this role.

As important for the shareholders as an outside impartial re-appraisal of their companies' assets is their ability to keep abreast of the ownership of effective controlling interests. Controlling shareholders who are directors have a duty to consider the position of other shareholders, not only at the time of an acquisition but at a later date, if changes in the share categories are being made by a successful offerer. The difficulty of maintaining the canons of take-over conduct rules were well illustrated during the battle in the late summer of 1964 over the footwear firm of W. Barratt. The unsuccessful bid by S. Phillips Shoes and Town and Commercial Properties, advised by Rothschilds, had valued a Barratt voting share at three shillings premium over the voteless 'A' and the market took due note; 'A' shareholders – had the offer been accepted – could rightly have complained that their shares were being treated at a discount. The Stylo Shoes bid for the company, partly in shares and partly in cash, of 18s 7½d for voting ordinaries and 16s 7d for non-voting 'A', was accepted by the key share-holding group of the Barratt pension fund, although a third bid for Clore's British Shoe Corporation was 22s for the ordinaries and 21s 6d for 'A' shares. The Barratt decision was justified by concern for their employees. BSC weakened their case by inviting the trustees of the pension fund to state the lowest cash price they would accept, indicating that this would not be available to other shareholders. Rightly enough, S. G. Warburg, advising Barratt, commented that it was 'most unusual and improper' to make such an offer, and when the pension fund consequently rejected it, Clore declared his intention of requesting the Stock Exchange Council to refuse permission to deal in the new Stylo shares needed to implement the merger. The Stock Exchange could only comment that its interventions were limited to cases where relevant information was withheld by the company. Having received acceptances of over fifty per cent of Barratt shareholders, the Stylo board went on to make its own company virtually bid-proof by increasing the voting rights of management shares so that the proportion would not fall after the merger, compensating shareholders for the reduction in their voting power by preparing to offer them a one-for-twenty scrip issue. On BSC initiative an attempt was made to challenge this in the courts, but was unsuccessful.

There were thus several breaches of the spirit if not the letter of the codes of respect for shareholders' interests, in particular the Stylo board's proposal to increase the votings and the somewhat cavalier treatment of BSC's reassurances on staff welfare. However, the Clore tactics justified Warburg's description, notably when a member of the BSC was quoted in the Press as saying: 'We do not have to observe the Queensberry rules. We are going in for all-in wrestling.'* What Clore's advisers, M. Samuel and Co., may have thought as they sent out circulars on his behalf is not, of course, on record, but some error of taste, if not of judgement, was evident in view of the fact that it was only a few months previously that Clore had been successfully challenged by the minority shareholders of British Shoe Corporation, led by the sturdy-minded Glasgow stockbroker, Mr Herbert Waddell, when an attempt was made to substitute their voting ordinaries by Sears non-voting 'A' ordinaries. In the absence of laws a sense of the proprieties is doubly important, and so too is the role of financial advisers in reminding all parties of the code. The Shareholders Protection Committee, in which Mr Waddell played the leading part, pointed out in their circular that no independent outside advice had been sought or given.†

There may, of course, be no opportunity to make formal offers to shareholders during contested bids where the situation is changing rapidly, as when the offerer is supporting his bid by purchases in the market, thus at the same time affecting the fundamental situation in

---

*The Guardian, 5 September 1964.

† This circular, sent out by Maclelland, Moores & Co., on 2 March 1964, is a model defence of a shareholder's position and rights.

which the shareholders have to judge whether or not to accept. The Issuing Houses' code therefore requires that if buying is taking place against such a background the offerer must without delay make a formal offer to the uncommitted shareholders at fair market prices. Nor should he attach special conditions to the purchase of shares of any class without making them available to all shareholders of that class. He must go further if he subsequently raises his offer price and make arrangements for all shareholders who have previously accepted his offer to receive the revised price.

Although the *Mirror*-Odhams contest of 1961 received maximum publicity, very largely because the Press itself was involved, the outcome did reflect a very strict regard for shareholders' interests. Odhams had already been broadening the basis of their operations in 1959 when they took over the Hulton Press and it seemed natural enough for the *Daily Mirror* to suggest to the Odhams Board in January 1961 that a merger would be advantageous to both. In rejecting the suggestion, Odhams turned to the then Mr Roy Thomson and together they announced a fifty-fifty arrangement. Challenging this the *Mirror* decided on a bid, lock stock and barrel, and made their appeal to the shareholders over the heads of the unwilling board. The offer was phrased to bear in mind the interests of all shareholders and a careful assessment was made of the profits which would result from the take-over. The final offer of five *Mirror* shares plus five shillings cash compares not unfavourably with the original offer of four and a half *Mirror* shares for each Odhams. Since the Odhams shares rose in value from 40s to 63s 6d, there certainly could have been no complaints.

The complications which can arise from making an unconditional offer illustrate the advisability of having an outside impartial guide. The calculation of future prospects, implied in the offer will be nullified if the total of acceptances received is much lower than the percentage figure named in the bid. This applies particularly when the consideration offered is in shares, and an offerer declaring his bid unconditional is under an obligation to disclose immediately the number of shares he has acquired and to keep his offer open for a reasonable period to allow uncommitted shareholders to make their decision. An 'unconditional' offerer consequently exposes his flank to counter-attack, as the board of ICI found to their cost in their abortive bid for Courtaulds and, in somewhat humiliating fashion, had to add fresh 'conditions' to the 'unconditional' so that Mr Paul

Chambers' 'Final, final, final!' resembled nothing so much as the Duce's pre-war *'Mai! Mai! Mai!'*

The ICI bid for Courtaulds, launched with inadequate assessment of the factors involved, was finally countered by Courtaulds revealing to their own shareholders the true value of their assets and increasing their distributions. It was a somewhat tardy, though fortunately not a death-bed, repentance. If a company which is the target for a bid has a clear idea of how it proposes to develop its assets, a defensive action is not difficult to plan, as when Watneys – advised by Barings – fended off the Clore attempt to take them over for the sake of their properties. The support of investors can be counted upon when directors make reasonable distributions of profits. Loan capital, even with the high rates of the 'sixties, is still cheaper than self-finance since the interest can be deducted before arriving at the profits liable to taxation. 'While it is proper to give reasonable protection to investors in the company's securities, the real security for these investors is the company's ability to make profits,' said Mr A. H. Carnwath, a managing director of Baring Brothers.* As he suggested: 'Before making decisions as to the amounts to be retained and the amounts to be distributed, boards of directors should apply to the investment of the amounts to be retained, quite as rigorous tests as they would apply when justifying the raising of fresh funds in the market or from their own shareholders.' The lesson has probably been learned and opportunities for 'stripping' companies are unlikely to be so frequent, while a too determined bidder may find to his cost that he has paid too high a price, as Tube Investments found with British Aluminium. Success or failure is thus not always – as the Press is too readily prone to represent – a question of who has taken over whom. The responsibility of the merchant banker is less to ensure that his client always wins but that he continues to make the best use of his resources. Some of the take-over 'victories' of the 'fifties proved in the narrowing industrial profit margins of the 'sixties to have been on the Pyrrhic side, and doubtless have been ruefully reconsidered in the boardrooms.

The Cautious Approach

The more cautious and open approach of latter-day bids – as against the legendary blow-by-blow behind-the-scenes contests of some years

* Address to International Banking Summer School at Oxford on 25 July 1964.

ago – is, perhaps, illustrated in the step-by-step offers made in 1964 by Trafalgar House for three other property companies, Consolidated London Properties, City and West End, and Metropolitan Properties. In its first abortive bid in November 1963 Trafalgar acquired a twenty-seven per cent holding in Consolidated London Properties and its two associates but, in the meantime, Capital and Counties, advised by Schroders, entered the field with their own bid for Consolidated. In June 1964 Trafalgar made a second move with a cash bid, backed by their bankers Kleinwort, Benson, for the remainder of the shares at sixpence more than their value estimated on the last valuation of the company's properties and 13s above the market price. But, as a result of cross-holdings by its first acquisition, it had raised its holdings by 9·4 per cent in City and West End and 7·7 per cent in Metropolitan. This situation had also been somewhat simplified by the repayment in the intervening period of the preference shares of the three companies which had been a complicating factor in the earlier bid.

The next step was a fresh offer of 48s for the one pound ordinary shares of City and West End, very close to their asset revaluation and some five shillings higher than the previous bid, at the same time offering an interim dividend to City holders. The directors of City recommended acceptance of the Trafalgar offer. The price was fair to City shareholders, and Trafalgar obtained the assets at a good discount and, in view of the anticipated dividend, could expect to cover its own outgoings on the money raised for its purchases. Since Trafalgar House's portfolio at the time of the first bid in June 1964 was worth only £2,700,000, the acquisition was in practice a reverse take-over since the company, without any increase in its equity, acquired a fresh portfolio of properties with both reversionary and development potential.

When, at the end of June, Capital and Counties Property Company on its side came out with a formal offer of 50s cash for the Consolidated London Properties holdings of City and West End, Metropolitan and Trafalgar itself, the three latter recommended acceptance and the bids for the property triplets finished up with Consolidated becoming part of Capital and Counties and City and West End of Trafalgar. Since Trafalgar thus owned thirty-five per cent of Metropolitan, and Capital and Counties about eight per cent, the stage was set for a final arrangement and, in the late summer of 1964, the intervention of a fourth party, the Freshwater Group of Companies, with a cash offer of 47s for the shares of Metropolitan enabled both Trafalgar and Consolidated to dispose of their holdings at a profit. So Trafalgar finished its take-over chapter not only having acquired the company of chief interest to it, but having made a useful profit of £458,000 from its other two tactical bids. The shareholders of all companies were at each stage given an opportunity of drawing clear comparisons on share prices and at no point were the terms such as to weaken the bidders. The merchant banking postscript to the whole operation was that Kleinwort, Benson, who at the time of the triple take-over bid were granted equity options in return for providing medium-term financial assistance, had these cancelled and received 150,000 shares in Trafalgar House and £150,000 in cash.

That shareholders are at times unable to make clear comparisons was illustrated, over the same period as the Trafalgar House bids, by the abortive attempts of Dufay Ltd and British Paints (Holdings) to obtain control of the share capital of Wailes Dove Bitumastic. British Paints offered cash plus nine of their ordinaries for eight of Wailes Dove while Dufay offered 25s cash. Since the latter's cash offer was conditional on a 'reverse bid' arrangement by which Wailes Dove would take over Dufay's paint division in exchange for 900,000 five shilling Wailes Dove shares and £100,000 cash, and that four out of seven Wailes Dove directors must be acceptable to Dufay, it was not surprising that the board of a £400,000 company should unanimously recommend the British Paints offer. On the advice of their advisers, Philip Hill, Higginson and Erlanger, they pointed out that on the estimated profits of both groups, after adjustment for a year's interest on the cash offer, the gross distributable earnings on £100 nominal of Wailes Dove shares would be about £27 11s. This would compare with £44 2s attributable to the ordinary stock of British Paints which an accepting holder of a hundred nominal Wailes Dove shares, would have received. However, on 27 June, after the expiry of their offer, the directors of British Paints (Holdings) had sadly to announce that as acceptances received up to the expiry time had not reached a satisfactory total, they had decided to let the offer lapse. In their view the failure was at least in part attributable to confusion. The sequel was an unsuccessful attempt by a group of Wailes Dove shareholders to remove four directors and demand explicit information on what had happened to the offer by Dufay, who had been advised by the merchant bank of P. P. Rodocanachi. The Chairman's reply probably left most of the shareholders still guessing. No doubt all the participants were doing their best in the light of what they conceived to be their responsibilities but the question which the simple soul among investors must ask is why such impossible or complicated offers were made.* The confusion also seemed to extend to the City itself.

Similar confusion seemed to surround the share exchange offer of the Rank Organisation, involving more than £30 millions, for the equity capital of Mecca on a basis of two 5s non-voting ordinary for each 5s voting ordinary in Mecca and five Rank non-voting for every six 5s non-voting Mecca ordinaries. Mecca shareholders would have been entitled to an interim dividend for the current financial year but the Rank 'A' shares offered them were not to participate in the Rank final dividend. At the time of the offer Mecca ordinary stood at 55s and the 'A' at 31s 3d so that the Rank bid valued them at 77s and 32s 1d respectively. The Chairman of the Mecca board, which controlled one million of 1,400,000 voting shares, in rejecting the offer said at their shareholders' meeting: 'What does this mean? A few shillings in paper money or values that fluctuate and which can disappear in a few hours on the Stock Exchange. . . . If this jewel is to be sold, it must be paid for in money we can understand, not something which will change its value before we receive it. If we are gambling in shares, which I am, then I prefer to gamble in Mecca.' While such sentiments demonstrated a touching faith in the kind of pound which the Bank of England promises to pay the bearer, they seemed for the investing public to reflect some quite unnecessary misunderstandings between participants in what was presumably a serious as well as important financial move.

Ideally, therefore, merchant banks prefer to come in at the earliest stage, and after studying the relative companies in detail, to be asked to make the offer on behalf of their clients, when they can get together with the financial advisers on the other side to find out whether the price is adequate and, if not, what would be. And, even if affairs are

---

* A sequel to the Dufay-Wailes Dove Bitumastic affair of 1964 came a year later with the news of the intended formation of a new company to take over all the issued capital of both as 'Dufay Bitumastic'. Under the terms announced on 28 June 1965, Wailes Dove holders were offered five shares of two shillings in the new company for every two shares owned, and Dufay holders six shares for every five. Prior consultation with institutional shareholders had indicated their acceptance. British Paints and the National Coal Board, advised by Schroder Wagg, came up somewhat belatedly with a bid of one 4s Ordinary and 16s cash for every two Wailes Dove shares. This worked out somewhat higher than the other offer. After buying W.D. shares in the market, where prices rose to 24s, Dufay was able on 20 July to announce control of Wailes Dove. This outcome certainly reflected firm guidance and careful handling by both Hill, Samuel and P. P. Rodocanachi.

arranged amicably as finally happened when ICI and Courtaulds agreed that the former should take over British Nylon Spinners, up to then owned fifty per cent by each, the presentation in June 1964 before the Chancery Division of the High Court of the 'Scheme of Arrangements' had to be supported by explanatory statements made in compliance with the Companies Act, 1948. The Courtaulds' shareholders were sent formal notification by Baring Brothers that in their capacity as financial advisers they had followed all stages of the consultations and had held their own discussions with the ICI advisers, Schroder Wagg, and recommended consequently that the proposals were fair and reasonable from the standpoint of both companies and their respective members. Since the disposal of the British Nylon Spinners' final dividend and the question of the use of the £10 millions ICI payment to Courtaulds were major questions for the shareholders, the courts rightly required an expert opinion. In arriving at their conclusion, Barings and Schroders were careful to stress that they had given more weight to the assessment of the commercial effect of the proposals on both companies than to comparisons of past earnings and market prices. Since the ICI chairman's circular to the ordinary shareholders may have appeared to some of the latter more like a declaration of faith than anything else the Schroder Wagg opinion came as a desirable reassurance.

Take-overs and mergers received less publicity in 1964 but the activity still continued. 'There is little to suggest that in 1963 and early 1964 there have been significantly fewer bids and deals than in earlier years,' says *Who Owns Whom* (UK Edition), 'but there have certainly been indications that defensive action has become more successful.'* The publication goes on to pay tribute to the merchant banks for playing a major part in educating companies in how to repel boarding parties. But it is also fair to say that directors and leading shareholding interests have become more alive to their responsibilities in this respect, although experience has also taught merchant banks new and effective ways of assisting their clients in countering unsought bids. The simplest method is to raise the value of the shares in the market beyond the price offered either by judicious purchases or often by the mere fact of publicity. The art of detecting attempts by the bidder to secure the shares by market purchases has also been refined. The target company can jump several moves ahead of the bidder by making their own revaluation of assets, by fresh long-term

* O.W. Roskill & Co., 1964.

114

estimates of future profits and forecast of dividends, and by hiving off subsidiaries or assets in which the bidder is particularly interested, and creating them as separate companies.

The remarks of the chairman of Mecca also underline a new factor in favour of the defence, namely, that since 1961 when the Stock Exchange witnessed its first great downward curve – apart from the Suez panic – a cash element is becoming a key element in most major bids. Although a share certificate in a first-class company is preferable over a number of years to a pound note in a cash box, the course of equity prices makes cash interesting for those who wish to have increased liquidity or at least some return on their holdings without necessarily relinquishing the shares. When in terms of present dividend yield and future prospects cash offers become attractive in comparison with market prices, the scope for the speculative 'stripper' is considerably reduced. Raising funds for legitimate take-over purposes also becomes tougher when share values drop: by November 1964, for example, Sears Holdings had seen the market value of their stock fall £64 millions from its peak while the Clore property company, City Centre, had suffered a market fall of £50 millions. Any merchant bank which is asked nowadays to provide short- or medium-term funds for company acquisitions as well as act as adviser, is thus more likely to find itself playing the role of gentle counsellor than that of tough bargainer. It may be that the Labour Party's preference for forms of taxation which encourage companies to hold back profits and build up 'hidden' assets will, in the 'seventies, again create an approximation of the technical conditions which started the take-over wave of the 'fifties. Would-be reformers tend to suffer from history's most recurrent phenomenon – the paradox of unintended consequences.

Questions of Public Interest

In the meantime both public and politicians have become more sensitive to the social implications of take-overs. The publicity and political agitation over mergers resulted in great part from the direct effect on share prices. They have, of course, brought both negative and positive benefits. Whatever the motives of some of the bidders, they did disturb the complacent financial ultra-conservatism of many boardrooms, and forced directors to re-examine the tradition, too widespread in Britain, of withholding maximum information from shareholders and setting their own convenience higher than the need to carry out periodic radical rethinking of where their companies were heading. It is somewhat disturbing that only as a consequence of professional bidders were shareholders in some of the biggest British companies able to learn of the true state of assets and of accumulated reserves far in excess of their market capitalization. The total of idle or under-used capital thus represented is in itself a side-light on the inadequate rate of investment which underlies the lagging British industrial growth rate.

The positive side of the mergers has been the creation of larger manufacturing and commercial units better able to carry rising overheads and to meet the heavy cost of research and development essential if British industry is to remain competitive at home and abroad. The most recent, and long overdue, amalgamations of this nature have been in the Lancashire cotton industry, where only large units, or even wholesale integration from mill to retail counter, can keep it competitive in the face of world-wide rivalry. A noteworthy example in 1964 was Courtaulds' acquisition of the ordinary stock of Fine Spinners and Doublers and Lancashire Cotton Corporation which, after major rationalization, will operate as part of the Courtauld group. In view of the strong financial position of Lancashire Cotton at the time, the long negotiations, conducted with Kleinwort, Benson and Baring Brothers acting as consultants, resulted in the Courtauld offer including a substantial cash element of seven pounds for every four shares in addition to the substitution of ordinary stock on a one-for-one basis at 54s 6d; Courtaulds' stock at the time was worth 82s per share.

Equally important for Lancashire was the Calico Printers' Association bid – also in July 1964 – for the Manchester-based mail order house of Oxendale. CPA shareholders had probably been more aware than most investors over the past three decades of the highly cyclical nature of profits in textile printing, and the post-war diversification and reconstruction of the group, which involved it in streamlining as much as in acquisitions, aimed at giving it an offsetting stake in stores, fashion shops, and steady mail order markets, particularly before the royalties on the Terylene licence and patents ran off. Here Kleinwort, Benson as advisers had to work out an elaborate scale of sub-offers to ensure that a parity principle was observed for all categories of shareholders, viz. one Calico Ordinary and 10s cash for every two Oxendale Deferred, eleven Calico $5\frac{1}{4}$ per cent Preference for every ten $5\frac{1}{2}$ per cent Preference of Oxendale, while to provide an exchange offer to holders of Oxendale's ten per cent Preferred Ordinary, a new Calico $7\frac{1}{2}$ per cent Second Cumulative Preference class was created to be offered on a basis of eleven for eight.

Yet, out of this complicated capital restructuring procedure came fresh hopes for Lancashire's traditional skills. Far from this being regarded as 'a plot of the bosses', the Northern Counties Textile Trades' Federation, representing 100,000 textile workers, said in its 1964 annual report, that mergers in the industry should have taken place years ago. As Mr Nicholas Stacey of Chesham Amalgamations, which specializes as an adviser on mergers, said in a Birmingham University Production Course: 'In countries where the number of large companies is increasing, growth and prosperity of the national economy is more apparent than in countries where the number of large companies has remained static or declined.'*

Concentration of financial power for its own sake and the deliberate policy of excluding investors from their legitimate say in company affairs are, however, indefensible. When successful bidders, having secured control of enterprises, proceed to offer non-voting shares in their financial holding companies in exchange for the ordinaries of companies they have taken over, the general public interest is clearly involved. It should be no business of responsible City houses to further this process and, if the merchant banks are taking seriously their role as investment managers, often for large institutions and pension funds, they too should be taking a long-term view and considering how a thoroughly objectionable practice by any standard can be blocked and past damage remedied. Even in the case of the Rootes' tie-up with Chrysler in June 1964, the breach of the code on the wholesale issue of non-voting shares was not justified – as Rootes' advisers, Lazards, claimed – 'because this is the only way it can operate to ensure that control stays in the United Kingdom'. If American investment in Britain is desirable, so is the continuation of democratic control.

Proposed mergers and take-overs may be held up under the Monopolies and Restrictive Practices (Inquiry and Control) Act

* 25 November 1964.

117

1948, as amended by the Monopolies and Mergers Act 1965. The Board of Trade continued to scrutinise mergers as they arose until this function was transferred to the Department of Employment and Productivity under the general governmental re-organization announced on 28 October 1969. The Board (and subsequently the Department) had to consider whether a merger fell within the scope of that legislation, and if so whether there might be a *prima facie* case for referring it to the Monopolies Commission. During 1969 the Board and DEP examined in this context some 110 mergers or proposed mergers and four cases were referred to the Monopolies Commission for investigation and report. Responsibility for government policy towards monopolies and mergers was transferred to the Department of Trade and Industry in the autumn of 1970.

So, apart from straightforward cases where an offerer pays cash for his acquisition from a willing offeree, take-over bids raise issues requiring more than an accountant's estimate of total assets and some legal assistance in drafting. The aptitude for the varied tasks involved is something which can only be acquired in the school of experience. The training necessary to read a balance sheet, an ability to spot important points in Articles of Association, an understanding of the elements of company law, and of the rules and guidance of the Board of Trade and the Issuing Houses Association, the habit of working out percentages and parities – these form the basic equipment which can and has to be learned during a young banker's apprenticeship. But all the rest is experience gained from one type of bid or merger to another. The general range of situations can be set out on paper but each will have its special aspect. A sense of how the market will react is only acquired over years and a feeling for when to call in a specialist – legal or actuarial – is probably more important than trying to be a specialist oneself.

In both issue and merger work the number one requirement is a sensitivity for men and affairs, an ability to recognize human strengths and weaknesses while keeping one's own counsel about the character of the people one is dealing with, who after all are rarely complete strangers to each other. Offers do not take place in a vacuum but in a financial and commercial setting where extraneous trading and industrial factors will eventually determine whether it was all worth it. Whether the aptitude, once aquired, will stimulate breadth of outlook in a merchant banker and set him on his own feet as a creative financier, or whether he will develop into a somewhat slick technician, hoping perhaps for pickings and favours from the personalities whose ambitions he has to serve, will depend on his own strength of character.

The Specialist Issuing Houses

This personality problem is one which particularly concerns the specialist issuing houses since they cannot offer the same wide variety of experience as the larger merchant banks. Some of them indeed figure in the financial pages of the daily press as frequently as the accepting houses, both the well-established ones such as Minster Trust dating from 1928 or new arrivals like Gresham Trust, founded in 1959. The story of Minster is one of growth and expansion: it was incorporated with a capital of £550 to manage an investment trust set up by Mr Austin B. Ferguson, still the present Chairman, and constituted in 1930 as an issuing house. Minster's interests now include three insurance companies, some £25 millions of managed investment funds, and a full 'after sales service' for its clients, including experts in take-overs and mergers. But while Minster can offer scope for wide experience and initiative in its special field of nursing small and medium-sized firms through critical expansion stages, the smaller issuing houses, skilled though they may be in basic techniques, have smaller opportunities in the first place.

Mr Charles Forte's reliance on Ocean Trust and on the Clydesdale Bank which helped him in humbler days in Glasgow may well be the result of failures in the merchant banking world to identify the small man with a future. The amalgamations of issuing houses during the 'forties and 'fifties doubtless added to their efficiency and profitability, but they may thereby have lost their more intimate touch and left a gap which in the 'sixties was being filled by new creations such as Mounthall Securities, founded by Mr John D. Robertshaw with the backing of stockbrokers, investment trusts, and accountants, and merged with Edward Bates – a partnership founded in Bombay in 1839 and in Liverpool in 1848, and turned into a limited company in 1962 – to form Edward Bates, Mounthall Ltd in 1967. The shares of the holding company, Edward Bates and sons (Holdings), were acquired by Atlantic Assets in 1970 in exchange for some of its own shares. Edward Bates maintains offices in London, Liverpool and Edinburgh, and a representative in Swansea. With the Hodge group

119

banking and issue work are dealt with by separate companies but, as Mr Julian S. Hodge puts it: 'In our case the actual issue is done by Gwent and West of England Enterprises Limited, but this is only because historically the latter Company obtained a Dealers' Licence from the Board of Trade before we had started Julian S. Hodge and Company Limited. For practical purposes the two Companies work together on New Issue work.'*

The needs which have brought the newer issuing houses into being exist mainly in new expanding industrial areas outside London, where firms requiring capital may be put off by some of the more irritating affectations of City institutions and may therefore be ready to turn to a man on the spot. Although many of Britain's economic and financial innovations derived from the Northern Kingdom, Scotland has since 1918 sadly neglected its own capital investment. The National and Commercial Banking Group has issuing house facilities available through Williams, Glyn & Co, the British Bank of Commerce has a connection with Seton Trust in London, and Edward Bates has issue facilities through Edward Bates, Mounthall. The Scottish issuing house, Glasgow Industrial Finance, was acquired by Industrial and Commercial Finance Corporation – a creation of the Scottish and English clearing banks – and renamed Scottish Industrial Finance.

Scottish Industrial Finance had in fact their first taste of take-over battle tactics by acting as formal financial advisers to Sir Hugh Fraser in his successful counter-bid against Lord Thomson for George Outram & Co. In practice, the battle – such as it was – was lost for Thomson at the beginning for his initial bid was dismissed as ridiculously low by the key Scottish investment groups. By the time they had examined the Outram situation and prospects, and as long-term investors they had no particular interest in realizing their investments, they were quite as ready as Lord Thomson and Sir Hugh to wait until future reorganization of the Glasgow press brought Outram's assets and profitability up to the later levels of the bids. To this was added a sense of virtue that they had somehow struck a blow for Scotland.

In the English provinces an active secondary issuing centre is developing in Birmingham with its surrounding complex of companies manufacturing complete equipment and components for the new techniques of the twentieth century. The locally established

* Interview with author, 1 May 1965.

issuing houses are Neville Industrial Securities and Midland Industrial Issues. Some London merchant banks also have offices in Birmingham and elsewhere in the provinces which may go part-way towards meeting the need of small companies for an adequate capital financing mechanism, particularly for those endeavouring to market and develop new techniques.

This was the opportunity which Julian S. Hodge has endeavoured to seize:

A very large public company can capitalize on its fixed assets by a mortgage debenture, but the smaller company finds it virtually impossible to find a market for any facility for a period of more than five years. At any given time, if money is relatively plentiful, there may be a few insurance companies prepared to grant mortgages on shops, factories and offices over a twenty or twenty-five year period, but such facilities are confined to two-thirds of the valuation of the property. I think the City goes a long way to meet these needs, but I also think that it ought to reach out to the provinces and get a more intimate understanding of local requirements, and this it might do best, perhaps, by co-operating with regional merchant banks.*

The Industrial and Commercial Finance Corporation with net equity assets of £51 millions in the 1970 balance sheet has borrowed some £81 millions by issuing debenture and unsecured loan stocks in its own name in an effort to make advances to and take investments in small and medium-sized firms. The ability of the ICFC to sell its quoted investments is limited by the size of the investment in individual companies, by undertakings which have been given in a number of cases as to the disposal of shares, and by market conditions. The lesson is that the public, either as individuals or through institutional savings, remains the main provider of risk capital, and that competition in the issuing world serves investors as much as companies. Indeed, one of the main features of the past ten years has been a noticeable loosening of client-merchant bank relationship, customers transferring from one bank to another in search of more efficient service, or continuing to use one bank for issuing business and turning to another for acceptance credits, and even contacting a third to make use of its particular speciality at home or abroad. The issue field has been the most fluid in this respect and the older accepting houses have risen to the challenge of proving to their long-standing top clients that they can service their capital require-

* *Ibid.*

121

ments and that they have survived the main test of modernity and flexibility of merchant banking. Indeed, for Julian Hodge it is the key: 'Once a merchant bank gets to the size where it cannot give personal attention to problems at principal level, it will lose some of the advantages normally associated with its somewhat specialized functions.'*

Lending 'A Good Name'

The service which merchant bankers offer and which so far has proved difficult for clearing banks and their subsidiaries to assume, is that of the role of financial 'father confessor', or as they prefer to put it, 'financial adviser', even to quite small firms. Instead of being consulted only when a special move, such as an issue or amalgamation is afoot, the merchant banks, if they have established a true relationship of confidence with their clients, find themselves constantly in touch with them, advising them perhaps on some foreign development, discussing some such contingency as the sudden decease or impending retirement of a family partner, looking over the pension fund investment portfolio, arranging a mortgage on factory premises with an insurance company, considering a share option scheme for employees. The small size of the merchant bank and the personal touch it is still able to maintain are here the main factors. An issuing house alone cannot offer the range of services, and while in theory the clearing bank can cover most of them, in practice it cannot do so with the same speed and informality. Not all the London accepting houses have brought themselves to the point of unbending sufficiently to see that in an era of bigness, one of their future tasks may be the cultivation of smallness. But at least most of them pay lip-service to the thought, and their services are available as financial advisers – notably Guinness Mahon & Co. – and 'experts' on how small companies can obtain the best return on existing capital, improve their liquidity, and expand by acquisition.

How 'expert' they prove to be in practice varies, and they thereby expose their own flanks when differences or difficulties arise over companies or industrial groups with whom they are associated in the public eye. The parting of the ways between Mercury Securities and the Minerals Separation in April 1964 naturally aroused curiosity

* *Ibid.*

after a period of active collaboration and joint promotion ventures. It would be surprising if, in a changing world, commercial and banking interests coincided at all points, and when in the early 'sixties 'Minseps' started selling off its Mercury holdings – wisely as it turned out as the share price dropped from 90s in 1961 to 49s in April 1964 – it was only doing what a judicious investment trust would have felt about merchant banking shares at the time. In the euphoric period of North American property ventures, the names of City Centre Properties and Philip Hill were happily coupled in the Press, but by 1964 the banking subsidiary of the latter was at pains to explain that it itself had no special holding in CCP, although it was obvious that the Philip Hill group as a whole had no option but to participate in the task of re-examining the management in order to safeguard its own and its client's investments.

Thus, in advancing into industrial promotion work and taking holdings in companies they have helped to launch, the merchant banks have to consider how far this reacts against the neutral and impartial role they must be seen to play in other banking and investment matters. In the public eye a merchant bank has only one good name, as was shown by the reaction to the collapse of Rolls-Razor; for, whatever the present statutory and customary definitions of an issuing house's responsibilities, no City institution will be able to dissociate itself from a venture to which it had once lent its name. Kleinwort, Benson who floated the Rolls shares when they returned to the market in 1962 treated the issue as essentially a speculative venture and offered it by tender. But, although they were not engaged by the company as their financial advisers, they acted on a second occasion for Rolls-Razor in the acquisition of a sixty-five per cent holding in Bylock Engineering and, when the crash came, their name was inevitably involved. Similarly, the brokers to the company, Fenn and Crosthwaite, although their functions were limited to carrying out share operations at request, found themselves reminded in the Press of one of their 1962 circulars in which the Chairmen of Rolls-Razor and Pressed Steel, Messrs Reader-Harris and Alex Abel-Smith, and Sir Isaac Wolfson as Chairman of Drages, were quoted as saying that the company was operating successfully and was highly solvent. Clearly a merchant bank, like any other bank, cannot reveal its views or make public statements about its clients, past and present, while to make formal requests for official investigations into the affairs of companies which are believed to be facing

123

difficulties might spell a death blow to a perfectly sound enterprise which was merely passing through a temporary trading phase.

It was, however, because of their very commitment that the merchant banks played a key role in opening up the overseas world to European endeavour. A deliberate choice now faces them. If, as many of them have apparently chosen, they propose to play the part of active partners in big groupings, this must be with the full anticipation of the consequences of seeming to lose their neutral status. There will be many compensations, especially for the medium-sized houses. The larger may have sufficient assets under their immediate control to maintain independence and to exert a wider influence through their management of large-scale portfolio investment. On the other hand, the Hambro family interests over several continents are now so extensive that the bank acquires the prestige of something akin to ascendancy rather than neutrality, of being above the struggle: as with the strong everywhere, their services are sought for their support.

By lending their good name for the placing of smaller issues to be held by the purchaser for a number of years, the merchant banker can also help to reduce the high yield normally demanded by institutions for unquoted issues. The merit of Close Brothers and Keyser Ullmann in this field is unquestioned, even if the concept of 'banking assets' has thereby become somewhat stretched. One solution, adopted a number of years ago by Kleinwort, Benson, is the creation of an investment trust specializing in unquoted issues. The Ionian Bank acquired its reputation by skill in ensuring that small companies in which it has an interest show a good return on their assets. As summed up by Julian Hodge:

The main function of a merchant bank must inevitably be the taking of measured risks, and this must always be to lend to the unquoted company, either in terms of equity or on some other basis, and then help to nurse and develop that company to the point where it is worthy of a public issue of its shares. This role of helping industry to grow, to foster new ideas, and to encourage them to develop, is worth-while work. For who else will do it? In nine cases out of ten, the people with the inventions and the ideas understand little else. It is the backing of ideas and of men which is called for, rather than established bricks and mortar, as the latter call for no special skills anyway.

Issue by Tender

Awareness of the inadequacy of the issuing mechanism prompted the controversial experiment first tried out in 1961 by Kleinwort, Benson for the issue of equity shares by *tender*. The system, which had been used by water companies for a number of years, aims at giving the benefit of the market price to the company offering the shares, and not to the speculator putting in multiple bids. It also gives the investor a certain flexibility of decision by fixing a price *below* which tenders will not be accepted. The minimum price is fixed in the judgement of the issuing house at what they could consider would be acceptable, if a normal offer for sale were made. The public applying for shares may put in higher prices if they wish. The determined will submit higher prices, the super-cautious will tender the minimum, but if the law of averages works there will be a concentration of prices within a reasonably narrow range. When the lists are closed the issuing house will fix the *sale price* (striking price) at such a level that the issue is at least fully subscribed and at the same time giving a sufficient spread of applicants. Those who applied at higher levels will pay only the striking price and have the excess refunded: some scaling down of the shares allotted to them may be necessary to arrive at the widest spread of the exact number of shares offered.

This procedure was introduced for new issues where it was difficult to estimate public demand. In the case of the water companies there had been no real problem as the shares were for practical purposes fixed-interest securities where the price could be determined very closely and the purchasers were generally professional investors. The Stock Exchange was at first reluctant to allow tenders for industrial companies. The main criticism made was that few applicants found themselves with shares at the exact price they were prepared to pay; while it was conceded that the vendor of the shares benefits to the extent that the difference between the minimum tender offer and the actual sale price accrues to him rather than to the 'stags', this only applies to the proportion of the capital offered. Since the issues by tender have been favoured by private companies going public, the shareholdings retained by them are often quite considerable and could be just as adversely affected if offered at a fixed price in a less buoyant market. The other objections are of a frivolous nature: first, that by resorting to this system the issuing house in some way abrogates its responsibility for price fixing; secondly, that the responsibility for pricing is put upon public investors who are incapable of assuming it; thirdly, that the system favours professional investors with their wider knowledge; and lastly, that it deprives the professional 'stags', who are said to play a valuable role in supporting the market, of their 'legitimate' profits.

The third and last criticisms are naturally contradictory and only require a brief swipe of Ockham's razor. As to the second, experience so far shows that institutional investors have tended to be too conservative in their price evaluation and have often been frozen out in favour of individuals. Any procedure which encourages the investor to work out pros-and-cons of his own is a step in advance. As to the responsibility of the issuing house, however, the proper working of the system requires that the issuing house should fix the under-written minimum price at a figure which is thoroughly realistic in relation to the state of the market and the prospects of the company, so far as these can be ascertained at the time of issue. The minimum price is thus a clear indication to investors of the appropriate subscription which they can only ignore at their peril. The sale price in tender issues has proved over the last three years to have been very much in line with subsequent market dealings, and growth potential seems to have been the longer-term factor determining the trend of the share levels, as should indeed be the case for serious investors.*

The value of a share is not the same thing to all men. The aim of the issuing house – whether it makes an offer by tender or at a fixed price – is to ensure a fair spread among the widest number of applicants at a price sufficiently close to the majority opinion to be acceptable. Part of the argument over issues by tender arises because of this failure to recognize that different investors have different objectives, a reality which complicates life for the professional over-simplifiers whose world is peopled by average investors consisting entirely of widows, orphans, and country vicars. There was thus an excess of *schaden-freude* when the Wilkinson Sword tender, arranged by Lazards in April 1964, was only just over-subscribed. While the minimum price was high in relation to the yield, the main adverse factor was the inclusion of non-voting shares in the units offered so that some institutional investors declined the underwriting offered to them.

If the tender procedure were really used extensively, applicants

* Of twenty offers for sale by tender in 1964 and reviewed by the *Stock Exchange Gazette* in January 1965, thirteen were still at that time commanding a premium over the striking price.

would require much more information in the prospectus in order to distinguish between the methods of scaling down different-priced applications by the individual issuing houses. Here the system is open to abuse. If an issuing house sets the underwritten minimum price too low and subsequently, to conceal its error, introduces scaling down merely to reduce the disparity between the mathematically ascertained striking price and the minimum price, this is a form of deception. In no circumstances can arbitrary scaling down be justified, except for the purpose of preventing an unduly large proportion of the issue falling into the hands of one investor, or for the purpose of securing a sufficiently wide distribution of shareholders. In such cases some form of statement should be made. The issuing houses have still to meet valid criticism on the question of the price the applicant is prepared to pay, and they may have to agree on some common convention on whether to treat the tendered prices as a maximum for each individual, possibly allotting shares at the fixing price as a percentage value of the money subscribed. Some residual ballot arrangement for the smallest applications would then be a necessary supplement. The tender system still requires considerable study and development but its extension to overseas territories, notably in South Africa, demonstrates that it does find increasing merit.

The Need for Reform

These criticisms of issue practice do, however, illustrate that the conduct of the market is continually becoming a matter of closer public concern, and the codes and procedures must be such as to stand up to public scrutiny. Political agitation against mergers and take-overs may at times have been ill-informed and ill-timed, but it must be met by better information and by a sense of appropriateness in the timing of operations. The loyalties and social assumptions of individuals who succeed in establishing a concentration of control over consumer goods and organs of opinion and publicity may not always accord with those human needs and aspirations which are the more valuable bequests of the European heritage. In the last century a too rapid concentration of new productive power and the neglect of social and emotional needs brought a series of political consequences, some of them disastrous, for those who thought that profit for themselves was sufficient justification. The debasement of human beings in a consumption intensive economy where profit is the only consideration must eventually result in a release of coarsened emotions with an equally grim outcome. If corrective measures are not taken early enough, the agitation will turn first against those who – justifiably or not – lend themselves most readily to the role of scapegoats.

No one expects the executive of an issuing house to introduce sociological considerations into his technical decisions on behalf of his clients. But the City, like other directing institutions of society, must always, because of the power it can exercise, largely unwittingly, in channelling both savings and consumption, be the first to ensure that its own house is in order and that the public interest is viewed in a wide perspective. There has been too much resistance to reform, too much insistence on the privileges of closed corporations, too many applications of white-wash by the usual Establishment-chosen commissions and too many excuses for non-action.

The growing unfavourable reception by private and corporate investors to non-voting shares found little reflection in the 1962 *Jenkins Report on Company Law* or subsequent legislative proposals. The Report's watered-down solution requiring 'full publicity' for restrictions on voting rights and the publication of detailed information on beneficial share holdings and participations throws a responsibility on the Press which the nature of libel laws and the exigencies of space, as well as of editorial preference, make virtually impossible to sustain. The decision, apparently based on the argument that old tried ways are the best, to leave stock exchanges to rationalize themselves and not to set up a supervisory body on the lines of the American Securities Exchange Commission, will probably be questioned should there be a fresh major disaster, and more drastic remedies are liable to be invoked next time. The almost total rejection in July 1964 by the investing public of a £2,000,000 Participating Preferred Ordinary Issue of one share in Rediffusion Television, sponsored by the Drayton Group, illustrated once more the basic hostile trend of opinion towards non-voting shares and similar attempts to raise funds from the public without yielding control.

Nor can the London issue market postpone for much longer the question of how to take formal cognizance of matters which are common knowledge in the City and which have direct bearing on invested savings. Under section 109 of the Companies Act 1967, the

Board of Trade – now the Department of Trade and Industry – may at any time, if they think there is good reason so to do, authorise any officer of theirs to require a company to produce to him forthwith any books or papers which the officer may specify. While such action may enable salvage action to be taken at an earlier stage, before a company is in deep trouble, it will not necessarily meet situations where the canons of share issuing have been ignored. Family trans-actions in shares and the use of company assets for personal use call for some restraining measure, such as a clause in contracts with issuing houses that promoters do not part with their own shares except after prior consultation or permission, or that they are held by the promoter for an agreed statutory period.

However, issue work still demands first and foremost the ability to form judgements on human character. The fear of missing out with 'a coming man' does remain, and every merchant bank has its legend on how So-and-So was turned away from the door when he was still in a small way, went round the corner to their rivals, and is now Lord So-and-So, the great tycoon. In the long run this risk may prove less embarrassing than that of going too far in the other direction. 'A man's worth and the strength of his character are quickly assessable,' said the late Mr Lionel Fraser, in *All to the Good*. This may often be so, but it becomes a dangerous myth when the City assumes that it possesses some special expertise on character assessment. The recent record shows rather the opposite, and the young aspirant in merchant banking will be wise to instruct himself in this art.

Tasks Ahead in Europe

If the British issuing mechanism is still capable of major improve-ments, even more does Continental Europe require effective means of mobilizing and allocating its capital resources so that its growth can continue. The industrial self-financing of the 'economic miracle' period is over and, in spite of a high level of savings, the private investor has not yet made his influence felt in Continental equity markets to the same extent as in the United States or the United Kingdom. While every European country has evolved its particular traditions, and the British have no claim to regard their own as possessing in every case some superior virtue, the lack of flexibility and diversification of European capital markets is nevertheless only too evident. Some of the features may be due to national tax structures or to legal restrictions on investment by institutions, and these may in turn reflect national social aims and objectives which outsiders have no right to decry. But even allowing for these, the absence of an efficient underwriting mechanism and of an issuing system which can distribute new issues fairly is an economic handicap by any standard, and there is a paucity of reliable information on the financial position of borrowers. Although the seven major European countries combined – United Kingdom, France, West Germany, Italy, Netherlands, Belgium, and Sweden – represent a more powerful productive potential than the United States, the latter's total of long-term capital obligations is three times as great. Nothing demonstrates more graphically than this comparison the outcome of restrictive policies, the isolation of European domestic capital markets, and the scope of the investment task ahead of the integrated European community of tomorrow. Whether Britain is a full member or not, its economy can never be divorced from Continental developments, and it will be a sad City of London which cannot in some way put its capital issuing mechanism to the service of European integration.

Europe is still in the throes of a new era of expansion. The largest single national economy, that of West Germany, continues to grow despite pauses in 1957–8, 1962 and 1966–7. The most backward of them industrially – Italy – is short of both equity capital and long-term loan capital. Yet even in Germany the new issues were for long subordinated to the maintenance of the financial supremacy over the money market of the three main credit banks and not by the needs of industry nor the readiness of the investor. Although Italian savers readily take up bonds even with the yields of less than 8 per cent which prevailed up to the end of 1969, industrial investment still lagged because of fears of tax discrimination against capital or capital earnings. Italian investors were understandably reluctant to pay inflated prices for ordinary shares when, between September 1960 and 1964, the daily index of share prices on the Milan Stock Exchange fell by one half. The Olivetti combine, a £100 millions producer of typewriter and office equipment, had subsequently to face at a crucial stage in a vast development plan (including a £30 millions acquisition in Underwood) not only family troubles but also the inability of the Italian market to take up unused shares priced in terms of the 1960

Milan boom. Nor could shares lodged as security over the years by the Olivetti family, which enjoyed as much but no more harmony than most families do, be put on the market. So, after an accumulation of short-term borrowings to tide over capital deficiencies, the main state industrial holding company (created originally by Mussolini because of Italy's capital weakness) moved in with a consortium of leading Italian companies to reorganize the Olivetti financial structure.

It is not only in Italy, but throughout all Europe, that great family empires are approaching this point of capital stress. The absence of an adequate issuing mechanism may thus prove a barrier to future economic growth. Paris and Amsterdam possess financing traditions and skills as old as London's but they are not equipped for the scale of the new ventures which an expanding Common Market will require. Whatever the inside tips and the excellent gastronomic judgement of the Daumier-like figures who, lacking only the folded neckerchiefs, sally along the rue du 4 Septembre after the closure of the Bourse towards their favourite restaurants, they have not the resources to underwrite Europe's future. Even if the US Government had not had to call a halt to the outflow of funds, Wall Street's listless periods and American share-pushing and allocation methods (whatever sense they make in a North American context), cannot be counted on to operate at all seasons to the benefit of European clients seeking to raise capital through New York. Europe will need a European capital market.

What part will British issuing skills play in this new European order? Our self-imposed exclusion from the formative years of the Common Market cut us out of the first stage of the process of consultation and integration through which EEC hopes one day to create a free movement of capital. London itself is still burdened with too many customs, stamps and controls, which offset the relatively flexible arrangements of the market to allocate equity capital at low cost. But if these can be removed, the British issuing mechanism may play its part in Europe. The dying order of princely absolutism with its lumbering bullion waggons and escorts apprehensively listening for the *sonneries* of French cavalry trumpets threw up men and skills which helped to create London's financial pre-eminence. It is now Britain's political life which is bogged down in the ruts of the concepts of 1789. But if the merchant bankers recall that their inheritance is a sense

131

of discrimination, of what is fitting, and that character is best judged by men of character, they can repay a debt of 175 years. They will find that they can step over many of the national barriers and inhibitions, and return history's compliments.

CHAPTER FIVE

Investment Management

A New Situation

Here some gesture of modesty is indicated. Within a British context the merchant banks may appear to possess vast international experience. But other countries can produce very sound reasons why *their* ways of doing things are perfectly satisfactory. British participation in their ventures is only welcomed if it is in *their* interest. The British are no longer loved – if they ever were – and where they still enjoy respect it is only where they merit it by their accomplishments. In the field of international portfolio investment, the power and influence of the merchant banks must basically be a projection of their strength at home and if, thanks to their traditional links with foreign banks and clients, they have extended their investment services, this has been primarily in the form of alliances and partnerships and certainly never in the form of domination or forced intrusion.

During the wave of fashion for European portfolio investment in the early 'sixties, merchant banks were too often represented as possessing some special mystique in this field, and their reputation consequently suffered with the fluctuations of the market. The picture bore little relation to reality. For, although some of the older accepting houses may have floated and dealt in the shares of the great European enterprises which launched the modern industrial era, their present portfolio investment role is now of quite a different order and owes its origins to new developments in our own time. The character of portfolio investment itself has been changing, perhaps even more than those who operate and preside over the institutions connected with it have recognized or would care to admit. The proliferation of inter-

133

national investment groupings, often with the prefix 'Inter-' or the suffix '-vest' and in which the British member is usually a London merchant bank, can mislead as to the significance of what has really been happening. For more is involved than a straight international link-up of national institutions or a simple extension of investment portfolios over national boundaries.

A new investment science has been growing up to meet a new situation and in each country a fresh foundation has to be laid. This has not always taken place or may be happening at different speeds. There are understandably enough often local conflicting needs to be reconciled while national characteristics find different reflections, even in concepts such as 'profit', 'dividend cover', and 'yield'. And to proclaim oneself part of something 'Inter-' or 'United', as we can see for ourselves in international political antics, is not enough.

Indeed, it is more than slightly anomalous that banks should appear to take part, much less to give a lead, in what, with every safeguard, is still a 'risk' form of activity. The merchant banks' role as pace-setters originated mainly from the need to arrange the orderly investment of the personal and private funds and trusts of families connected with the bank; by gradually extending this service for other clients, individual and corporate, they have in course of time come to act as managers and advisers for leading investment trusts and institutional funds. Foreign investment interests in turn may have shown some preference for extending their British portfolios with the help of merchant banks well known to them, particularly as the clearing banks were debarred from such operations: but they could have, and to a great extent do, make direct use of the services of British stockbrokers.

In practice, in pre-war days and up to the time of the 'economic miracles' of the early 'fifties, portfolio investment operations between Britain and Europe were on a relatively small scale. The traditional policy of old-established Scottish and other investment funds in their overseas selections was to give almost exclusive attention to North-American securities and those of other English-speaking areas. This was partly because of higher interest rates overseas, but also because of the absence of language problems and the presence of connections kept up between emigrants and friends at home. Under changed conditions the policy has continued. The combination of a political climate favourable to investment in the United States and of attractive double tax agreements between Britain and the United States and

Canada, has encouraged the older funds to continue to expand their portfolios in countries where their investment managers now feel as much at home as in the United Kingdom.

Nor has experience proved them wrong in their judgement. Differences in the taxation and accounting procedures of the 'non-Anglo-Saxon world' – to reverse President de Gaulle's simplification of the problem – as well as currency and transfer questions, are daunting obstacles for the accountants of Edinburgh, Dundee, and Perth, to say nothing of the difficulty of assessing European political factors. And at times of political and economic uncertainty at home, as in the 1964 General Election year, the traditional overseas investment outlets receive fresh attention, in spite of the handicap of the high premium to be paid on dollars available to British investors – 'the investment dollar'; North American, South African, and Australian shares can be judged on their own merits as long-term savings media.

There was also a flurry of new investment and unit trusts to provide yet another illustration of the City's lemming-reflex whenever it thinks it is on to a good thing; and when there loomed up the possibility of income from American investments being affected by Labour's corporation tax proposals, there was a corresponding series of anguished yelps before any blows had fallen. Under the surface, however, the established closed-end trusts had been steadily increasing their holdings of United States securities as a result of their assessment of improving American investment prospects. According to Bank of England statistics these amounted to £46 millions in 1963 compared with £18 millions in 1962. In addition, prior charge money had been raised in the United States over the twelve months preceding the election by some of the older Scottish investment trusts. Most of this switch to American securities was by means of funds of overseas origin which were eligible for investment in foreign securities, by the sales of Canadian stocks, and by the reduction of cash balances awaiting investment.

Although it is impossible to trace back directly to the workings of the Exchange Control Act 1947 any material improvement in UK balance of payments over the years, the Treasury decided that UK investors should be further handicapped from April 1965 by having to surrender one quarter of any investment dollars arising from the sale of securities in the non-investment dollar market, thereby forfeiting the dollar premium on a quarter of their capital. This led to the

135

invention of 'back to back loans' and 'offshore funds'. Back to back loans involve in principle an American company lending dollars to an 'English' company registered outside the UK in exchange for an English company lending sterling to an American company in England. Offshore funds are basically unit trusts registered in 'tax havens' not subject to the 25 per cent surrender rule and which can therefore follow more relaxed canons of management.

Overseas portfolio investment thus follows its own course on behalf of a steady clientele and is backed by long-standing experience. The misleading gimmicky picture, for which the Press is only partly to be blamed, serves to underline the element of myth and fiction which has come to surround the whole sphere of portfolio investment, although it might be thought that here is one activity which should be based on facts as far as they can be established. Some of the City institutions may themselves help to maintain the myths, partly out of self-interest but, since their origins lie in the days when the legend had the support of reality, partly from the English penchant for play-acting. The *dramatis personae* of the play are the stockbroker who is in the know, the outsider with money who wants to be put on to a good thing, and the director with a store of boardroom secrets about his companies, while as background to the drama is the Stock Exchange with its 'shunters', who buy shares in one town to sell them in another, 'jobbers' who deal only in their own specialised stocks and not directly with the public, 'bulls' who hold shares on a long-term view, 'bears' who sell shares they haven't got in the hope of buying them back cheaper later, and 'stags' who apply to buy new shares only to sell them again almost as soon as dealings begin. In the folklore of the Stock Exchange, a 'stag' is supposed to resemble 'a nervous bull'; and it is possible that a person who bought shares intending to sell them within a fortnightly account – thereby avoiding having to pay out the full consideration for his purchase – may, several decades ago, have been called a 'stag'. The Spanish concept of '*alcista a corto plazo*', or 'bull for a short while', applies to a person who only buys and holds shares while the price is rising and who sells them when the price turns downwards, whereas an '*alcista*' or proper 'bull' holds shares for the long pull of a company's good management over the years and he may pay relatively little attention to minor news items or short-term price fluctuations. The legendary way to underpin the price of a share was to overload the market with shares; this was supposed to stop the price of the shares from rising so rapidly as to attract a herd of 'short-term bulls', or 'stags', who were liable to turn round and sell on the slightest pretext.

In fact, the broker 'in the know' and the man who has been put 'on to a good thing' are nowadays as fictitious as griffins. The market mechanism of the world's leading stock exchanges is not much more than one hundred years old and is a historical growth born of circumstances which have now completely altered. The brokers are no longer likely to be the first to hear of some new development which may affect share levels; indeed, they are liable to be among the last. The specialist knowledge required for satisfactory investment management is now of such an order that few brokerage firms are able to give it adequate assessment and the investor himself may have a higher level of knowledge and sophistication as to the factors which will determine the asset value of shares than the professional stock exchange practitioners.

The 'jobber', to whom the broker goes to deal with on behalf of his client, quotes a double price and is prepared to buy *a limited number* of shares at the lower price and/or sell *a limited number* of shares at the higher price. Without disclosing whether his order is to buy or to sell, the broker may obtain quotations from several jobbers before going back to the first jobber who made the best quotation from the client's point of view. The number of shares in which a jobber is prepared to deal on his original price depends on how much of his order the broker has already carried out with another jobber, partly on how much of his own capital the jobber has committed in his business, and partly on the normal size and frequency of bargains in the particular security being quoted. If the broker has a larger order than the jobber is prepared to carry out on his original quotation there is a sophisticated dealing etiquette which – if used properly – tends to protect both the jobber and the broker's client from being landed with an unfair bargain. However a broker who has an order to 'buy at best' is expected to deal at the lowest offered price he can find in the market at the time, irrespective of whether that price may have risen substantially in the previous hour or so. In theory the broker's client may protect himself by placing a 'limit' order at a price which provides the broker with ample scope to carry out the order unless there has been a change about which the client is unaware. In practice members of the public may be reluctant to place this kind of instruction because they fear that the broker may deal with the first jobber he approaches without checking the market to find out whether he might be able to arrange a better deal with another jobber. A spate of orders to buy at best, or a spate of orders to sell at best, can all too easily accentuate short-run fluctuations in share prices and provide opportunities for jobbers specialising in them to buy shares when they are 'cheap' and sell them when they are 'dear'. The amount which a jobber lowers his price to meet a preponderance of selling orders and raises them to meet a preponderance of buying orders depends partly upon how much of his own capital he has available to take a view on the possible future course of share prices. Unfortunately the standard rate of income tax has for three decades hardly enabled even the ablest young jobber's dealer to build up an adequate amount of capital to keep the business going on a proper footing when his elders retire. Amalgamations and take-overs of jobbing firms have been the inevitable consequence.

In recent years brokers have experienced some difficulty in doing sizeable orders through the jobbing arrangement to their own satisfaction and sometimes make enquiries with their larger clients in case one of them may wish to deal the other way. If the broker manages to match his order, then he puts the transaction through the market so that the jobber in the stock gets something out of the deal. The commission the broker charges has to be commensurate with the cost of doing most of the work so that under such circumstances the institutions are effectively subsidizing the jobbing arrangement to keep it alive for the benefit of the general public. Even so the number of jobbing firms has declined from about 324 before the war to about 30 at the present time and some 114 institutional investors are making arrangements to use the computerized telexed order matching service which Fourth Market Systems of Luxembourg hopes to have operating by the autumn of 1971. Jobbers may become even more reluctant to take on large orders because they may feel that somebody else has already tried the business and that they have little or no chance of finding somebody with whom to close their initial transaction.

This does not mean to say that the London Stock Exchange no longer serves a useful purpose or is out of date in all respects. The mechanism, dependent basically on the Dutch auction technique of the jobbers dealing on their own account, has proved to be a unique combination of free market with a relatively stable price basis. It has been thoroughly tested in peace and war, crisis and prosperity, but it is difficult to see how the present institutions of the London market can be maintained on the existing basis of personal taxation in the United Kingdom.

The Institutional Investors

The institutional investors hold about a third of domestic holdings of quoted securities, but as they trade their holdings – in the light of changes in economic and market expectations – they may account for something like half the turnover. The market value as at 31 March, 1970 of all securities in 'The Stock Exchange Daily Official List' and 'The Monthly Supplement of Quoted Securities' amounted to about £120,000 millions.* Members of The Stock Exchange, London, are free to deal in any stock quoted on another exchange so this total may include for instance the market value of shares in a company which is more actively traded on Wall Street than in London. A breakdown of the figures shows the market value of fixed-interest securities of local and central governments (both overseas and domestic) at £19,820 millions, companies registered and managed in the United Kingdom at £42,734 millions, and companies not registered and managed within the United Kingdom at £57,487 millions. The company figures include fixed-interest securities with a market value of £4,489 millions.

Institutional investors include 'gross funds' which are broadly speaking charitable institutions endowed with capital, the income on which may be applied tax-free for the purpose for which charity was formed. Gross funds have a considerable influence on the fixed-interest market where tax-free or 'gross' yields have, in the main, been sufficient to compensate for the rates at which the purchasing power of sterling has been declining. By and large the 'net funds' have not been able to obtain a sufficient after-tax yield to allow them to amortize the declining real value of their capital. In the face of this latter difficulty, the old private investors, who were once the backbone of the market, appear to have lost interest and, as they die, their holdings have been sold by their executors to meet death duty. They have been replaced by a category of private investor who appears somewhat less inclined to take quite so much interest in company

* Figures from 'Statistics Relating to Securities Quoted on the London Stock Exchange for the year ending 31st March 1970.' This is an annual publication issued by The Public Relations Office, The Stock Exchange, London, EC 2.

affairs and who would rather pay someone else to do the job for him. Putting a company which is going wrong, back on the right road is daunting even for the institutions in spite of their absolute and relative growth in importance. In practice it is easier for the managers of institutional funds to sell the shares.

And while in days gone by a relatively few individuals, in whose hands capital was largely concentrated, determined where this should be invested, the institutional funds of today are largely concentrated in the hands of salaried managers. The boards of insurance companies and pension funds have a predetermined, although far from inflexible, basis for the investment policies pursued by their fund managers. For they have minimum requirements to meet. A policy holder or an employee is guaranteed a minimum sum on his life policy or a minimum pension on retirement, and these requirements are calculated on an actuarial basis to show the minimum return which the managers must obtain from the funds available to them. The larger part of the funds will therefore be invested in fixed-interest securities such as gilt-edged – or government – securities, debentures, and mortgages, the yields of which may be calculated· with as much certainty as is possible. The policies of investment trusts and unit trusts are not limited in quite the same way by actuarial considerations.

A company needing a million pounds or more is unlikely to find it from any one source and for an issue, debenture, or mortgage involving £5,000,000 as many as fifty institutional investors might provide on average £100,000 each, thus spreading their risk, and might look to one City House to arrange such requirements for both offerers and takers. Every institution has a need to try and improve on its minimum commitments, mainly to protect policy holders and pensioners against inflation, and will thus earmark some proportion of its funds for investment in ordinary stocks. 'Rights Issues' are particularly favoured since the offer to shareholders will be outstanding for at least three weeks, during which there may be changes in the market price of the shares resulting in existing shareholders being unwilling to take the new shares to which they are entitled. Institutions are therefore ready to consider proposals from issuing houses to come in as sub-underwriters for a rights issue, not only receiving a portion of the issue but also part of the commission paid to the underwriters. Their support is not negligible; it guarantees to the company concerned that it will raise the money it requires.

Britain seems, therefore, to have followed a path similar to that followed by the United States. Between 1949 and 1963 the proportion of New York Stock Exchange-listed stocks held by institutions rose from 12·7 per cent to twenty per cent with pension funds making the running. By 1970 the institutions held about a quarter of the stocks, with some preference for the 50 to 180 largest issues which afforded them a manageable size of holding. The Security Studies Committee of the Investment Bankers' Association of America in autumn 1964 reported that fifty-five per cent of all corporate debt was being placed outside the market and that forty per cent of these negotiated deals failed to use investment bankers even as agents. The reasons were partly the expense of complying with the regulations of the Securities and Exchange Commission in the case of public offers, secondly the size of the funds available to institutional investors which mean that large placings bring a better return, and finally, as a result of competition for mortgages from savings banks and loan associations, insurance companies have been forced to enter the capital market in search of alternative long-term investment.

Prospect for Investment Banking

What does the analogous trend in Britain portend for the merchant banks? Will they hold their own or be by-passed as seems to be the threat to American investment banking?* Investment advice and management is not a service peculiar to them nor even to banks in general. It becomes increasingly a task for big organizations and if independent counsellors enjoy a continued existence, this is largely a question of demand still in excess of the supply. All banks can arrange for the purchase and sale of shares for their clients at the same cost as when they use a broker directly: on average the bank takes twenty-five per cent of the broker's commission in return for passing him the business and makes no charge for passing on his investment opinions – 'without obligation or commitment' to themselves. Their trustee departments will also undertake full-scale portfolio investment management, see to the collection of dividends, deal with the paper work arising from 'rights' and scrip issues and on the basis of the

---

* A warning of some relevance came from the 1964 report of the American Investment Bankers' Association: 'Many smaller dealers have done little to develop research departments or other expertise but have relied on their Ivy League connexions to bring them into underwriting syndicates and to peddle the allocations they receive.'

141

powers given them by the client, alter holdings within his portfolio. Normally a charge of between one and two pounds a year is levied on each £1,000 of capital.

But while the clearing banks are reluctant to give a full advisory service since the celebrated case in which a client successfully sued one of them for wrong advice,* the merchant banks are prepared to do this and offer their own investment studies and opinions and through their nominee companies make the administration of portfolios as simple an affair as possible for their clients. That they happened for historical reasons to be the best organized houses in the field of investment management at the period of the growth of institutional saving has been a major factor in their successful advance in this field. A number of the oldest investment trusts, even those of 'Scottish' origins, are in fact managed by London merchant banks while remaining registered north of the Border, or at least, as the composition of their boards shows, have access to the banks' advisory services. By becoming the managers of the pension funds of some of the largest companies in the country, they gained a head lead in both market influence and placing strength. Their ability to keep it will depend on sensing the changing needs of such funds, not only in meeting the requirements of pensioners' income calculated on an actuarial basis, but also in countering the depreciation of the currency in which actuarial calculations are made.

This in turn requires imaginative ability of a high order and, not surprisingly, where merchant banks face fresh demands for investment talent they have been supplementing their resources from outside. The Board of Hill Samuel, for example, includes Mr G. H. Ross Goobey, who was for many years investment adviser to the Imperial Tobacco Pension Fund, and Mr Douglas S. Allison, who was one of the leading investment officers of the Manufacturers Life Insurance Co. of Canada until he joined the bank in 1964. The merchant banks of course learned long ago that it is just as hard to keep a fortune as to make one, and the senior partners – who bore the brunt of the responsibility for managing the portfolios of their families – had become expert in the hard school of experience. However, the collation of detailed information about companies is a time consuming process and, between the wars, Kleinwort, Sons & Co. Ltd, set up a research department to analyse investments, checking the balance sheets of companies whose shares had been suggested for portfolio

* *Woods v. Martins Bank* [1959] 1 Q.B. 55; [1958] 1 W.L.R. 1018.

investment, establishing statistical comparisons of profitability, arranging further investigations where necessary, and building up records. By 1961, at the time of the amalgamation with Robert Benson Lonsdale, the department already totalled some twenty-five analysts and researchers.*

The influence of merchant banks is not confined solely to the total investment assets they manage or control by name, such as Hambros Investment Trust, Philip Hill Investment Trust, or Kleinwort Benson Investment Trust, but is diffused further by the wide spread of their

*Investment analysis is basically a problem of striking comparisons. The ability to read a balance sheet, supplemented by on the spot investigations together with a reasonable knowledge of the economic and industrial environment, should enable an investment expert to form an opinion of the soundness or otherwise of a company and estimate its business prospects. But to select the shares of one company rather than another as a portfolio investment, requires an agreed basis for comparing their main financial features. These are usually:

    Recent Price
    Earnings Yield per cent
    Dividend Yield per cent
    Earnings per cent
    Dividend per cent
    High and Low Market Price over past 12 months
    Capitalization: Debentures, Bonds, Mortgages
                Preference Shares
                Ordinary Shares
    Book Value per Share
    Net Current Assets per share
    Trading Record (usually over 7 years)
    Earnings and Dividends (over same period)

'Cash flow', an expression much used in investment analysis, is usually defined as: 'Net earnings available for the Ordinary shares plus depreciation' [this includes funds retained by the Company as provisions, etc., as well as those which it intends to pay by way of dividends]. The use by analysts of this concept enables them to assess the ability of a Company to finance its expansion programmes and also to compare Companies in countries where the net earnings figure is more or less meaningless for analytical purposes in that only a figure sufficient to cover the agreed dividend is shown. The cash flow figure is likely to provide a much clearer indication of true profit. A variation of cash flow analysis – Discounted Cash Flow – is being used increasingly by large industrial concerns in an attempt to forecast capital flows in relation to projected expenditures and rates of return.' A further breakdown is sometimes made into 'Gross Cash Funds' including funds earmarked for dividends, and 'Net Cash Flow' excluding these funds.

Certain tools of analysis thus provide a specific, if limited, guide to the likely behaviour of individual companies, share market groups, and within narrowly defined limits, the market as a whole. General systems of stock market analysis, whether of the graphic type or not, may supply a broad historical guide if taken over a long enough period of years. But the irrational aspects of human motivation and the uncertainty as to the presence and significance of current factors mean that care must be used in applying them within the time scales which have to be considered by portfolio investors.

clientele throughout the whole investment world. An accurate estimate of the total portfolio in whose management members of the Accepting Houses Committee have some direct or indirect say is hardly possible, but a very conservative 'guesstimate' might be in the neighbourhood of £6,000 millions. There is a whole series of delicate shadings between 'managed by' and 'associated with'. Most investment trusts managed by the merchant banks themselves used to be of the closed-end variety, as until recently few of them cared much for the complexities and overheads involved in the technical administration of unit trusts. They may act as selling or paying agents for North American mutual funds and Continental unit trusts, largely for the prestige element or as an obligation to European ally, while Kleinwort, Benson are 'associated' with the oldest unit trusts in the world, the Municipal and General Group who started their first in 1931; Baring Brothers and Robert Fleming are shareholders of Save and Prosper Ltd, Edinburgh. In recent years merchant banks have become less inhibited in sponsoring open-ended unit trusts. There is certainly justification for trusts with a regional emphasis where advisers on the spot can give good local investment guidance, such as Singer and Friedlander's 'Midlander' Unit Trust launched in July 1964, or for those designed to meet the conditions imposed by a particular clientele, such as Hill Samuel's The Trades Union Unit Trust, which, for the benefit of some thirty-four trade unions, assembled a portfolio of shares without a single steel stock. But in an investment field where the small man has some £350 millions at stake, accusations of 'stuffiness' are to be preferred to the headlines of gimmickry. For the merchant banks as a group the important long-term factor is that they too should retain a large enough stake in unit trust management to ensure that they preserve status and influence throughout the whole investment world. Provided they train and recruit the necessary talent, they need not be a prey to the same fears as the American investment banks.

Their chief concern should be to demonstrate that they can lead in continually readapting the investment machinery to meet the wider social and economic demands which are being increasingly made on it. *Caveat emptor* can no longer be a maxim where the solvency and growth of institutions has become an affair of the widest public concern. The precepts and rules for security issues have taken the place of the jungle law which existed up to the 'twenties. The Issuing Houses Association and the Stock Exchange may be able to prevent 'bucket shops' from deceiving the public but whether the whole investment mechanism and the store of expert knowledge which accompanies it are being directed in the most constructive direction is more questionable.

The Stock Exchange and Public Interest

The Stock Exchange mechanism is proving its worth – as a mechanism. But as a presiding institution the Exchange itself is frequently under fire. Its control over its own members is effective and an excellent machinery of consultation with the issuing houses has been evolved. But when the English are busy making a self-conscious virtue out of arrangements which were mainly intuitive in origin, it is time they were submitted to rational scrutiny. The American institution of a Securities and Exchange Commission may not be exportable in its entirety – no national institutions ever can be – but the SEC power to demand information and to enjoy legal protection for its published opinions is clearly something which would serve the public interest in any society. And in matters financial, as well as industrial, Britain does tend to follow the American pattern. Since our standard of living, in spite of the set-backs of stop-and-go, has now reached a point where in the next decade or so the numbers of investors, either as individuals or indirectly through institutions, will double to seven million, it is high time that the fitness of the existing City investment machinery for tomorrow's problems was examined. The merchant banks, being at the point of intersection of domestic and international investment, as they are in banking and credit matters, are most deeply involved.

When 'irregularities' have reached the point where they almost overshadow 'orthodoxy', it is a sure sign of inadequacy in a concept or institution. The growing volume of securities' business, particularly that with an international flavour, which by-passes the Stock Exchange is one of the main indicators of this. It is natural enough that orders for overseas securities are placed directly with foreign brokers or finance houses, some of whom even have their own offices in London; for, particularly in the case of 'riskless' transactions, British brokers' commissions seem unnecessarily heavy. The brokers' argument, that their services include the protection provided by the rules of the Stock Exchange, is hardly sufficient to justify the client being charged materially more than if he had dealt directly with a good name abroad. It may be noteworthy that when in June 1964 the Minster Trust put out its own circular offering to sell at favourable prices large lines of shares which they were in a position to secure from their financing of take-overs, there were no demonstrations of sympathy for the stockbrokers. The reality is that if a new market is developing outside the Stock Exchange and is offering services at lower rates, the brokers have in the long run no option but to reduce their rates and improve their own service. The international security issues raised through London have in turn reinforced direct links between institutions, trusts, pension funds and merchant banks; if the London Stock Exchange has not itself become the main market for such issues (which would have been the natural and satisfactory corollary) this is not merely because domestic purchases are few or because of exchange control but because non-resident investors believe, rightly or wrongly, that London commissions are too high and that they may be in some way subject to British taxation or official restrictions. So although the trade in these is quite considerable nearly all of it is secured by merchant banks and foreign brokerage houses with London offices. Even when a member of the London Stock Exchange does receive an order, it is not always transacted on the floor.

The reasons for this are probably two-fold: first, that jobbers are not fully *au fait* with the technique of trading in bonds for delivery abroad; secondly, the merchant banks have in recent years acquired just this experience and can conduct their operations on extremely fine margins through Continental partners who were in the original placing syndicate and can find sellers without delay. As Europe progresses slowly but surely towards the harmonization of its security trading and investment practices, and eventually to the creation of the institutional framework of an integrated capital market, the problems of the London security trading mechanism will become even more acute.

Not that the merchant banks are consciously trying to take business away from the London Stock Exchange. For normal security dealings they are dependent on it and in issue work their services are essentially complementary to that of the stockbrokers. Stockbrokers have had to go through an uncomfortable process of adjustment to survive in an adverse climate of high taxation and small retentions, and the composition of their House has altered as the need for concentration became stronger. During the past three decades there has been a continual reduction in the number of broking firms. Before the outbreak of war in 1939 there were nearly five hundred; by 1970 the number had fallen to one hundred and eighty-eight. The downward trend was reinforced by a policy decision by the Council of the Stock Exchange in 1962 to place a lower limit on the amount of capital per partner which a firm must maintain if it wishes to continue trading, and which gave one-partner firms five years to amalgamate or cease trading. Unless there are very substantial changes in the tax environment the process is liable to be extended, as investors call for more statistical background information, economic reviews, and studies on domestic and overseas investment possibilities which can only be provided by brokers who are adequately capitalised.

Because merchant banks do not undertake any activities peculiar to themselves but have grown and progressed by doing them better than others, and by creating new roles for themselves before others caught up (as they have always done), these developments are highly relevant to their own survival. If the investment world is changing character, enterprises are found to be doing each other's jobs, some being swallowed up and others uncertain of their tasks, and when national and international operations are developing outside institutional supervision, some new concept is ready to be created. And if there is said to be nothing so irresistible as an idea whose hour has come, the master of the particular moment of history is he who knows how to give it the first creative expression.

The public interest, in so far as investors can express it coherently, requires clarification and information to take the place of mystery cults. The workings of the Prevention of Frauds (Investments) Act and supervision by both Board of Trade and Stock Exchange Council can have some deterrent effect. But the investor requires more positive expression of how company affairs are conducted and more details of the Stock Exchange's own methods of operation. The inability of shareholders to obtain the former under normal circumstances is well enough known and the weightier influence which institutional investors can bring has still to be effectively felt. The Association of Investment Trusts, formed after the 1929 crash to protect its shareholders in the various redemption moratoria of that time, and the British Insurance Association's Investment Protection Committee, also created in the 'thirties, have recently been showing some interest in joint action to examine financial proposals of companies in which they have an interest as investors. In some cases they have even suggested amendments to the companies' proposals and, if this did not appear to be having effect, the Association has advised its members not to support them. That more companies are now prepared to consult the two bodies before making far-reaching financial changes is a testimony to their fairness and impartiality. Since their motive is only the protection of the savings of millions of small investors, industry is beginning to accept that consultation with them need not imply interference.

The mere fact that this development is taking place highlights the need. As the Master of the Rolls said in his judgement on the Selfridge case (even if this particular appeal was critical of the support by the two Associations of the Selfridge capital reorganization):

> It would obviously not be business for a company which is proposing to put forward a scheme of this kind, to go to all the trouble and expense and spend all the time necessary to prepare and present a scheme, and then find that owing to the opposition of important and experienced shareholders, the scheme is going to be rejected. Therefore, it is wise, prudent and useful for everybody concerned that the attitude of shareholders of this character should be ascertained before the proposals are put into their final shape and submitted to the general body of shareholders ... it is, I think, by no means a bad thing that shareholders should be informed as to the views taken of a scheme such as this by responsible and experienced bodies such as those in question.*

Shareholders' protection groups can usually, however, only wade in after trouble has started and it is only on rare occasions, such as Mr Herbert Waddell's move to block Mr Charles Clore, that they are effective. Without some more orderly procedure backed up by the influence of organized investment management, the public is left with that dubious spokesman for the common weal, the back-bench MP, who tends to discover the claims of widows, orphans, and country vicars at those moments when the Chief Whip is looking round for someone to take over as Parliamentary Under-Secretary of 'Ag. and Fish', and who, once he is in office, just as quickly forgets about them.

The Stock Exchange Council's request to companies with listed shares to give the fullest possible information in half-yearly statements,

* An appeal had been made against the capital reorganization proposals for Gordon Selfridge Trust and Selfridge Holdings, and the appellant had criticized the statement in a circular to the effect that the Association of Investment Trusts and the BIA Investment Protection Committee were recommending that the proposals be supported. (Court of Appeal, 1946.)

rules aimed at stopping the creation of 'false markets', and the Council's monthly estimates of turnover, were useful first steps. However there are still many bargains which are not marked and investors could be all too easily mislead about the approximate market worth of their shares or debentures by the published prices at which they were marked on the previous business day. Institutional clients could insist upon their own bargains being marked by their brokers in order to rectify an absurd situation in which small bargains in as few as a hundred shares are marked while bigger bargains in many thousands of shares are too often omitted from the markings. Marking of all bargains done after hours could be compulsory.

Looking further ahead, the Stock Exchange Council should take note of the fact that specialists survive on the New York Stock Exchange despite the publication of detailed daily figures of turnover. The etiquette of the London Stock Exchange does not necessarily require jobbers to be 'on' at their earlier quotation if a broker's dealer has spoilt an order by trying to do a small part of a bargain a penny or two better. Publication of daily turnover figures in individual shares in London would be a very welcome improvement, but it is difficult to see how this can come about unless jobber's dealers are to feel free to explain to a broker's senior partner why the jobber is not 'on' to the broker's dealer when he comes back sometimes. In the long run the London Stock Exchange is a free market or it is no market at all.

American Lessons

The published Stock Exchange returns for 1969 showed monthly turnover varying between £1,910 millions and £3,678 millions with the number of bargains in a month varying between 373,341 and 701,233, and whether there can be effective policing under the present arrangements of the ten thousand daily deals covering some nine thousand quoted securities involved must be the first question. With only sixteen hundred quotations in New York the Americans feel a need for a more systematic approach. The second question, even if the great mass of business is honestly and efficiently conducted, is why the share prices – as pointed out by a prominent banker* – published

* Lord Latymer, Director of Coutts and National Provincial, quoted in the *Evening Times* of 1 September 1964.

149

in the Stock Exchange Daily Official List, are too often at variance with the record of business done. Citing the case of ICI shares, shown at a selling price of 44s 4½d and a buying price of 46s 10½d on a day when the only business recorded was at 44s 5¾d and 45s 6d, Lord Latymer pointed out that the published prices are important for the valuation of estates. The Stock Exchange Council, still opposing publication of daily turnover and of 'real' prices – although this is New York procedure – continues to defend the existence of a jobbing system which has lost much of its claim to be regarded as such.

So, in calling on public companies to furnish fuller statistics on trading results, subsidiary participations, and methods of calculating depreciation, the Stock Exchange must begin by putting its own affairs in order. The Conservative Government, after many delays, produced in July 1964 a milk-and-water version of company law reform, picking the most innocuous points from that most anodyne of documents, the 1962 *Report of the Jenkins Committee on Company Law*. The substantial matters, such as the acceptance of the concept of equity shares of no par value and the indefensible practice of non-voting ordinaries, were still evaded. 'Fuller information' remained the Tory theme, but given the obstacles, not the least those of the technical jargon which baffles the comprehension of the average lay investor, this avoided the main question facing the twentieth-century world of investment – how far the shift from the 'risk' to the 'social security' sector is paralleled by the mechanism of control. Both government and Jenkins Committee failed to face up to the principle that shares should carry the 'rights' their names imply. The concept of shares with built-in special privileges, 'founders' or management shares, or other categories with conditions which maintain control in family or selected hands, is not consistent with that of a public company.

The merchant bankers, as institutional investment managers, can be challengers or reformers, or they can conform and compromise. Sooner or later some affair, even if not of the Hatry or Kylsant order, will reveal the inadequacy of measures to protect public interest and there will be indiscriminate harrying of all those who had identified themselves with the old order; the outcome will be an extension of official intervention or supervision. The contrasting views in 1963 and 1964 between the American Securities and Exchange Commission and the National Association of Securities Dealers, following the poor performance of the New York Stock Exchange after the Kennedy murder, showed that an artificial spread of price quotations by quasi-regulatory bodies, who are themselves involved as dealers, becomes less acceptable than ever. The sheer weight of institutional pressures will continue to create, *de facto*, a new mechanism separating myth still further from reality.

Here again American events, moving two or even three decades ahead of us, can be a signpost and a warning. The increase of large corporations brought about by a more generous system of depreciation allowances – an inherent necessity in societies where economic growth is consciously encouraged – has resulted in some cases in more cash being generated than can profitably be employed by the companies themselves, while in other cases there may be a passing need for extra cash; the consequence has been a by-passing of the market and investment bankers by corporations dealing directly with pension funds, insurance companies, and other institutions.

In 1963 more corporate bonds were privately placed in the United States than were offered to the investing public. The upward trend in private placements that began in the 1930s reached a peak of $8,150 millions in 1965. The growth in private placements reflected the demand for corporate debt securities by insurance companies and pension funds until 1966 when these institutions began to put a larger proportion of their new funds into equities instead of debt to hedge against a rising tendency in wholesale and consumer price indices. Public offerings rose as corporations were subjected to a programme of accelerated tax-collection and rising unit costs from the beginning of 1966 which bit into profit retentions. According to a graph which appeared in the annual report of the Federal Reserve Bank of New York for 1969, internally generated funds of non-financial corporations fluctuated between $55,000 million and $65,000 million between 1965 and 1969 while their fixed investment rose from about $52,000 million to about $82,000 million.

Towards a European Capital Market

If Europe follows the American path of growth – and this is now the proclaimed aim of the Common Market states – roughly parallel developments will occur. Since the Continental issue world has been mainly *dirigiste* and controlled, the transition may well take place by

151

adapting the existing institutional investment framework with the support of both national and EEC planning bodies. Even within the freer Dutch and Belgian systems, as the investment officers of the pension funds and insurance companies develop fresh confidence and experience, they will be increasingly ready to apply their own judgement independently of stockbrokers and private investment banks. The growing standardization of the procedures of investment analysis and the agreements on definitions now being hammered out within the newly-formed European Federation of Financial Analysts, mean that the investment officers of institutions will have available a common pool of knowledge for evaluating shares by earnings comparisons, by employment of capital, and from investment tables. The Federation, according to the reports on its Third Congress, is now discussing with EEC officials in Brussels, the uniform requirements for capital issues. The new European investment framework, within which such conscious skills will be applied to the problems of growth and size, will leave little room for the jolly atmosphere of prep school rags which characterizes the London Stock Exchange at its high festivals, or for eye-catching 'Euro' or 'Inter' gimmickry.

Europe will still have its own deficiencies to make good. Given the present state of growth, Continental Europe will have by 1975 a standard of living approaching that of the United States, an increased average output per worker of seventy per cent compared to 1960, and an increased gross output of ninety per cent, while the population of Western Europe will have risen by twenty-nine millions.* The investment needs of such a society and the mobilization of resources on a European basis to meet them will be beyond the capacity of the present capital markets. The inability of the German and Italian bourses to prevent the foreign buying sprees of 1960 and the selling rushes of two years later produced exaggerated fluctuations in share prices and illustrate aptly enough the existing inadequacies. The overall Common Market stock index doubled between the beginning of 1959 and mid-1961 when the annual growth rate was believed to be twelve per cent, but slumped from June 1961 to November 1963 although the growth rate was still an impressive six per cent per annum. Although the German capital market accomodated DM 6,176 millions worth of foreign fixed-interest securities in 1969, the largest in its post-war history, and the Swiss capital market some Sw. Frcs.

* Estimates from *The New Europe and Its Future, Twentieth Century Fund, July 1964.*

10,148 millions, other traditionally capital-exporting European countries, such as the Netherlands, continued to discourage the issue of foreign securities on their markets.

During 1969 most of the bonds issued in Germany by foreign borrowers were bought by residents despite some occasional speculative foreign purchases on revaluation hopes, residents' net purchases of foreign bonds coming to DM 5,320 millions, or about 86 per cent of the total amount of foreign and international bonds underwritten by German syndicate banks. In the same period net sales of domestic bonds (after allowing for changes in issuers' own holdings) amounted to DM 12,382 millions while new money raised by share issues amounted to some DM 1,722 millions. In July 1970 there were Deutschmark bonds with a total nominal value of some DM 167,955 millions outstanding with average yields of between 8.5 and 8.8 per cent. At the same time the shares of 563 public limited companies were officially quoted with a market value of some DM 113,216 millions and an average yield of about 4 per cent.

The German capital world is dominated by banks, insurance companies, and *bausparkassen* whereas, in the United States for example, investors outside the banking system take up whole issues of corporate or financial bonds. This feature has its historical justification in the nineteenth-century expansion of German industry, when banks had to hold the shares of their clients in their own portfolios until the businesses were on their feet, and released them only to the market when they were thought to be free of speculative risk. Unkind commentators may remark that the German bankers took the best for themselves and gave the investing public the leavings. The tendency may have been accentuated by the moratorium of the 'thirties when frozen credits became, in practice, participations. But the final outcome is that there is no real distinction between underwriting and marketing in Germany: the banks as underwriters purchase the entire issue from the company and sell it at an agreed price to the public, as against the British system where the underwriters take over only that part of the issue not placed within the stipulated period.

The supply of new shares to the German capital market has then been small, both compared with the supply of bonds and compared with the total financial requirements of trade and industry. The Report of the Deutsche Bundesbank for the year 1969 suggested that, among the reasons why no greater use was made of this source of risk capital, are the tax considerations of public limited companies, as financing through the issue of new shares is still disproportionately expensive. But other motives, too, are certainly of no little importance, such as reluctance to adopt an issue price appropriate to the price level of the shares already in circulation – a reluctance frequently due to disinclination to change the existing pattern of holdings in public companies. It can at any rate be observed that some companies whose ownership is firmly established expand their financing with funds from outside sources in a way that sometimes raises problems. On the other hand, the growing domestic supply of capital for equity investment was clearly illustrated by the great increase in the purchase of foreign shares and of saving by investment in domestic and foreign share funds. The fact that so little use is made of shares in Germany as a means of financing, whilst the desire for investment in such securities is widespread, could lead to substantial tensions in future in the ratio of supply to demand on the share market. The Bundesbank reported that the Ministry of Economics and the commission of stock exchange specialists appointed by it to examine this and other problems are seeking solutions and suggestions as to changes, tax questions naturally being of particular importance.

The Paris Bourse, although its tradition is as old and honourable as that of London and looks back to halcyon periods during France's rise to industrial and imperial power, has to cope with a series of laws and regulations concerning marketable securities dating from 1801, and a corps of 'Agents de Change' enjoying the status of 'Officier Ministeriel'. The agent de change, who is a trader only by virtue of carrying out his charge as a government-appointed official, is the outward symbol of a long-established State priority of access to the capital market. There is governmental control of rates of interest, and an officially regulated queue of new issues. The state has made repeated calls on the capital market while industrial and commercial enterprises have been forced to turn to 'auto-financing' and the Paris Bourse has remained a strange stagnant side-pool over the years. Companies, even those highly regarded by the investors, have found that *any* issue of capital seems to depress the price of their shares. This may also lie in the Frenchman's congenital mistrust of any institution where he suspects his government is active, but also in the ethos of the Paris Bourse, its domination by several investment syndicates and banks who direct effectively the course of trading, the tight hold on great blocks of the most important shares by leading financial and industrial families, the secrecy of companies evading or profiting by tax regulations, and finally by a tax structure which penalizes distributed profits. The Frenchman has tended to invest in 'a hole in the ground' like a copper mine or gold mine or an oil well because he regards these as safer places to put his savings than bonds whose real values has been eroded by rising retail prices in the past, and the shares of French industrial companies whose prospects are difficult to assess on sparse data. Since the decline in cash flows forces industry to look again to the capital market, and the Government has apparently realized that a regular flow of private investment is also essential for its planning, a change may come, but it may also highlight other inadequacies. When in mid-1964, as a gesture to the potential beneficial influence of a broad-based corps of investors, the Ministry of Finance authorized unit trusts, there was little reaction. Yet a potential interest of the French in equity investment is continually demonstrated by the good performance of *foreign* shares on the Paris Bourse and by attempts to obtain new North American listings to stimulate the small and medium-sized investor.

The historical factors in these national situations can be readily accepted and there have been compensating advantages, and Britain can only envy Germany and France their post-war career of modernization and expansion. But a fresh wind will undoubtedly blow as integration of capital markets becomes reality within the Common Market. The alignment of grain prices and the removal of tariff barriers at the end of 1966 will, in effect, bring about further price adjustments and the introduction of units of account, if only for international bookkeeping purposes. The European Investment Bank will be making truly international issues and, in theory, provided the right of establishment has also advanced, there will be nothing to prevent any European company raising money by whatever means it chooses in any Common Market country where it does legitimate business. There will be obstacles and difficulties but, as integration approaches, there will be new areas of freedom within the wider regulatory European concepts and the merchant banks now striking out into Europe with imaginative plans may well be those who will most profit from the new liberty of action.

Here the study groups formed by groups of European banks to enable their investment managers to work out agreed principles of investment analysis are likely to be the pioneering step in creating a common vocabulary from which to develop new concepts. The next

155

requirement – already in evidence – will be for better co-ordinated machinery for portfolio investment. The existing loose groupings, some of them including stockbrokers and dealing companies as well as banks and investment houses, do not yet go far enough, and their studies and analyses inevitably reflect the many sectional compromises of shifting alliances. An agreed formula for an earnings-capital ratio may be possible among Dutch investment experts, while in Germany the Cologne private bank of Herstatt and the Frankfurt house of Georg Hauck & Co. have done their best to pierce the abracadabra of German balance sheets and offer indices of a sort. But generally there is a lack of the facts and figures for the type of international comparisons on a basis of which orderly portfolio investment can be planned. Running an international fund or trust still involves techniques more akin to espionage than to information gathering and analysis, even though the privileged position of bankers and leading stockbrokers has given them courage enough to launch ventures in this field. There is still a long way ahead before even the embryo of a true European investment market has taken shape. But eventually enough company information may become available for common European investment criteria to be properly assessed, and when national bourses begin to harmonize their practices as an essential preliminary to European integration, the influence of the criteria will become apparent in dealings.

As we have seen, European markets are largely primary bond markets which need to be backed up by resilient secondary bond markets to enable holders to sell their bonds with less difficulty than at present if they come across an opportunity to back an alternative project with a higher if less certain potential yield. Attempts to shave the yield on new bond offerings, whether by restricting the amount of new bond issues or by making potential issuers queue up, do nothing to improve the resilence of the secondary bond market in subsequent years. Although clearly not a sufficient condition, a necessary condition for the creation of a more resilient secondary market may be the creation of an international service for bond holders, making investment comparisons of bonds across European frontiers. Although it is doubtful whether such a service can be operated profitably from London until the Exchange Control Act, 1947, is repealed, INTINCO of London did set out some years ago to provide such a service with a team, including computer experts, an investment analyst and a taxation expert who, once a week, worked out their tables on a basis of the lists of bonds sent in by the participating European banks and taking into account current factors such as ease of dealing, dollar premiums and cross-frontier tax arrangements. The actual computation took five hours and the results were mailed to subscribers to give them each Monday morning the information on the previous week. In making regular estimates of the value of long-term bonds for international investors, who play their part more effectively as they become better informed, the comparisons brought out the relative significance of the annual decreases in the purchasing power of various currencies. Leaving aside price indices of agricultural produce which are liable to display seasonal fluctuations of irregular magnitude, between July 1969 and July 1970 investors would have to show an increase in the money value of their capital of 4.4 per cent in German marks, 6.1 per cent in American dollars, and 6.8 per cent in sterling in order merely to maintain the real value of their capital assets.

The concept of an international dealing mechanism for listed securities may still one day be shown to be realizable. The development of telecommunications has gradually put an end to the older type of security arbitrage transactions, which was one of the Helbert Wagg specialities of the 'twenties, and the obstacles are now mainly fiscal and political. Will our delayed entry into EEC reduce the City to a minor role in this or will, as has so often happened in the past, high finance find a way over and around diplomatic obstacles so that, even with an ambiguous political status, we shall play a major role? It is apparent that some of our self-imposed handicaps can be removed, for example, the abolition of British transfer duties and the liberalization of rules on bearer securities with negotiable coupons. The more far-seeing British stockbrokers, profiting by the London Stock Exchange's belated general sanction to the principle of overseas representation, have set up some 31 offices overseas.

This development is a recognition that the underlying issue is not merely one of profiting from safehaven funds, whether in Switzerland, Luxembourg or elsewhere, with the rather 'unethical' connotation attached to this activity. The international spread of large corporations, the accumulation of 'homeless' funds by interests obliged to withdraw from or cut down their operations in Asia and Africa, the steady growth of oil royalties in the hands of Arab rulers, have created a new pool of funds on which national jurisdictions have no legitimate claim, and to which 'parallel loans' notions resting on the premises of national capital resources are irrelevant. National authorities may continue to tighten up their tax regulations so as to reduce the attractions of tax havens, but the steady internationalization of manufacturing organizations, the transfer of royalties, the aeroplane which makes the concept of 'residence' a matter of timetable interpretation – all these combine to blur parish boundaries. Even the British 'Big Four' tacitly accept that there is now a field of activity which is no longer to be left to 'gnomes', from Zurich or anywhere else. The Westminster's participation in the underwriting syndicate of one of the international loans raised in Germany, and the Midland's entry into the 'European Advisory Committee' of German, Dutch, and Belgian banks, put them on a road, which if it is to lead anywhere at all, takes them into active international investment banking.

By establishing 'free' ports and entrepots throughout the world, Britain was able to make its sterling and its bills as good as gold. In the same way our scientific discoveries and their world-wide application have helped us to retain some semblance of ascendancy in economic affairs. And a role in Europe's new endeavours can be won for Britain by our financial techniques. Here, however, the British are not the only ones on the move. Branch operations in major European towns by New York banks and reconnaissances by smaller American banks presage a more active role and American stockbrokers, who first appeared tentatively some years ago in Paris and Frankfurt to serve their own countrymen, now offer their services to all. The monthly investment plan which gave Merrill Lynch their dominating position in New York and made them 'the world's largest firm of stockbrokers' is now being offered to the new prosperous 'small men' of Europe. Competition in the older European techniques of banking and finance may not have looked very attractive to Americans in 1945; but now they can see Europe moving into the path they have followed. Their experience of the process of modern economic growth and their massive resources make them formidable competitors. White, Weld & Co. have played a leading role in the Eurobond market and in the foundation of a secondary market in Certificates of Deposit, and, more recently, the introduction of Euro-Commercial Paper – basically a negotiable form of promissory note. And in keeping even one jump ahead, only the most rigorous professional training and mental toughness will ensure a future for British banking institutions. Indeed what is at stake is our very capacity to direct our own financial affairs.

CHAPTER SIX

The Men in Charge

'Wear Their Brave State Out'

After nearly two hundred years of such a history, after so many fresh starts, so many old ventures wound up, so many unforeseen new ones, one would expect to find merchant bankers possessing at least their fair share of 'British' qualities, good and bad, and not a few of the strengths and weaknesses of that oft-discussed though vaguely defined 'Establishment'. The definition always remains vague. For if one can identify the outline of the crests and even recognize some of the supporters, the quarterings and devices are never quite filled in. And among the heraldic beasts, the shadings run from the truly mythical to the utterly phoney. In close up the merchant bankers appear not only as the 'heirs to adventure', to quote the title aptly lifted for the history of their bank from the Tudor poet, Nicolas Breton, by Brown Shipley, but also as the only too human inheritors of all the strands and episodes of our rough island story. Their counting houses range from the panelled and crusty in unblitzed and pleasantly under-developed back courts of the City to the steel, concrete, and chromium skyscrapers of our time. Their homes, too, bear record of past struggles of social climbing and of safe arrival at the summit in a land whose fondest illusion is that the Domesday Book is the basic social register. The pawnbroker's three balls, we are reminded with a slight cough, was the Lombard coat of arms.

Thus it is that the boards of the leading accepting houses range from those which are pure *Debrett* to others which, with an effort, might make Pears' *Encyclopaedia*. When the first edition was written the Chairman of the Accepting Houses Committee and senior managing director of Baring Brothers, the oldest bank, was Sir Edward Reid. His courtly manner is appropriate to the son of one of Queen Victoria's Maids-of-Honour, the Honourable Susan Baring, and of the Queen's physician. The gestures and remarks which turn a meeting into an occasion will be remembered next day by others who will kick themselves for not having had the grace to have thought of them first. And in the older style of the City he began in his family bank as a clerk and, in forty-two years of banking, learned every professional and human problem which could concern his own generation in the counting house.

Yet a straight numerical count of senior members of even the older accepting houses could be produced to disprove the charge of a closed Establishment preserve. A growing number are probably men who rose by merit and without benefit of family connection, while the basic English litmus test of accent might reveal a broader social base than the boards of a similar number of companies in other economic spheres. The picture of progressive 'democratization' may perhaps begin to fade once some more qualitative test is applied, such as that of Jewish preference if not exclusivity. The number of Abel-Smiths may seem to be increasing rather than diminishing. But there appear to be such striking exceptions that any attempt to prove a rule is soon abandoned. While it is easy to sneer at social orders where the young master rather self-consciously mingles with the tenants, Sir Edward Reid and his generation grew up in a much less self-conscious and consequently a blessedly more human world; in the Edwardian hey-day human relations still possessed virtue in themselves and 'service', 'duty', and 'responsibility' had not quite become debased verbal currency. For all the paternalism implicit in a system of private partnerships, the merchant bankers were insistent that their progeny should learn the trade from the bottom up, lick stamps, look up entries in company registers, keep ledgers, check bills, and so learn what were the responsibilities of each member of the staff and on whom at a later stage they could call for information, advice, and decision. By its very nature, banking must be a meticulous craft and the document issued in London can be seized upon in Athens or Beirut by a lawyer whose livelihood consists in finding profit for his clients in a missing comma or a wrong date.

Then, after the routine, there was a grand tour, as when the 'young' Kleinworts were sent round the world in the early 'twenties to meet the local correspondents and the main clients of their family bank before they settled down to the task of accepting bills, for at that time every bill of Kleinwort, Sons and Company was personally accepted by a partner belonging to one of the families of the bank. If some traditions have lingered longer in merchant banking than elsewhere in the City, it is not because they were held to have some inherent virtue but because they were part of the training in responsibility. In retrospect this seems to have been one of the most important contributions of the accepting houses between the wars, when less edifying City practices at times threatened to replace older norms of personal conduct. Today the cheques and bills may still be brought in for signature during the later stages of boardroom lunch while the guest copes with a port of rather sweet character for the palate of the Pall Mall clubman. If the gesture has now little more meaning than the Changing of the Guard, it nevertheless remains as the outward token of the assimilative power which turned Central European Jews, Yankee merchants, and Bombay traders into pillars of the City.

When it would have been so easy for banking dynasties to relax, follow the Barsetshire hounds, and never be seen in their banking parlours, they deserve credit for upholding this tradition of personal responsibility. But if they had been made thoroughly aware of the risks of idleness, they may have overlooked another peril. Too strict instruction in the minutiae of double ledger entry and in the office routine of banking can produce something akin to ritualism. Among groups who unwittingly isolate themselves by a specialized media of communication, as well as by the rules and rotes of family clannishness, the small change of minor issues becomes inflated into a currency which looks spurious to the outsider. This particularly afflicts 'Establishments' who take themselves too seriously. The older merchant banking training, which concentrated on the basic procedures of banking and on the human relations of counting house and partners' room, was perfectly adequate so long as the universal gold sovereign and its first cousin, the bill on London, provided the stable elements of continuity. Coupled with a certain shrewdness about men and affairs gained by experience, this was sufficient to ensure success, as was the analogous British training of district commissioner, military column commander, and consul. A conscious framework of concepts was not required when the British were in a position to direct events according to their own liking.

But when faced in the 'twenties by the historical paradox of unintended consequences, the weakness of an upbringing where

161

critical analysis and concept formation had been neglected betrayed itself by a continual misreading of cause and effect in world affairs. If our motives had been so, therefore, in spite of evidence to the contrary, the outcome must be so too. The comforting habits of routine and social division bolstered up the illusion that the world of Edwardian ascendancy could be re-created. The merchant bankers were not the only ones. 'The world's great age begins anew,' pontificated George Nathaniel Curzon, moving the congratulatory address to the Crown on the victory achieved over the Central Powers; and out came the toppers and round went the sweetish port.

Since the majority of all classes of British society were doing their best to maintain the illusion, it worked – for a time: the bucket shops and City scandals of the late 'twenties and early 'thirties were generally dismissed as the intrusions of cads and outsiders. Improvisation, coupled with the extensive knowledge of personalities and firms throughout the world, could still work wonders. The nineteenth-century practice of endorsing an incoming letter with some comment drawn from memory or experience seemed to serve as well – and sometimes even better than – systems of card indices and tagged files giving background and precedent. An essential part of the mystique was that the merchant banker had a phenomenal memory and a capacity for split-second judgement and decision. But in a world where Britain was ceasing to enjoy any sort of supremacy and where narrower professional competence had to be supplemented by an understanding of the potentialities and limitations of general situations, even the highest sense of responsibility was not enough. The introduction into the banks of friends of the family and sons of the friends was imperceptibly loosening the cement of personal responsibility without providing a more imaginative professionalism. Although, in the partners' room, the daily small change could be passed round for approving comment, there was an irritating world outside which was insisting in doing things in an un-English way. Asked what had been the toughest problem he had faced in banking, Sir Cyril Kleinwort replied: 'As a member of the Joint Committee of British Short-Term Creditors to Germany, attempting to persuade my colleagues that Hitler could meet his obligations but was using the available foreign exchange to rearm.'

Yet, compared with other sectors of British finance between the wars, merchant bankers stood out by their insistence on strict standards of professional competence. The thorough training of every new entry – however he may have been introduced – was part of their tradition. And the standards of those selected for higher posts were in theory those demanded of the whole personnel of the bank. A code of professional conduct, if it is observed, is still better than the rules of shop-stewards' handbooks, while human relationships, if they can be preserved, are preferable to the gimmicks of 'man management'. Even two wars and vast economic and political changes have not obliter-ated the features of British society from which such codes and relationships have been derived. The myth of the Edwardian leisured gentleman – at times in rather strange versions – still remains the approximation of a social goal for the majority of Britons who have some conscious notion of 'bettering themselves'. Sad though it may appear to 'progressives', Britain has not yet found another to take its place. Any rival model tends to be presented with such an air of self-conscious defiance that at the outset we can guess that its life will be short. The outside world has been surprisingly tolerant of the English and their myths, perhaps because they only do harm to the English themselves, but perhaps also for the same reason that they have treasured the papacy, as being at least something to believe in.

Tradition as an Asset

Possession – when this means both wealth and the brains to make wealth work usefully – is nine-tenths of the law of further acquisition. The accumulated capital assets of one hundred and fifty years of British ascendancy have not all been entirely dissipated. It is not empty myth-making which maintains S. Pearson & Sons, the £100 millions industrial and financial empire of Lord Cowdray, whose interests, ranging from Lazards and great engineering enterprises to Chessington Zoo, still go on expanding, and which, through its subsidiaries, Standard Industrial Group and Industrial Selection Trust, is moving into transport, whisky, gin, and property. Prior to August 1969, S. Pearson had no stock exchange quotation and many of the constituent companies of the Cowdray group and its nominees remained private, so it is not surprising that round Lazards itself there for long hung an aura of mystery.

There certainly seems to be a solid core of unpublicized assump-tions in a bank when, after fifty years of being presided over by Kindersleys, Viscount Hampden was appointed Chairman in 1964.

Soon afterwards three new managing directors of Lazards were named, none of whom were over forty. They may have been well-connected, but they were also well-equipped professionally as research economist, lawyer, and accountant respectively, and had proved themselves as able bank executives. Lord Poole became Chairman of Lazards in 1965 and has continued to appoint the under-forties to the board which now numbers twenty-four. There is an ease and flexibility about Lazards' methods of operating which seem to combine the older British manner with a fresh view of the world; this was reflected in a new conception of export finance which aroused the baffled envy of Britain's main industrial competitors, and has subsequently been developed by other merchant and clearing banks.

The convenience of common assumptions is in fact the 'magic' of Establishment. It enables the newcomer who shares them to get the feel of the house in twenty-four hours and there is no problem about spelling out the lowest common denominators of conduct, efficiency, honesty, and all the rest. If a higher quotient is required, it is more readily developed in a familiar form of life than in some strange species fished out from some other environment. And as he climbs the ladder it is so much easier to present him to a wider public: if he is rather ordinary, he becomes 'approachable' or 'modest', if he makes no mistakes he has 'shrewd judgement'; and without being Galtonians we can concede that he will develop whatever innate ability he may possess rather quicker than would more inhibited outsiders. 'Old Stinky was like that at school' disposes of the black sheep. If in addition merchant banks, such as Lazards or Morgan Grenfell, have clients of the standing of Rolls-Royce or Ford, why should they look further afield and why should Kindersleys, Cattos, and others not follow in succession? They will in due course bring the additional bonus of directorships in the other companies connected with their families. Apart from that they are such nice chaps!*

The catch about it all, and it *should* keep members of any oligarchy awake on at least one night a week if only because others depend on them for their daily bread, is whether the process is truly one of fresh acquisition or merely a redivision of old spoils? What if the magic circle is broken into by someone who does not believe in the old spells and simply sacks Stinky for being an infernal nuisance? The founders

---

* *Author's Note*. They are too! The affairs of Rolls Royce however have proved to be less so!

of the accepting houses themselves set the example of what upstart intruders with different accents could do. For the world is changing and, in the last analysis, the world and its wife are not prepared to support the English love of myths at the cost of their own pocket, any more than most of us allow workaday necessities to be subordinated to the precepts of the Sunday sermon. The merchant banker may excel in his skill, and his staff, however he recruited them, be superbly trained: but if someone starts changing the rules, it will all be of no avail.

The great virtue of Sir Siegmund Warburg in the post-war world was not that he broke any rules but primarily that he forced his fellow-bankers to think out consciously what was their role in the changing world, while he himself demonstrated how London could profit from the new rules being consciously devised by the new Europe. His rivals had been slow to realize that, on the Continent, other games than cricket and polo were now in vogue. The Warburg interests in Breda provided an inside understanding of what was afoot in the whole complex of Italian parastatal industries, his exploratory sallies revealed fresh banking and financing possibilities in the new industrial areas of Germany which others assumed to be mainly inhabited by bearded dwarfs hammering out cuckoo clocks in underground smithies. Added to that, the years between his flight from Hitler in 1933 and the moment in 1946 when he was able to establish a full-blown finance house afforded Sir Siegmund Warburg opportunity to evolve a coherent philosophy of merchant banking adapted to the needs of the second half of the twentieth century. The period when he was limited to currency arbitrage and barter work was also one of fruitful reflection.

And for S. G. Warburg the international aspect of merchant banking remains part of its distinctive character. 'There is no major piece of business conducted for any sizeable client which does not have its foreign angle,' maintains Sir Siegmund. 'The disinclination of the British for solving problems by structural arrangements is one of their strengths. Even if the Continental approach has its virtues in arriving at logically formulated conclusions, the British contribution can be an important factor in separating the essentials of a problem from the unessentials.' And as for domestic business? 'The role of the merchant banker is akin to that of the Harley Street specialist' is the favourite Warburg analogy. 'His advice is still sought even where he is not the man who actually orders the patient into a hospital bed.'

There need in theory be no fear that, as advisers to industry and commerce, merchant bankers will one day find that the finance directors and the investment officers of great enterprises have learned all the answers and will dispense with their services. 'When any major operation is pending, one surgeon always calls in another for an independent opinion,' says the resourceful founder of Warburgs. In slightly different form, some of the older dynasties say the same. 'I rather doubt if the law of size for survival will apply to merchant banks,' suggests Sir Cyril Kleinwort. 'To a very large extent they sell personal advice and certainly to this extent, size is of little importance.'

But if Sir Siegmund Warburg refuses to see merchant banking skills as wasting assets, it is because he believes that feeling and instinct underlie them, as well as professional competence, and these are born afresh with every new generation of mankind. While this is perhaps not so remote from the British Establishment belief in 'character', he prefers his own, somewhat mysterious, notion of 'professional dilettantism' which may possibly be interpreted as delight in work combined with thorough competence. He rejects, however, the notion of a City 'mystique' as something which has only done harm to its standing with public and politicians. If merchant banks resort to publicity, it should, in the Warburg view, be to improve the general picture of the City as a whole, rather than to overwrite individual banks. Others may perhaps feel that the Warburg reputation has seemed excessive in relation to the capacity and resources of the house but it was, nevertheless, on a similar basis of skill and good name that the merchant banks made their main break-out a century ago.

However, by themselves there was nothing discreditable in the more traditional methods by which the older accepting houses concentrated after 1945 on restoring their time-honoured links abroad. The recovery of a sense of history and the rebuilding of tradition were as essential needs for Europe as the material advance into a ferro-concrete and chromium world. The first post-war visits by the late Sir Charles Hambro to the cities of Piedmont and Lombardy, where his bank had once assisted Cavour and Mazzini to hold government together at a time when the *risorgimento* might have collapsed, was for the Italian business and industrial community also a symbol of their country's return to the wider world of trade and sanity. Not all the inhibitions and hesitancies of the old code, as compared to the eagerness of the new men, were unjustified: there was a natural reluctance by the older merchant banks to reaccept as clients those who for a decade had profited commercially from the torture of men's bodies and the breaking of their minds. Gestures of 'forgiveness' had to be balanced against obligations to those who had put their trust in Britain at the time of our national need, and some discrimination had to be made between the competing claims on the skills and limited resources of the City. In the longer perspective the loyalties of the merchant banks will probably be seen to have yielded their own dividends.

So some of the myths which are woven into reputation are not lightly to be abandoned and tradition, even in terms of annual profits, can remain an asset. When Sir Charles Hambro died, his family successors moved almost as of dynastic right on to the boards of a network of manufacturing firms and mining finance corporations spread across several Continents. This family connection alone represents for Britain a powerful factor of influence and control over the development and use of key industrial materials for perhaps many generations to come: it is not to be rashly discarded however much the ascendancy of merchant banking families may seem an affront to the proponents of 'meritocracies'. It can be legitimately debated whether some other walk of life would have revealed the families as average, good, or geniuses, and whether Eton, Oxbridge, owning racehorses, shooting, and 'art collecting' add up to an enervating or a fortifying process. It may be that others can and will one day perform their tasks better. But so far it cannot be said that they have performed them badly. They cannot be complacent, however, for the next generation will not only have to meet professional standards far in advance of any hitherto demanded of them, but display them in a world where the going for the British will be tougher than ever before.

The New Men

At first glance the generation of the late 'thirties and early 'forties which should be moving into the top level of executive direction looks less colourful, but flamboyance is not in accordance with the *zeitgeist* and we are certainly better without some of the too carefully cultivated eccentricities of the past. In our time toughness and

167

quietness are popularly associated and it is consequently not surprising to find Mr Peter Guinness at the age of forty, after wartime minesweeping and long training in the United States and Norway, being hailed by the scribes as typifying the new wave of the 'sixties, even with six generations of family banking behind him. Nor must the role which some of the scions may be called upon to play be underrated. Since attacks on currencies, from whatever direction and for whatever reason, inevitably start buying sprees in the gold markets and finish up with selling ones, Samuel Montagu as the world's largest bullion dealers have a vital part in the ordering and control of the currency media of Britain and its friends. There is thus every reason for wishing to believe the chroniclers of contemporary City faces when they record hopefully of the Honourable David Montagu, great grandson of the first Lord Swaything who founded the bank, that his quiet manner accompanies both a strong intellect and an underlying gusto for expounding ideas in public forum as well as boardroom. It may well be in the smaller banking houses that 'character', as traditionally understood in Britain, will be most likely to persist.

However, merchant banking itself now requires such a variety of professional qualifications that no family can remain self-contained. The tightest partnership has had to bring in outsiders. The immediate cause may have been given as 'specialist knowledge' or 'wider experience', rather than 'fresh ideas' or 'new blood', but the outcome will be much the same and the pace seems to be quickening. The Hambros Board has continued to expand and included thirty-two directors with a low average age and with one exception, all working members in 1970. Most of the newer directors are divisional or departmental heads. The Rothschild partners' parlour was opened in 1960 to Mr David Colville, who became personal assistant to the Partners, then Anthony and Edmund de Rothschild. This may not at first have looked like the dawn of a new era of Rothschild history, but it was still an innovation in the merchant banking world; in 1961 Mr Michael Bucks, having made his way up through the bank, joined the Rothschild partnership, and he was followed by a barrister who had been acting as taxation adviser. 'I should not like to forecast the future' commented Mr Edmund de Rothschild, 'but a pattern has been set'. In September of 1970 N. M. Rothschild & Sons became a private limited company. The partners therefore retired before joining the new

168

board of twenty directors and four non-executive directors of N. M. Rothschild & Sons Limited. In 1964 William Brandt's Sons and Co., the last family accepting house closed preserve, admitted Mr Frank O'Brien Newman, a specialist in industrial management, now on the Board of National and Grindlays. Experts can no longer be shown in and out of the servants' entrance – as the musicians were in their time – but now claim the status as well as the rewards of power.

But it is when there have been mergers and public issues of shares in the banking groups that there develop these clashes of wills and antagonisms which throw up new ideas and men. Even a small minority holding by outside investors requires public explanation and justification, and whatever the precautions taken to maintain the family majority or controlling interest, a process of weakening their ascendancy begins and proves to be one which permits no reversal. The merger which produced Hill, Samuel and Co. pointed in only one direction: no Old Moore was needed to prophesy that the Samuel family, the Philip Hill Investment Trust, the First National City Bank, and Charles Clore would not for all time share identical views on the conduct of affairs, to say nothing of those who may acquire the shares available on the market. Public participation in merchant banking equity will certainly not diminish: whatever take-over and other chances, the capital needs as well as the ethos of the time require it. The families who have withdrawn to the bastions of a holding company, leaving the way open for the evolution of the bank as a professionally-managed subsidiary, have perhaps found a more grace-ful way of making a virtue out of the necessities presented by time, death, estate dispersal, and changing allegiances. For the individual the opportunity will still be given to prove his worth – as an individual. To their credit not a few members of banking families are ready to do this.

More recent comers to the City seem to have accepted that it is by welcoming change and by offering wider participation in top direction that they will secure the foundations they have laid: their own initial success probably gave them a sobering insight into the vulnerability of some of the older family dynasties. The small but highly capable investment bank of Leopold Joseph and sons, started after World War One by the London manager of a Swiss bank, and up to a few years ago managed by his three sons, was reconstituted in 1963 with fresh British partners and Sir Hugh Weeks joined the bank as Chairman in

1966. Following the changes from 1963 to 1966 the pace of the bank's advance quickened. Leopold Joseph, in fact, restarted almost as a new bank with a widened range of investment and stock arbitrage business.* In the same spirit Sir Siegmund Warburg resigned in 1964 as Chairman of Mercury Securities and of S. G. Warburg, commenting: 'Leaders of industry and commerce are often inclined not to step down before the decline of their capacities becomes manifest, holding on too long to their position thus preventing the formation of a strong chain of successors.' And handing over to Mr Henry Grunfeld as Chairman and Mr Gerald Coke as Deputy Chairman, he left the advice: 'They in turn will in due course want to make room for other colleagues.' Whether Sir Siegmund's oft-publicized creed of training up a competent management team of young directors and senior executives will in practice turn out to be as consequential as his own dominating presence is another matter. The Warburg requirement is for non-conformers and he himself is not discouraged by the national reputation for conformity. He believes that sufficient exceptions can be found. But wisdom in any event allows no option. The succession must be passed on and its basis made as broad as possible.

Image or Loyalty

The London merchant banking world may therefore be less in danger from the atrophy of establishment and from those who challenge its assumptions than from the cult of the phoney. Both tradition, if backed by solid worth, and 'dangerous' new ideas can combine to play their part in creation. But the representation of merchant banking as something it is not, and has never been, can be destructive. The ever-growing dominance of the 'pseudo' in the presentation of men to each other is becoming such an entrenched feature of society that it is increasingly difficult to distinguish between genuine and counterfeit. Deception is nothing new and it exists in nature's preconscious order. Nature, however, allots it a special role in her

* 587,354 of the 1,560,000 £1 shares of Leopold Joseph Holdings in issue were offered to the public at £1.70 per share and a Stock Exchange quotation granted in January 1971. A few days after dealings commenced, a sizeable buyer entered the market and, by dealing somewhat aggressively, caused the share price to rise rather rapidly.

automatism and its unnatural misuse usually results in the destruction or disappearance of the species. It is not likely to be otherwise with human creation. Our American cousins have developed conventions for accepting the phoney as the phoney and discounting it. The older Edwardian establishment play-acting possessed a certain quality of unself-consciousness and consequently of innocence. The artificial image-making of the Ad- and PR-men has no such saving grace and, once committed to it, escape is not so easy.

It is bad enough to have the tycoon informing us that his aim is 'service' when we all know it is profit. But while a banker can survive by being traditionalist or by being dynamic, a too obvious pose would undermine the trust and confidence which are the essence of his profession. At the beginning of the 'sixties some of the merchant banks were skirting perilously close to the phoney, overplaying personalities, representing the normal overseas services of banking as some esoteric skill, and exaggerating the scope of some short-term and short-lived operation. In a field where a client requires discretion such presentation is apt to be counter-productive, and by 1964 there seemed to be some change of front. This may have been due to the embarrassment which arises when pseudo-body meets a pseudo-body coming through the lie, or merely the belated discovery of the correctness of Brown Shipley's partners' view a hundred years ago when it was suggested to them that they should engage a 'publicity man' to push their steamship line: 'He would very soon get into the habit of smoking cigars and drinking brandy and water with the passengers if he had not more firmness than most of them.'

Any phoneyness in their public presentation becomes doubly dangerous for the merchant banks when the changing family circumstances and the expansion and complexity of their operations have necessitated an increase in the number of executive directors, either drawn from their management or as a consequence of mergers. The ethos of the corps of senior executives has its effect on the attitudes of all the servants of the bank and fashionable attitudes, whether cynical or loyal are damnably catching. Finding a new internal 'ethos' is difficult enough when bringing together modern methods of issue work with traditional banking procedures. The former activity tends to create a professional attitude which, at its highest, is akin to first-class diplomacy while, at its lowest, it may have something of the mentality of the barrow boy; the other breeds a sacerdotal outlook ranging from scrupulous regard for the secrets of the confessional down to a love of hocus-pocus for its own sake. The reconciliation of thrusting and scrupulous natures is only possible in an atmosphere of genuineness and personal trust. Loyalty and truth are the first two casualties when all are roped in to maintain a conspiracy to deceive.

The merchant banks have a responsibility to see that the public are informed of their activities; they are now involved in too many matters of public concern. If they are misrepresented or their role is not understood, they are liable to find themselves targets of political action and eventually subordinated to forms of control both harmful to themselves in the short run and, in the long-term, equally noxious to the public interest. Information about themselves, however, should be clearly differentiated from the PR-created image; and the picture which is most likely to find favour with public and politicians will be one which shows the merchant banks as joining in the managerial revolution now in full swing in Europe. Indeed, the retreat in Western Europe from the doctrines of collectivist social-democracy is mainly due to the resurgence of efficient and progressive capitalism, in both production and management, and on the Continent both family concerns and public companies have been fairly successful in carrying out their individual 'revolution'. True identification with progress is not achieved by lowering the tone, a regrettably prevalent notion of English 'progressives', but by demonstrating that men can rise. Setting an example by opening wider avenues of advancement to skilled management and broadening the basis of top direction form the best public relations policy.

Here, fortunately, the family ascendancies which have in so many cases persisted through into the post-World War Two world, may have enabled, albeit unwittingly, the majority of merchant banks to avoid one blind alley into which so much of Britain's enterprise has landed itself. The high professional demands they made on themselves meant that they had little patience for that stultifying corps of half-pay soldiery, admirals trained in sail, political has-beens, and civil service pensionaries who have spread mental sclerosis throughout so many British boardrooms. It has been a strange and disastrous interlude, this heaping-up of a top layer collected from the debris of professions where concealment and suppression, rather than tackling and solving problems, have been the essence of lifemanship. In its lack of logic it is a peculiarly British phenomenon, since it implies either that boards do not matter or, if they do, that neither capacity nor knowledge are required for them. The consequence has been to drive the rising technician or trained executive away to other fields of effort, usually overseas.

A bank, particularly if it is a public company with wide ramifications throughout industry and finance, may well require directors with advisory functions, as Sir Siegmund Warburg noted when he passed the chair to another member of the board, although his philosophy seems to be that even those who take up back-stage positions should in future be drawn mainly from the executive directors. But a decision to widen board representation by taking in outsiders, either because they are expected to bring with them some fresh expertise or because they can advance the bank's interest with firms with which they are associated, is also a decision as to the future nature of the bank. Smaller banks which increasingly identify themselves with industrial and commercial holdings groups may need to extend their councils in order to expand their business. For the medium-sized bank it may seem acceptable to sacrifice some independence in order, paradoxically, to retain at least some freedom of decision within the boardroom. The family may feel that their own weight is not enough. But at no time can merchant banks afford to discourage their own rising executives. As one of the new men, Mr Julian Hodge has no doubts about this:

I think it is important that those people who make a career in a merchant bank can see the ability to achieve board status. Too many businesses in Great Britain, in past years, have drawn directors from family connections, or from outside, and good managers have been completely frustrated in their undoubted ambition to become directors. On the other hand I do not think it is a good idea to have a board which consists entirely of *working* directors. Outsiders can bring valuable additional experience and objectivity to deliberations in the boardroom. Often the enthusiasm of those working in a business prevents them seeing the wood for the trees.*

The 'school solution' may well be that each time an 'outside director' is brought in, a senior manager is offered an outside boardroom post which is in the gift of the bank. Even if 'company directors' have replaced the prewar 'majors' as all too familar figures in courtroom cases, while the bank manager still enjoys an unsullied reputation, no captain ever turned down a majority.

If the economic metamorphosis ahead of Britain and Continental Europe is towards greater entities with a continual American infil-

* Interview with the author on 1 May 1965.

tration, and if there is to be a new creative phase of merchant banking, the advancement of the new professionally trained executive class becomes doubly important. Though the talk of 'service' by the button-holed, toilet-watered, Mayfair tycoon may rightly seem suspect, there still is a question of a wider interest, and this not only in the narrower sense of the technical success of share issues or the investments of institutions and individuals who have entrusted their savings to the bankers.

The growth and prosperity of merchant banks depended basically on the progress of a sturdy island stock from pioneering and settlement to a world-wide role. For the Rothschild family to make its 'killing' from Waterloo, the 'scum of the earth', as their commander-in-chief dubbed them had to stand firm in their infantry squares; and history so willed that, in April 1943, 77 Field Regiment R.A., in which Mr Edmund de Rothschild was serving as a battery officer, found itself surrounded and under enemy attack: it won through, as the British seem generally to do. Seeking their profit today the bankers have still to reckon what the preservation and reinforcement of national character add up to as assets. Some fifty years ago – in 1914 – the 'German' character of some merchant banks made them suspect but they all proved their loyalty. In our time the preponderantly Jewish character of others may give us cause to wonder to what strains they may be put if the Israeli *raison d'état,* in a still uncertain struggle for survival, makes demands which clash with Britain's needs to maintain its kith and kin in a world of assertive human diversity. But, whatever their past origins or their present associations of cult, their independent existence depends as much as ever on the competitive vigour of Britain. If this goes, so does their own *raison d'étre.*

Loyalty to the British people has been too often breached by its politicians and civil servants over the past two decades, particularly in the six years of the Macmillan administration. It was a betrayal which brought both economic and moral detriment and something of a breakdown in trust. 'The British people have lost the will to govern', said Mr Duncan Sandys, according to Sir Roy Welensky, and Lord Alport went into the night to be sick. When, in the Commons, Sir Frank Soskice announced that it must be accepted that Britain had become a multi-racial society he was cheered by the Labour ranks, presumably applauding our impending genocide. Lest merchant bankers think such matters are not their concern they need only recall the descendants of the *k und k* bankers peddling British Forces Vouchers in Viennese back streets. They had no choice when circumstances overtook them. It remains the task of all members of the directing institutions of society to ensure that 'circumstances' never break in on them and that for the British people, as well as for themselves, there is always scope for choice.

CHAPTER SEVEN

What Sort of Career?

The Staff Requirement

Since it will be the vision and ambitions of the top executive grades which will determine what choice is eventually made, how are the men recruited and trained? How may a young man hope to rise to the highest level of this profession and what are the number and range of top jobs open to him? If a merchant bank does nothing which is not done by someone else, how does he equip himself professionally? What awaits him in the interim as he jostles for his share of whatever elbow room is available on the way to the top? If from time to time he looks across at those struggling up neighbouring paths, how will he seem to be faring age for age or diploma for diploma with his contemporaries in the civil service, law, medicine, industrial manage- ment, or even in the dubious trafficking of politics? And in the intangibles – the human interest, the range of activity, the pleasure in learning and applying skill, the excitement of action, the satisfaction of accomplishment – will he feel 'stretched' or will he sense an aching void which the responsibilities of family life and the substitutes of hobbies fail to fill? What will hold his loyalty?

Obviously there is no six-monthly departmental hand-out of honours and awards as in governmental bureaucracy, no assured consolatory knighthoods, nor the headlines of politics and the law. The limited number and size of merchant banks demonstrate that, as a sole whole-time occupation, it is a top profession for the few. Admittedly the total number of directors of the Accepting Houses in December 1970 was 363 compared to the hundred or so Permanent and Deputy Secretaries who head the Home Civil and Foreign

Services. But, while there are some 2,750 members of the Administrative Grades of the Civil Service ordered in a rising hierarchy based quite largely on seniority and for which the Civil Service Commission has annual recruitment targets of approximately eighty and thirty for the Home Civil and Diplomatic Services respectively, the annual intake of young banking aspirants probably averages some two hundred, with no certainty for any of them that they will rise above a purely clerical level of tasks. The comparison cannot, of course, be taken too far since merchant banking offers a range of senior managerial posts – difficult to estimate numerically – with salaries and other emoluments decidedly more advantageous than those of the medium and senior grades of the Home Civil and Foreign Services. In addition the wastage is high, reflecting in great part the haphazard methods of recruitment. Even in a 'good' year, the seventeen Accepting Houses probably lose about 25 per cent of their younger men, either because of unsuitability or because they have found attractive alternatives. Some of the houses admit ruefully that they have lost annually up to four times the number of their intake. The consequence is in turn a tendency to over-recruit. But even allowing for this, the base and peak of the profession suggest a comparatively broad pyramid.

The merchant banks have also to compete with the recruiting posters of the clearing banks: 'You Could Be A Leader Among Men', 'Our Sort Of Man?' The clearers can hold out the promise of a salary of at least £1,600 per annum at thirty-one, for outstanding men of twenty-nine some £2,000 per annum, including prospects of managerial status by the early thirties with an annual salary of close to £2,400. One of every two entrants will achieve the latter, say the staff managers of the main clearing banks, who these days lack only the red sash and cockade of the recruiting sergeant, and they suggest that the majority of entrants will go further and no one with 'A' level GCE or its Scottish equivalent is barred by birth or education from top executive positions up to and well beyond £5,000. The school-leaver entrant to a clearing bank can have study leave to prepare for his Institute of Bankers' examination; although the university graduate is welcome his degree confers no special guarantee of speedier advancement or favour.* The branch manager in an expand-

* The Diploma of the Institute of Bankers can be passed in three years but on average it takes between five and six. It consists of two parts. Part I has papers in English, Economics, Bookkeeping, General Principles of Law, and Commercial

177

ing industrial economy is clearly a person of considerable status in the community; in our century, as against the nineteenth, he doubtless rates higher in the social scale and in public esteem than minister, dominie, or doctor. The salary scales and working conditions of merchant banks must thus pivot round those of the clearers and they will not find the men they want by offering less. In practice, if an applicant has special qualifications or experience in, say, languages, he can probably succeed in bargaining for something higher than the equivalent clearing bank salary for his age. A salary scale running from £1,200-£1,400 at twenty-five years of age to £3,000 at thirty-five for an outstanding man would not be unusual in merchant banking.

Banking in general has not always seemed so attractive a profession. In the 1920s there was over-recruitment, and the consequences were acerbated by the many mergers and amalgamations between the wars. But few banks, clearing, overseas, or merchant, foresaw the consequences of the removal of official credit restrictions in 1958 – the rapid growth in the number of accounts, the opening of new branch offices (911 by the clearing banks from 1960 to 1964). Meanwhile the extension of the range of banking activities placed new tasks on the senior executives and general managers of the clearers for which, it must be admitted, few of them were qualified by temperament or training. Inherently this points to a need for something on the lines of the Civil Service division into Administrative and Executive Grades. An approximation of this seems already hinted at by the growing practice of banks recruiting men in the twenties with experience of other professions and the introduction of 'special merit grades' with appropriate salary addition or merit bonus, which may be as much as £300 a year, for the promising young bank clerk. The complete step has not yet been taken, however, a factor being perhaps that clearing bank experience with university graduates has shown a high wastage, mainly, it would seem, because their qualifications were not put to early use.

Geography. Only two of the papers have to be taken and passed simultaneously, and exemption is allowed if 'A' levels are held in the subjects. Part II covers Commercial Law, Monetary Theory and Practice, Accountancy Finance, Foreign Trade and Foreign Exchange, and Practice of Banking. Candidates for the latter examination, which is two parts, generally study at evening classes or by means of correspondence courses. Failure rate is as high as forty per cent but the pass rate has recently been helped by the action of some of the clearing banks in introducing a Day Release scheme offering examinees half a day off a week or about two weeks a year at a revision course. Banks generally aid candidates with the cost of their studies by providing a tax-free bonus of £30 after Part I and £100 after Part II.

The reason is that the clearing bank system demands basically a thorough training in the routine of counter work, just as police forces claim that ultimately there is no substitute for experience on the constable's beat. Overseas banks, on the other hand, always had a special entry category of 'management trainees' but this derived its justification from the need to manage 'native' employees, not – as would no doubt be asserted in these days of the maudlin cult of human equality – because of any assumed inferior local capacity, but because of the importance of knowing the 'mind' of the London head office.

With the merchant banks the staffing problem is of a different order. There is no volume of counter work: 'business' is with other banks, with finance houses, with the financial departments of every type of company, and with brokers in the various fields of money and securities. Where a merchant bank has private clients, these tend to have something 'special' about them – either they are resident overseas, possess mainly overseas assets, or have some very compelling reason why their banking requirements do not fall within the framework of normal clearing services.

Superficially the appearance of a merchant bank is misleading. The banking hall's similarity with those of other banks extends to a counter and guichets; the paper being checked at the sea of desks in the rear looks much the same as in any other bank and a sharpsighted observer may spot much the same forms and revenue stamps. There is the usual background clatter of typewriters. But at the counter there is no irritated queue waiting to cash cheques for five or ten pounds while the teller, ever so conscientiously, counts out the grimy notes and dulled coins paid in by Bloggs' Supermarket, whose messenger lounges at one side blowing tobacco smoke into the faces of the unfortunate. In the merchant bank, notices over the guichets say: 'Bills For Collection', 'Inland Bills', 'Documentary', etc., and the commissionaires and other visitors waste neither their own nor anyone else's time in collecting the packets prepared for them. At the hatch or counter section where the top-hatted representatives arrive and depart, the eavesdropper would at most catch references to 'Old cock ...', '... on the wireless last night ...', the names in the latest City joke or scandal, or technical references to the bat-and-ball game customarily played south of the Border in summertime. The history of merchant banking shows that, although counter work and checking of names and dates on bills, cheques, and payment advices, and verifying them against books are necessary for control and have to be meticulously conducted to avoid disastrous consequences, these are not the essence of the profession.

Clearing bank managers have little latitude for decisions over requests for credit and must recommend any departure from agreed lines to their superintendent of branches at Head Office or to their local boards of directors, however rapidly the system may work in the era of telephone and telex. But a merchant bank manager learns early to take responsibility himself – even where formal endorsement has later to be given by a director. The most thorough knowledge of banking procedures and definitions will not by itself enable him to come to even a tentative opinion on acceptance credit lines, advances short or long-term, issue prospects, or investment possibilities. In fact it would appear that the ideal aspirant merchant banker should be a fully qualified accountant and a brilliant linguist, passing from Arabic to Finnish without batting an eyelid, who has found time to pass the examinations of the Institute of Bankers and, while able to do the complicated mental arithmetic of spot and forward rates in any currency, has also acquired some acquaintanceship with company law and conveyancing. Ideally he should possess a knowledge of Stock Exchange practice equal to the most accomplished stockbroker, be ruthless in his assessment of his fellow men and withal remain a sympathetic human being, putting at ease both Cabinet Ministers in their moments of muddlement and the man who has come in to fix his phone.

Since no such paragon exists, most merchant banks aim in practice at building up their staffs as teams of first-class specialists in these various fields of accomplishment, while their organization problem is to ensure that they do function as a team. Where the tradition and ethos of the bank has developed a practice of informal consultation and easy harmony, this may be no problem at all, although the organization charts and 'spiders' – if any could be produced – would turn an efficiency expert's hair grey. Where an organization has to be created consciously, either because of a merger or the deliberate expansion of the bank's activities, the problem is less easy of solution – if indeed there is an organizational solution at all. Satisfactory answers to merchant banking questions are usually the result of mutual professional respect developed round the basic skills of a quick grasp of percentages and a capacity to read a balance sheet at sight, then demonstrating in lucid terms its relevance to the problems under study. For the latter skill, the implications of what a balance

180

sheet does not reveal are at least as important as what it discloses. Credits, issues, take-overs, mergers, portfolio investment – all require the ability to make a quick and accurate judgement on the resources, liquid and fixed, of a company; what its obligations are, what possible 'concealed' assets exist, and what could be embarrassing liabilities under adverse business conditions or if confidence sagged through no fault of the firm itself.

This is not in itself difficult to learn, not even for those who have never had a professional training as auditors. But the context in which the balance sheet is read determines the significant points for the banker. Is it advisable to add to the firm's indebtedness by an acceptance credit? Does the cash flow warn of reefs ahead for future dividends? Is there an item which should cause a would-be bidder to think again? The accountant, the investment analyst, the credits manager, and the legal adviser see the balance sheet from different angles and their judgements, jointly or singly, should determine the decisions of the bank. A well-run merchant bank is one where there is an easy but frank interplay of views between the members who specialize in all these subjects. The hierarchical organization is secondary to this.

Problems of Responsibility

And who will bear the formal responsibility of decision? In theory the partners or directors, in between moments of taking off for Johannesburg, Sydney, Montreal, and New York. This would hardly seem to leave time for reflection. Even where they follow more sedentary modes, it will probably be on the manner and method of presentation of the problem that they will make their decision and not on its substance: they will rarely be able to rethink it all out in detail for themselves. The form and practice of the role which partners and directors see themselves playing are in any case as myriad as the concepts of 'merchant bank'. Some actively exploit their outside directorships to bring new business to the bank so that matters already agreed in substance between themselves and their outside colleagues require only executive implementation from the management. Other directors bury themselves in such executive detail as to be barely distinguishable in function from the managers. At the other extreme are merchant banking boards whose members pursue their own profit or pleasure in ways which may or may not benefit the bank, leaving its running to the managers who can in their turn either follow the minimum required routine or boldly take the initiative in developing the bank's policy. The fluctuating fortunes of the merchant banking fraternity are largely a reflection of the various shadings and combinations of these three basic situations.

All of them have, of course, their meetings of boards, committees, and sub-committees which proliferate in the courts and by-ways of the City as much as they do in Whitehall, but since the system of following precedent – supported by previous minutes and tagged files – has barely penetrated East of the Temple, their resolutions are forgotten as soon as the meetings have broken up. So decision – and this applies to all the City and not merely to accepting houses – depends on putting partner or director in a corner where he can only say 'Yes', 'No', or 'Leave it till I come back', if he wants to escape and catch the plane for Tokyo. Does the senior manager or departmental head drive the old boy into a corner or not? Will he deploy a formidable array of logic or follow the example of the character in the pre-war Aldwych farce who found that the only way to make the rustic simpleton take action was to challenge him with: 'Gertcha! You can't do that.'

The question is one which goes beyond the City, and probably concerns the whole business world. 'It is probably the most difficult problem which the merchant banks have to face,' considers Sir Cyril Kleinwort:

> It arises largely because in Britain the concepts of direction and manage-ment have become all muddled up. In simpler days the partners really were directors and while theoretically the latter should under modern conditions have a considerable knowledge of the working of the departments of the bank, there has been no time to build this up. Under the circumstances main emphasis must be given to building up a management which will eventually steer general policy. The formulation of the latter should then theoretically be the function of directors. A solution along the lines of the German division of *aufsichtsrat* and *vorstand* is one possibility. But in most institutions I am in favour of higher executives having a seat on the board whilst they hold their executive positions. In the last analysis I see no cut and dried solution because the differences in the merchant banks are determined by the differing nature of their business.

Mr Gordon Richardson sees a less clear-cut distinction between senior categories:

Before the second world war, merchant banks consisted essentially of partners and clerks, the latter being organised by one or more managers. The decision was a question of risk and it was the partners' own money which was being committed; once the decision was taken, the subsequent conduct of business rested basically on the clerks. Today the business of a merchant bank and the decisions it calls for are quite different. They require professional expertise in both directors and staff. This means that directors must be operating professionals; it means too that the division of responsibilities between the directors and their senior staff or managers is less abrupt than it used to be. While the directors must remain responsible for the pattern and nature of a bank's business, I should look for ideas and initiative from the senior staff as well. We should not get high-grade managers and senior staff if we did not make this clear. Ideas are not things which are thrown out at the top, but develop from doing something. I therefore expect the generation of ideas and the practical conduct of business to go hand-in-hand at the levels of both directors and senior staff. Merchant banking is thus a job where personal capacity and creative talents can be employed.*

Apprenticeship in responsibility is, therefore, for the aspirant in merchant banking ultimately a question of getting to know his men. His elders have their own lifemanship for intimidating the young and the apprentice is liable to have early experiences which may shake his faith in his own capacity or over-impress him with the legend of merchant banking mystique: for example, having his senior draw his attention to some bankruptcy in the morning paper and telling him to look up the files to see that some years before the apparently sound firm had had an application for credit turned down. He may at that point despair of ever developing a nose for financial affairs until perhaps after many months he realizes from the records or from gossip that the senior in question had opposed every application from potential customers for the past thirty years.

Given the range of tasks, this is the absorbing aspect of the profession: it is all about people and there is nothing more interesting to people than other people. Like the clearing banks, merchant banks have been increasingly prepared to accept diplomas and qualifications of other professional bodies, not necessarily because this will add to the number of technicians in the banking halls or upstairs parlours, but because they have sensed the benefit when coping with the wider variety of persons and entities involved in their new ventures at home and abroad. The concept of the balanced team of specialists is therefore decidedly a post-1950 one and it is not by any means

* Interview with author on 29 April 1965.

accepted as a conscious staff policy in all the main merchant banks. A tradition of engrained habits which appear to derive virtue from the mere fact of their existence does not readily yield to the notion of responsibility born of specialist expertise.

Since, however, the old tradition cannot itself cope with all the new problems, the compromises with specialist efficiency take as many forms as there are accepting houses. They all possess a common underlying feature in that the Sunday theology that decision is for those at the top is preserved by a weekday practice which in fact reduces their options. This has the same consequences as in other sectors of our national life, that there is plenty of room for manoeuvre, for ambiguity, for face-saving, for human success – and failure. It is – and will remain so until they cease finding universal values in their mirror images – the English way of doing things. Those ready adapters, the Scots, have long since decided to leave well alone and not push too far their own national predilection for logic.

However the working level of pre-war accepting houses tended to have a cosmopolitan character and this, paradoxically enough, was not due to their German or Jewish origins but was the result of the anglicization of the founding families and the consequent shortage of younger British key personnel with the requisite linguistic and other overseas background. It was easier to engage a German, Frenchman, or Spaniard to handle correspondence in their mother tongue and deal with desk matters about their countries. Not surprisingly, since foreign exchange dealing and securities arbitrage between main European centres constituted a large part of daily business, the trilingual Swiss were to be found in charge of these departments and sections. The ascendancy of 'foreigners' at the working level may not have been the happiest feature of merchant banking between the wars. There was an absence of the old clan loyalty and of that formerly shown by the protégés sent to London by the uncles and cousins in Hamburg, Berlin, or Vienna. The 'foreign' wave of the 'twenties constituted its own network within the City and had its own contacts overseas: their virtual monopoly of the international telephone, which like most new-fangled things was making slow progress in the face of English resistance, and their dominance of indigenous juniors gave them greater freedom of action than the partners would have wished – had they known. And they certainly did not neglect their personal interests in the process.

This is not a blanket condemnation. There were faithful servants in every bank. Mr Lionel Fraser has described the pleasant atmosphere and the sympathetic coaching he was given in the ways of the world by Helbert Wagg's foreign managers. But this interlude, prolonged by the wartime years, did mean that there was a passing scarcity of British managerial personnel to handle the executive responsibility of the multitude of new tasks facing merchant banking after 1945. It had also the fortuitous consequence that, to remedy the deficiencies, it was necessary to bring in from outside a stronger leavening of professionally-equipped men. In particular, the strong quota of demobilized servicemen after the war injected into merchant banking a corps of men who, after completing in their spare time the various professional training courses interrupted by hostilities, still retained the habits of responsibility and command which the wartime services offer to those who by nature are fitted to exercise them.

Rewarding Competence

How are the merchant banks planning to encourage and reward professional competence, especially since their own future as well as the economic viability of Britain itself depends on a conscious grasp of purpose and not on the preservation of old nostalgia about 'Empire' nor on current cant about a universal 'Man'? The dealers in their securities sections must not only be familiar with the range of technical situations of Stock Exchange jobbery but also understand the general framework of investment policies required to meet the institutional needs of funds where the public interest is involved. Their issue departments must consider what wider events can react on the fortunes of the clients' companies they are helping to launch, and what may be the effect on the reputation of the bank. The credit and foreign exchange departments have to take into account how far political controversies may alter the country's international financial standing. All this demands imagination as well as skill. Nor is it only with the clearers that the merchant banks must compete if they are to build up a generation of young executives equipped for the world of tomorrow; they must offer a professional attraction to the cream of young accountants, economists, lawyers, and linguists. A full human being will not be satisfied merely with his pay cheque. The satisfaction of work comes in great part from the application of his knowledge and from the stimulus of daily co-operation with inspiring colleagues.

185

Rather than following the concept of a team of specialists, Sir Siegmund Warburg believes he can find the answer in developing 'all purpose' bankers with original ideas, who will not be deterred from action by the fear of making mistakes. The specialist role is seen as something for non-action fields such as research. The development of something akin to 'special merit grades' seems workable enough in the Warburg *weltanschauung*, which holds that every spur should be applied to ambition and, if a younger man of ability is seen by his contemporaries to be advancing, they will be encouraged to emulate him, and where the case is proven they will accept his leadership. Since Sir Siegmund Warburg prefers that 'properly qualified insiders' should take precedence over outsiders in the composition of boards of merchant banks, their comparative smallness should not therefore be a career disadvantage. Indeed his firm view is that merchant banks of the future should not be too big: what is the 'optimum maximum' may be difficult to define, and probably discovered only when it is too late.

The Rothschild staffing philosophy is a fairly pragmatic compromise. 'We need one or two all-rounders', says Mr Edmund de Rothschild. 'But the pure banking side and investment management are each in themselves too vast and complex for one man to be expert in both. We try, however, in each branch to move men around so that eventually they will find their own niche.' Some occasional exception may be made for a man with specific professional qualifications but as a rule Rothschilds set no particular store by university graduates. 'A suitable school-leaver who is taken on will be encouraged to go to evening classes and equip himself with, say, foreign languages, as well as being given facilities to study for his Institute of Bankers' Examination, but it is not only the question of finding them. There's also the problem of those who leave.'

If the City has not always drawn from the best output of the nation's educational and professional institutions, this has been due in no small measure to the reputation acquired by the older – and one hopes nearly extinct – tradition of pulling off 'smart ones', of dirty jokes, and of bridge-and-golf in Darkest Surrey as the *summum bonum* of human existence. All this seems to be dropping down the scale along with the jokes which were regarded as funny merely because they were dirty, and the City is all the better for their disappearance.

Nevertheless the requirements of the new situation do point to the need for the merchant banks to follow the clearers' example and work out some more orderly arrangement of promotion. Provided it is never allowed to become too rigid and is operated with sufficient discretion left to the senior managers and the staff manager, it will be a decided advance on the older, more haphazard, even if human, basis of entrance and advancement. Compromises are doubtless inevitable during periods of transition. 'In the first instance recommendations for promotion must come from top management', suggests Sir Cyril Kleinwort. 'I think these recommendations should go to one director who should, to a certain extent, specialize in this and have immediate recourse at all time to a management committee.' An age whose concepts of right and privilege derive from union contracts, employers' agreements, welfare laws, and administrative regulations, may dismiss the methods employed under family predominance as 'nepotism' or 'favouritism'. The dismissal may at times be too easy. But against that, customary arrangements will only operate satisfactorily if they are generally acceptable and, when they cease to be so, those who ignore the change do so at their peril.

The banking families have with rare exceptions been relaxed enough to accept change as soon as the need for it was brought home to them. They had, in common with the rest of the City, abandoned the apprenticeship concept which a hundred years ago required parents or guardians to deposit a substantial surety, while the young entrant received five pounds per annum in his first two years, ten pounds in his third, and rose to twenty pounds in his seventh and final year. The bright young man is now offered pay and conditions which initially seem as attractive as in any other main profession with a slight added-glamour element. The main problem which is likely to face merchant banks will be to keep men of real ability under conditions where either the family has not yet retired into neutrality or a bottleneck has resulted from the pre-war paucity of indigenous managerial talent and subsequent over-recruitment in the post-war demobilization period. Even though boardroom tables become longer or more elliptical, it will not take a young professional long to calculate his numerical chances of acquiring a seat at them as he counts the family, its protégés, checks the age groups of the senior executives, and considers the expectation of life. His actuarial conclusions will soon enough have their consequences on morale at the working level and thus on the efficiency of the bank itself. And outside prowl the management selection agencies, growing in size and importance in a Britain which has too long neglected professional training,

G

who are not averse to piratical methods in securing promising executives for their clients in commerce and industry.

How far have the accepting houses foreseen and prepared for this? When a new chairman has been brought in from outside, particularly from some other profession, new ideas of staff selection and handling are unlikely to be long delayed. Coming from the law via the Industrial and Commercial Finance Corporation to be, at the age of forty-six, chief executive of the newly-merged bank of Schroder Wagg, Mr Gordon Richardson was quickly enough confronted with the necessity of an objective reassessment of staff policy. Indeed, by itself a merger can bring the issue to a head and one of the first consequences, as with Kleinwort Sons and Co. and Robert Benson, Lonsdale, has usually been the appointment of a full-time staff manager to handle the immediate problem of double-banking and the longer-term one of ensuring that justice will be seen to be done over appointments and promotions. Theoretically the increased spread of interests should help in equating opportunity and capacity. In the case of the newer 'merchant banks' established by financial holding interests, these have still to determine the extent of their business before they can forecast what sort of career they can offer to talent; their longer-term success may in fact depend on how quickly they can do this, and if they are to live up to their promise they have probably to give at least the same attention to investing in young men as they do in acquiring participations. How far the majority of them have grasped this is difficult to judge from their appointments to date.

Even where the family still dominates, the need to put pension schemes on a sound actuarial basis is in itself a powerful factor in bringing order into recruitment and promotion, although frequent exceptions, less from 'nepotism' than as the result of a 'bright' idea of a partner, demonstrate the persistence of the idiosyncratic in the assessment of merit. And if it is the family which pays for the idiosyncrasies, who can gainsay it? However, in the perspective of the generation coming to manhood in the 'seventies, the chances of an able and qualified entrant to a merchant bank becoming its chairman are certainly higher than they were for the late Mr Lionel Fraser or the existing Sir George Bolton when they started the hard way as exchange dealers in Helbert Wagg. It would be a loss if the obstacles and barriers of early years ceased to be part of life's experience, even though in later days extreme individualism may create its own romantic illusion that toughness is all. *Pro tem* no school-leaver nor university graduate with the right qualifications and enthusiasm need be shy in applying to a merchant bank: it would be surprising if he or she did not get at least one offer from the thirty or so houses legitimately claiming the title. Whether he or she writes in 'blind' (a normal custom these days) or whether they answer an advertisement in *The Financial Times,* their applications setting out their scholastic and other qualifications will be carefully studied and their references (which should not be overloaded with prestige names) will be taken up.

Indeed, the personal predilections of potential employers even increase the chances of recruitment. If 'non-conformism' is the Warburg cry, that of Sir Cyril Kleinwort is: 'Commonsense first – brains second'; in case the latter sounds a little too like the dangerous English preference for safe mediocrity, he qualifies it with: 'I think new staff should always be taken on a probationary basis. The decision to take him on to a permanent staff should be based on his competence without particular reference to his education.' Mr Gordon Richardson, the Chairman of Schroder Wagg, strikes a note at the other end of the scale:

If I am forced to say what I am looking for in a candidate, I would put it somewhat crudely as 'excellence'. By this I mean that I should look at his past record to see if either in his studies or in a previous job he has done something positive to offer. I of course also attach importance to a candidate's manner and impression in an interview in forming an assessment of his character and temperament. A large part of merchant banking is involved in the provision of a service: the staff should consist of people able to supply such services to our customers. Specialist qualifications I regard as important though not vital. I would expect our intake of young people to include a fair proportion of university graduates. A large proportion of the abler young men and women go through the universities today; to ignore university graduates would therefore be to exclude from our selection some of the best available talent.

Mr Julian Hodge looks for:

intelligent people with enthusiasm and an unlimited capacity for attention to detail. I think it is important to test the capacity for detail in a new entrant, because this shows whether he has a tidy or untidy mind. One is looking for a combination of reliability and ambition. It is not easy to find both.

Paths to Advancement

But whether or not the young merchant banker starts off with the average salary of £700 a year which a GCE or Scottish Leaving Certificate entrant might receive or with something tailored to his specialist qualifications, he will find himself at a desk checking details on bills, verifying them against ledgers or letters of credit, looking up names in Dun and Bradstreet, issuing travellers' cheques for staff going overseas on business, checking application coupons for issues, or writing in yesterday's prices in stock lists. He will from time to time be given initiative tests, usually in some messenger or similar capacity to find out whether he is likely to be a 'steady' or if he possesses some special aptitude. The 'steadies' can, after all, look forward to a lifetime of banking hall tasks in congenial company, with frequent summonses to the parlours to sit in on a meeting with representatives of the clients whose affairs they have been recording and with whose financial officers they have been in daily communication. As they advance in age and seniority with their opposite numbers in such firms, they will join in luncheon occasions to partake of the sweet port. Those with an aptitude for figures, a reputation for carefulness, and a natural curiosity in the doings of the City, may have a prolonged sojourn in the cash department with its daily contact with bank messengers, money brokers, and all those who make use of short-term funds. The daily round seems less a common task when the transactions are in millions rather than singles or tens. The trustee department, in addition to being a haven for those who prefer routine and precision, requires sympathy and interest in human problems. For those in the clerical stream, salary on retirement at sixty-five on a purely routine basis of advancement by age and years of service should be in the region of £2,400.

The increased scope of merchant banking activities since 1945 has inevitably complicated staff management beyond anything other similar-sized institutions have to face. While the banking departments must never be so rigid as to bar extra advancement and selection on the basis of merit or specialist qualification, they must still remain fundamentally a hierarchy of responsibility, with their assistants, with the 'half-signatories' allowed to sign *per pro* and the 'full signatories' signing proudly 'for', and the boardroom as a clearly defined summit. An issuing house on the other hand is essentially a group of go-getters often given director status at a comparatively early age as a reward for a particular coup, and supported by a large clerical establishment in which the individual carries only routine responsibilities. Promising assistants will be picked out quickly enough and given an initiation into 'go-getting'. There is consequently a relatively young stratum in the issuing world and in itself this is no small factor in the success of specialist issuing houses such as Minster Trust where one managing director is fifty years of age, another forty, and the three directors are in their thirties. But then the problem arises of what prospects can be held out to the next generation of subordinate executives, while in a merchant bank proper, to equate experience and skill in issue work with the same qualities in banking and produce an acceptable quotient for salary and promotion purposes raises still further questions which can only be answered by a large-scale turn-round in staff over a relatively short span of years, or by some major new development in the bank's activities.

The better and more widely qualified the new entrants are, the easier it will be to create a fully interchangeable corps of future executives. Understudying a senior executive in issue work brings insight into company financing and gives first-class opportunities of meeting a cross-section of key men in British industry and commerce, but the issuing techniques and procedures of company finance in themselves can be narrowingly repetitive. Mr Peter Cannon, as managing director of Minster Trust, is ready enough to try out young recruits straight from school or university but forcibly expresses the view that his executives must somehow gain experience of how profits are made in business 'even if it is only from running a whelk stall'. In practice this means giving preference to men who have already shown elsewhere that they can make their mark. The young banker on the other hand has a continual challenge to widen his horizon in the field of foreign and overseas affairs; he has to take account of an ever-changing kaleidoscope of political and economic factors and, if he is noted as a man who takes readily to responsibility, he will be given a spell as learner in Paris, Brussels, Düsseldorf, New York, or in the financial departments of old-established overseas clients of the accepting house. From the stimulus of this foreign experience should develop a broadened interest in the work and a greater *savoir-faire* in dealing with his fellow-men.

For the initial stages of his career, of course, a *konzernbank* may look a more attractive proposition to a young man. Mr Julian Hodge puts it thus:

As our bank forms part of a very large industrial group it is possible for us to train our future merchant bankers in all aspects of business life – from manufacturing to retailing. This we do, and we are able therefore to earmark fairly early the bright young men and move them around within our group, transferring those more suitable, ultimately, to the merchant bank. Not unnaturally we are inclined to favour chartered accountants, cost and work accountants, lawyers, and economists who want to train this way. It is astonishing the number who do. The work should prove to be certainly as varied, but more exciting and worthwhile than private practice and more remunerative. There is also the attraction of a certain security which cannot possibly exist in private practice. But while there must be teams of specialists, it is also important to preserve a balance by having good all-rounders, as I would suspect the growth possibilities of an organisation that consisted merely of technicians.*

Modern requirements for accurate intelligence on domestic and international commercial and financial questions, as well as on individual sectors and enterprises, have also extended the scope of banking research sections. The collection, collation, and presentation of information for the use of all departments of the bank requires a training as thorough and a background as comprehensive as those of government intelligence departments. Not only economics graduates but those in other disciplines can fully engage their intellectual bent. Perhaps only the largest merchant banks can afford research departments which in themselves offer a promotion path up to at least assistant managerial status. Even where such departments have been set up, the older board members may still continue to set more store on who tells them rather than on the substance of what they are told. But gradually and inevitably organized 'deep' research is being accepted as an essential ancillary and the research staffs have to be offered career and status prospects equal to those of other members of the bank. The solution devised in the United States of admitting analysts to the rank of 'vice-president' may not lend itself to transplantation but semantic ingenuity should be able to produce a British equivalent. The standardization of methods and definitions of investment analysis throughout Europe requires that the researcher and analyst should enjoy at least the same standing as the managers in the banking and other departments. Ultimately 'research' is as much a function of management as the determination of 'going' rates, and no banking house can depend on a quick opinion based on something read in today's *Times* or yesterday's *Figaro*. One of the sadder

* *Ibid.*

aspects of modern times is that the speed of communications has not been matched by an increase in the reliability and honesty of news reporting, while the angled reports from propaganda and public relations departments, both official and commercial, make the distillation of truth a more difficult process than ever before.

'Perks' at the Top

So there will be a widening range of departments through which a man can rise to the senior managerial status which will put him in the middle four-figure salary category. Once the step to the board has been made, the rewards increase rapidly and the initial £8,000 or so annual salary for an executive director should mean a fresh progress to a gross basic salary of £15,000 or more at retirement in the larger merchant banks. Here, however, rewards of a different order begin to open up like spring flowers to those who enter the paddocks and meadows. Custom has ordered some of those. Although fees from outside directorships which come to a member of the board by reason of his banking status are paid into the bank's profits, they are taken into account in determining whether he will get something more than the basic salary of an executive director.

The code about 'declaring one's interest' and not profiting from confidential information about the affairs of a client is well enough understood, although there may be fringe situations where arguments on what is the spirit, rather than the letter of observance, may be quite legitimate, as, for example, the repercussions of some banking development on investment portfolios managed by the bank. But the issuing house practice of allowing its members to participate in interesting placings at favourable rates is nowadays subjected to growing critical comment. Originally it was justified as one way of ensuring that the shares remained in safe hands for agreed periods and senior executives who participated did so, theoretically, at their own risk, even if their position enabled them to make a fairly safe judgement and also afforded opportunity for raising the resources required. When, however, the issuing house is linked to a banking department which is extending financial facilities to the company for whom the issue or placing is being arranged, and even more if the bank's equity is held in part by the public, either directly or through a holding company, any appearance of special perquisites for privileged

193

groups will raise wider questions. If the bank also manages investment portfolios, ethics require that these be given first consideration whenever there are attractive placing possibilities.

The concept of public interest, the changed role of financial institutions, and wider investment participation thus present not only merchant banks, but the City as a whole, with problems which are liable to become harder rather than easier of solution the longer they are evaded. For the City, however much it may deserve the eulogies at annual banquets and in the commercial and financial supplements of the Press, remains in the last analysis a temple dedicated to greed and all acolytes enter in the hope that they themselves will one day be full-blown high priests. The public ethos may impose a decent modicum of restraint on greed, but material ambitions and the healthy desire to emulate and surpass those around him do help to bring out the energies in a man. He too will want his due share of the pickings and perquisites available to those at the top. So a reconsideration of the public interest has still to be tempered by the need to provide incentives for the individual.

Bonuses, of course, are justifiable, particularly for those who succeed in bringing in new business in the highly competitive fields of issues and placings. Some of the older merchant banks exceptionally allow their managers to act as principals and pay them commissions on successful deals, notably in foreign exchange or commercial credits. But this practice has been disappearing steadily since 1945. Stock exchange firms have perhaps a longer tradition in arranging such matters: authorized dealers, unauthorized clerks, member brokers and partners can count on well-defined conventions for commission-sharing, risk-bearing, and profit-sharing. Merchant banking is in some need of similar guidelines, for younger men will be less patient than were their forebears. To some extent the ascendancy of families has up to now prevented the issue from becoming acute: they could order – and usually did – the payment of special bonuses, and take into account the human needs of some ambitious and promising young man. The loyalties they inspired, their concern for personal welfare, the favours they could confer, helped to blur the basic issue for a time. But growing self-consciousness has also created hard shells of selfishness and 'fair shares' require the objectivity of laid-down regulations rather than the inconsistencies of humanity. The outcome may not mean more happiness, but the requirements of efficiency probably leave no alternative.

Some internal ordering of the system of rewards should not reduce merchant banking to a drab profession. It should in practice bring a desirable stimulus to the junior working level. The 'gimlets', as – following Bank of England practice – young men are labelled who are selected for testing out in assistant managerial responsibilities, are inevitably few in number; those not so selected may prove to be late developers who would respond to other forms of encouragement. While merchant banking is blessedly free of the more ostentatious forms of 'expense account' living, it does require that executives representing their houses maintain an appropriate style, whether they are visiting potential clients in Birmingham or calling on the historic banking firms of Flanders, the Rhineland, Lombardy, and Tuscany; and for return visits traditional City hospitality is also required. This is something to which the aspirant rightly looks forward as part of the dignity of his profession.

The profitable 'tips' and 'inside' hints which are popularly supposed to be the prerogative of the man in the City are perhaps not quite what outside legend would suppose nor so frequent. In general the man who is 'something' in the City is in a position to make a better assessment of the technical factors which can make an investment opening more than usually attractive; he can discover more readily when some share is 'sold out' after a prolonged price fall, when a 'floor price' is likely to emerge, and what is the relative strength of buyers and sellers. But for the general criteria of share-buying he is at most only a few days ahead of those who base their investment decisions on published material. If it is his bank's policy to permit the holding of outside directorships he will certainly receive offers, although whether they will be acceptable is another thing, and it is probable that in future few merchant bankers, if any, will finish up with the thirty directorships of Sir Mark Turner or with the spread of board representation of the members of the Hambro family.

If ultimately, through no fault of his own, the rising merchant banking executive finds himself being left behind in matters of preference, he will discover that in industry, finance, and trade there exists a ready seller's market for his unique combination of experience in banking, trade finance, investment management, high level negotiating, and trustee work. Nor need his 'au revoir' always be a painful one, for up to a point merchant banks accept a certain loss, knowing that allowance has to be made for ambition and personality and hoping that by letting the bread drift off on the waters the

195

one-time member may return with new clients. And so it often works out. In something of the same spirit they accept 'learners' from both British and foreign firms to reforge personal links between their own rising generation of executives and that of their clients. The outcome has sometimes been that firms taking advantage of this arrangement decide that they have learned the skills well enough to dispense with the services of an accepting house. But over the years the gestures reap their harvest, and the maintenance of an international atmosphere in the banking hall is like virtue, not without its own rewards. The continual demand for learners' places, particularly from Germany, which is still remedying the personnel deficiencies of the Nazi period and the years of post-war chaos, is tribute enough to the value of British merchant banking training.

So far the merchant banks have been able to draw on human material above the City average and equip it to a professional standard too often lacking elsewhere in Britain. Yet if their post-war record demonstrates that family inheritance has not been an obstacle to initiative and new ideas, the era ahead requires even greater change and adjustment. The mergers, the outside participations, the wider range of activities and also the disintegration of traditional operational boundaries between City institutions, all require a consciously planned concept of merchant banking. If a compromise can again be effected between humanity and loyalty on one side and the needs of creative effort and efficiency on the other, the historical names will still figure on the City's active list. But to ensure this the banks will have to do better than the general group of professions and institutions known as 'the City' which has not particularly distinguished itself in producing coherent explanations of its role and functions. Collective platitudinizing at banquets on past glories, or trite exhortations for future effort are not enough. The concept must be in valid relationship to the new era which is emerging in outline; in helping to clarify and define it, the merchant bankers will be serving not only their immediate interest, but contributing to the much-needed clarification of Britain's own role in the world. For Britain too is badly in need of a new concept about itself.

CHAPTER EIGHT

Wanted — a Concept

Conditions for Independence

If, then, the merchant banks hope to maintain their independent status, they must again take up their role of pioneers; and for this they must be prepared to recruit and develop high-grade youthful management which can be offered a clear path to the top. Alternatively, they can seek the security of alliances, either with American banks or as the *konzernbank* within holding groups. Where family resources are large enough, the decision can perhaps be deferred but in the end it cannot be evaded.

For every field which was once their special preserve is being invaded by rivals, British or foreign, and being subordinated to some consciously conceived plan; if they postpone decision too long, the one-time pioneers are liable to find themselves playing at best a fringe role. Their standing within the City establishment and their own resources could doubtless enable some of them to amble along, but they would lose their brightest and most thrusting executives. Cut-throat competition among the accepting houses themselves would be no substitute for a forward drive into new fields of endeavour. For if foreigners still place large amounts of call money in London or buy its bills and other short-term paper, it is because the London market in itself has been a better guarantee of both security and liquidity than can be afforded in their own markets.

So, whatever the early saga of Rothschild ruthlessness, today's requirements are different and piracy must yield to some ordering concept. Growing community consciousness requires loyalty and confidence. If Freiherr von Kauderwelch can no longer turn up from

Weissnichtwo and employ the latest Central European skills to oust the old and established, neither can the latter count on PROs thinking out new publicity gimmicks to keep the old firm afloat. The change, we saw, came in the crisis of post-World War One. 'A City,' wrote the *Financial News* of 17 July 1929, 'which for six months can obey a sanctionless ordinance to refrain from issuing foreign loans, or to maintain the market rate of discount at a fixed level, is no mere agglomeration of banks and brokers, but an organism knit together by bonds of finer fibre than the common desire to make money.'*

Yet, in searching for a future concept for merchant banking, one basic lesson can justifiably be drawn from the past. And it applies not only to the older accepting houses but also to the more recently created banks associated with industrial and financial holding groups and to the new institutions established by the clearing banks. The merchant bankers attained wealth, influence, and even power because the founders had foreseen possibilities where for others there was only the unknown beyond the horizon. Like the rest of the British Establishment they may be afflicted by periods of doubt and hesitation, but their world is in no greater state of convulsion than was that of the Rothschilds at the end of the eighteenth century. The Rothschilds anticipated the needs of princes. A few decades later the Browns and Morgans sensed what tasks the opening up of the West would impose on merchant and banker. Greed may well have been their motive but creation was the outcome. As soon as others moved in to imitate and profit from their creations, the merchant bankers, although accepting the flattery of imitation, rapidly moved on to new tasks. Now their post-1945 innovations have been taken over by others, and it is time to move on.

Predicting the future is not usually a very profitable activity, except for those who print the almanacs concerned with prediction, but assessing the potentialities within a given situation is legitimate enough and permits at least a guess at the range of probabilities. The partial closing of the New York loan market in 1963 could hardly have been predicted a decade earlier, but the continued refusal of the merchant banks to accept that the international loan market in London would never return did enable them to move rapidly into action when the unexpected did occur. It is even more important that they now do not mistake every false dawn for the beginning of a new

---

* Quoted by R. J. Truptil, *British Banks and the London Money Market* (Jonathan Cape, 1936), p. 197.

era and that they learn to curb the City's lemming instinct. If at present the main weight of their banking business is within the United Kingdom, the greater becomes the necessity to look ahead to credit and investment needs which are as yet but barely sensed, but which are nevertheless inherent in the constituents of the future.

The American Challenge

The big battalions, who will not only force a change in the strategy of City financiers but even in the whole deployment of European financial resources, will be the American ones. If, in the immediate post-World War Two world, New York did not straight away take the place of London, this in retrospect seems natural enough. The London bill market and the acceptance mechanism were the products of a particular combination of historical circumstances which, like all events in history, were unique. But the size and dynamism of the American evolution has created a special sort of bigness – one which must go on expanding, rationalizing, and driving forward. For the big corporations there can be no nostalgic resting on laurels and in their wake – in spite of restrictions dating from Old Hickory's régime – American banking has created the essential logistic-financial follow-up, like the 'Red Ball Routes' of the United States Army – so that where American industry invests, the banks will follow.

Even economic nationalism cannot by itself halt the weight of the American advance, largely because of the revolutionary technological content of the investment. The growth sectors of every industrial economy require fresh know-how and, whatever the resources of European inventiveness, the American industrial giants provide the readiest short cuts of proved applied techniques. So the growth of United States private investment in Europe, rising from $1,000 millions per annum in 1960 to $2,500 millions in 1963, contains a dynamic element greater than the totals would appear to suggest. At the same time, a less obvious, but on that account no less powerful, ascendancy is being established by the enlightened ideas of the US Treasury and Federal Reserve offering European monetary authorities willing to accept their co-operation massive resources to ease their national problems, whether of liquidity or of stringency.

Consequently European central banks have seen American banking activities in a kinder light since the 'sixties when the United States

199

set out to develop – through the Federal Reserve Bank of New York – a network of relations with other central banks originally designed to protect the dollar in the exchange markets against speculative attacks from any quarter. Federal Reserve reciprocal currency arrangements with European central banks, Bank of Canada, Bank of Japan, Bank of Mexico and the Bank for International Settlements amounted to $11,230 millions in September 1970. For better or worse, both the American banking system and United States credit policy now dovetail into the European financial world.

As the United States Treasury pursues the policy, firmly enunciated by Mr Robert Roosa at the 1964 Tokyo meeting of the International Monetary Fund, of adding to the supply of international credit facilities, the need to solve the financial problems connected with growth will probably prove more compelling than national pride. There will be setbacks as well as advances. In the late fifties the United States had low investment and high savings, while the other industrialized countries had high investment and low savings, and the less developed countries characteristically had both low investment and low savings. It should not have been expected that countries under three fundamentally different sets of conditions, all pursuing further expansion, could have achieved equilibrium in the flows of payments among themselves by following identical policies. Yet the conventional wisdom of balance of payments adjustment assumed, in addition to free flows of capital, that fluctuations in wages, prices, employment and output would bring about balance among the payments of the industrialized countries. Since modern economic policy is weighted towards limiting the downward slide of such fluctuations, once current account convertibility had been largely achieved by the end of 1958, much more of the actual burden of effecting balance came to be placed upon capital movements.

The significance of this was hardly realized while the United States pursued the tax-reduction strategy of the early-sixties. The wholesale price index (total figure) remained remarkably stable between 1958 and September 1965, the annual growth of gross national product in real terms advanced considerably and the volume of savings expanded further, assuring an abundant supply of capital funds to finance rapid increases in investment by private enterprise and local governments. The government deficits that remained, though declining year by year, were all financed, in effect, from the same enlarged volume of savings that was amply financing the new high volume of investments. This American strategy was abandoned in the end of 1965 in the face of external payments difficulties. By 1970 consumer prices were rising by about six per cent per annum and output had flattened out. President Nixon's administration was struggling with the handicap of not being able to issue long-term government bonds with a coupon sufficient to resume the previously successful American strategy. But in the meantime American banks had not only found means of meeting the overseas needs of American industry and of drawing in short-term into the United States itself, but were even offering new credit possibilities to European borrowers and lenders.

Just as, for nearly a century, the sovereign and the bill on London determined the global ascendancy of the City, so the world-wide organization represented by the extension of American banking will create its own mechanism of power even if in Washington itself the advocates of tighter US credit policy enjoy interludes of political favour. The Interest Equalization Tax did not after all block American sponsorship of international bond issues; it merely brought US houses increasingly into European selling syndicates, and President Johnson's measures may have some similar outcome. Even in pre-tax days only about two-fifths of any foreign loan was actually taken up in New York itself so that – not for the first time in history – an intended restraint based on an out-of-date concept had the paradoxical consequence of liberating a new truth.

Thus, measures which might have been expected to clip the wings of US underwriters in the end stimulated them into finding ways of offsetting them. A tried skill and procedure can overcome national restrictions, and the unfortunate difference between the situation of British and American finance houses is that the former have to take weakness into account, while the latter operate from the basic strength of their national economy. So, while official US agencies and boards compete in laying down what type of foreign acquisitions American banks may make, or what overseas operations they may or may not conduct, the houses themselves have found ways of profiting from the emergence of an embryo federal Europe just as easily as American corporations were able to develop structures suited to the needs of modern production and consumption, in spite of 'trust busting' myths and the fiction of states' rights. The currency swap system of the United States Treasury creates in practice a powerful support for

American overseas financial and commercial expansion so long as the dollar remains a reserve currency and national governments fail to agree on a major overhaul of the Bretton Woods system. There comes a time when the Banque de France must urge the virtues of restraint on even its most Americanophobe head of state. Not only the British accepting houses, but other European banks as well, will find the American challenge ever-renewed.

Whether it is Dundee, Stuttgart or Milan, the American banks are found to be actively at work. Although each of them, as it opens a fresh European office, is careful to explain that it has no desire to upset the local correspondent banks with whom it has maintained connections for many decades, it can and it does take business away from them. In fields such as airline finance, oil exploration and drilling projects, pipeline and refinery construction, they possess experience which gives them a decided advantage over European banks with their basic philosophy of mortgage-secured overdrafts. As corporations such as General Motors, the Ford group, Chrysler, IBM, National Cash Register, and Procter and Gamble steadily expand their overseas operations, it is to those banks who already understand their financial problems that they most naturally turn. When an industry finds its optimum rate of expansion, the credit possibilities must be created to match it. In establishing a fresh link with their American progeny, now grown to gianthood, Morgan Grenfell have made a timely decision. The lesson has not been lost on all Europeans, and was probably a significant factor in hastening bank amalgamations in the Netherlands, where First National City and Bank of America have arrived in force. First National City had by 1970 about 250 foreign branches compared with some 97 for the Bank of America and 53 for the Chase Manhattan, while in Europe alone it had some 28 branches spread through ten countries.* During the years 1950 to 1962 direct United States investment in Europe had expanded by four and a half times to nearly $4,000 millions and since then, as we have seen, the investment rate has increased still further, shifting significantly enough in favour of the EEC countries away from the United Kingdom, whose annual share over the same period dropped from sixty per cent to almost fifty per cent while EEC

* *The Financial Times* of 3 June 1964 quoted Mr George Moore, President of the First National City, as saying: 'With the dollar the leading currency and the US the leading exporter and importer of goods, services and capital, it is only natural that US banks should gird themselves to play the same relative role in international finance that the great British financial institutions played in the nineteenth century.'

proportion rose from twenty-four per cent to forty-three per cent. It is not surprising that the United States banks have resurrected an instrument bequeathed them from President Wilson's administration, the Edge Act amendments of 1916 and 1919, which permit them to form an 'Edge Corporation' or 'Agreement Corporation' to conduct international operations including those, such as equity investment, which they may not undertake at home.

Long dormant – in 1955 there were only six Edge Act or Agreement corporations in existence – the practice has been revived with some vigour and by the spring of 1964 there were thirty-six, operated by twenty-three American banks and bank holding companies. That formed by the First National City in 1961, the First National City Overseas Corporation, undertakes equity investment abroad, mainly in finance companies and development institutions. Its agreement corporation, the International Banking Corporation, extends its interests to Canada, South and West Africa, and to the tax-haven operating groups in the Bahamas. The major operations of the United States banks in London, so far mainly felt in the Euro-dollar market where they were the largest depositors after 'Swiss accounts', are therefore likely to extend still further. Chicago, Middle Western and North Western banks are beginning to follow the example of the Eastern seaboard institutions. They can to a great extent justify their plans by claiming that their presence in an overseas country tends to attract American capital and so to develop fresh loan business. This may be arguable but, after the American fashion, they are likely to test their hypothesis by action rather than by dialectic, and we shall find them increasingly in our midst.

In the meantime American investment houses are pursuing their own path. Some have always maintained their special links with London merchant banks and stockbrokers, but others are perfectly prepared to set off on their own, collecting allies by success. White Weld & Co. has, in a short space of time, already created its own placing power in Europe for dollar bonds. In 1964 they broke fresh ground by being the first American investment bankers to head a consortium for placing a dollar loan outside the United States.* When First National City announced in May 1966 that its London office

---

* This was an $8,000,000 debenture issue for the Finnish Kesko Oy. The British members of the underwriting group were Kleinworts, Montagu, and Warburg. In the latter part of the year White Weld followed up with a $15 millions fifteen-year loan at $6\frac{3}{4}$ per cent for Sumitomo Chemical.

would issue Dollar Certificates of Deposit* in negotiable bearer form, White Weld simultaneously announced that it would provide a secondary market through its international network of offices.

Is Britain Big Enough?

Nor can the merchant banks any longer be certain of holding their own even where mainly British interests are involved. The more active clearing banks have not only seen the possibilities of medium-term export finance but have moved into more formal associations with foreign and overseas banks who operate beyond the traditional limits of their domestic activity. Bigness, of course, brings its own handicap and, in the short term, the clearing banks, with their boards of vague 'top people' who are presumed to have 'connections', may be slow to redeploy their efforts, while their increasingly unionized staff structures can hold up the initiatives and bright ideas of their top management. But their wholly-owned overseas subsidiaries, which can operate in the City as independent banks, have taken up the bidding for flexible rates. They, in the face of the world-wide competition of American banks, are in turn being obliged to extend their lines, as in July 1964 when Barclays DCO took a one-third interest in the Bank of London and Montreal, whose capital had hitherto been held equally by the Bank of Montreal and the Bank of London and South America. A regional basis is becoming too narrow even for British overseas banks. Lloyds Bank Europe had built up a network of twenty branches in Belgium, France, Holland, Monaco and Switzerland by the time the merger with the Bank of London and South America was announced in 1970. Within the limits imposed by restrictions on credit and exchange controls, Lloyds Europe and Westminster Foreign have been able to bid actively for deposits and so to provide short-and medium-term loans, in Euro-dollars and other currencies, to their customers in the United Kingdom, Europe and elsewhere. The same applies to the 200 or so foreign and Commonwealth banks with offices in London, particularly the French: those from the EEC countries, while profiting from London's

---

* Certificates of deposit are usually referred to as 'CDs' and an individual CD is an instrument issued by a bank evidencing a deposit of monies for a stated time at a stated rate of interest. A large number of domestic and foreign banks are now issuing CDs, and several other investment bankers and dealers have joined the secondary market.

business, appear to be forming combinations among themselves to run banks in Africa and elsewhere with the undoubted intention – whether successful or not – of by-passing London.

Big business, too, is poaching, and trying to find its own access to the world's money markets. The treasurers and finance officers of large corporations, American, German, Japanese and others, have started paying their own visits to brokerage firms, and even to each other, to find the most profitable employment for their surplus funds and to obtain credits at special rates. The financial departments of such companies are now beginning to produce men fully capable of dealing in foreign currencies themselves; sometimes the existence of a *konzernbank* under their control enables them to give the form of a bank transaction to their operations, sometimes they can dispense even with this. The merchant banks may frown on these developments but they cannot reverse them.

In spite of the inventiveness and initiative shown by merchant banks in home affairs, many of them may be excused if they wonder how far the United Kingdom will continue to offer a satisfying field for their types of individual enterprise. In their more vigorous days the English were individualistic pioneers preferring action to ideas; in their weary moments they profess a preference for 'pragmatism', for 'give and take', for 'compromise', all of which nowadays sound too much like excuses for inaction. Euphemisms, such as 'partnership' and 'new dimensions in relations between government, industry and finance' may be used by one political party while the other may talk of 'national priorities', but whether the national administration be Conservative or Labour, the country's economy requires increased public intervention and control. Practical issues cannot be solved without them. The location of industry cannot be accomplished without development grants and any redirection of resources requires forward planning of capital expenditure under official sanction.

Ultimately some central direction, some coherent realization of ideas, are, therefore, necessary to ensure steady investment, industrial growth, and broad enjoyment of the profits. The inability of the British educational system to produce minds which can formulate and apply broad ideas has its unfortunate economic consequences. The failure of the National Economic Development Council – in the original form conceived by the Conservatives – to draw in a wide informed body of leadership, to produce an adequate calculus for statistical work, and to do more than publish generalized papers on the desirability for growth reflects this limitation. Labour's more centralized scheme, by which forecasting and planning were brought inside the government policy-making machine, was at least a more logical step but the practical outcome was a limping process where national output never came up to expectation and hopes have once more to be cut back.

The general nature of the cure is always easy to formulate. At home a faster rise in productivity and efficiency, greater stability in costs, increased exports, more economical stockpiling and holding, and better manpower training; abroad, the scrapping of outdated and unrealistic commitments. Since, however, each political faction finds its own justification for evading the domestic issue, and some piece of verbal self-flattery is found to justify fresh government expenditure overseas, the cure is never undertaken. Possibly it never will be. The process, of which the 'stop and go' procedure is but an outward symptom, may be the only one which now accords with the British temperament. Its comfortable fatalism enables society to adjust to the consequences of each step backwards. It may be that as a nation we shall slip behind in material matters and allow others to set the pace and do our thinking for us. By 1969 the United Kingdom had fallen back from first place to thirteenth place in the race towards higher gross national product per capita. We have got used to living off the sterling area reserves and having our trade deficits financed by others. 'There is a lot of ruin in a nation', said Adam Smith.

This has meant that sterling has steadily lost its status as a reserve currency, that other countries now decide our credit policies for us, that the City may gradually cease to be an earning factor in its own right, and that merchant banks who live by initiative and expansion will have to look to a wider world. Morgans have decided to align themselves in the American order of battle. Hambros, Kleinworts and Schroders may feel that they command a wide enough spread of international assets for a decision to be taken in their own time. Lazards is part of a financial group strong enough at home and with enough influential overseas connections to hold its own even within what could be a declining national economy. Rothschilds feel that opportunity may still beckon anywhere in the world and conversely that any dawn may prove false: the experience of the house does, after all, range from Labrador to the Antipodes. Smaller banks are building themselves into holding groups, or being taken over; if in the long run this limits their freedom of action, it ensures an immediate staying power. The present generation of Warburg directors will certainly have strong enough nerves to venture where others fear to tread.

Even in a world of bigness Sir Siegmund Warburg flatly refuses to accept that the next decades will see the end of merchant banking as conducted from London. He foresees that there will always be a role for the small bank with mobile resources and adventurous minds. 'Money-lending will play a secondary role', is his view, but the problems of capital-raising and general investment will, over the next twenty years, call for the type of skills which merchant bankers are most likely to develop. If sterling's status as a reserve currency continues to decline and Britain's general credit policy becomes dependent on the decisions of others, he still sees London maintaining ascendancy through its expertise. 'Lloyds is the parallel', he maintains. 'Although similar insurance underwriting could be carried on at other centres, it remains in London, because London does it so much better.' The techniques of long-term capital-raising can similarly be improved; the skill can be developed. Under full economic European integration and within a unified EEC capital market there would, under the Warburg philosophy, still be a role for mobility. But without some forward-looking concept all will find themselves playing a secondary, if not a tertiary role, in tomorrow's world.

Tomorrow's World

How do we see this world? The expansion of merchant banking was only part of the wider outward military and economic thrust of Europe, while the accompanying political vocabulary was derived from eighteenth-century European rationalism with its notion of a universal 'Man'. The power of the European thrust, the successful revolt of Boston merchants and Virginia planters, the effectiveness of the slogans of liberty, equality, and fraternity in enabling ambitious middle-class politicians to gratify their hopes of power and office, gave 'Man' an air of corporate reality for a century and a half and fostered the illusion of grand human convergence. That is now over. Growing self-consciousness has caused a reassertion of human diversity and the eighteenth-century notions are shown to be narrowly conditioned in time and place with no contemporary validity outside Europe and the areas of European settlement. If the now self-conscious races of mankind prefer the security of their own sense of identity to the universality of 'Man', this means rejection of all the concepts of legally safeguarded privilege which gave reality to European 'liberty'; 'equality' enjoys a passing fashion among Asians and Africans as a useful slogan for despoiling their former masters, and 'fraternity' is being replaced by the kind of brotherly relationships which have been normal since the episode of Abel's priggishness and Cain's jealousy.

Western techniques may continue to spread and be imitated, as techniques always have been since men started to chip flints; but they have never brought unity and are likely to do so even less in the service of self-conscious divergent aims. Where banking and credit techniques can be used as autonomous skills or ordering methods – and to a surprising extent they can – they will continue to be employed by non-European peoples with great adaptive capacity such as the Chinese or Japanese, particularly where their societies possess conscious ordering notions. The notion of contract will continue to be maintained, even if contracts are not always observed, in societies where human relations are regarded as subject to higher sanction, as under Islamic Law: keeping a tally and exchanging the record of a promise are as old as civilization. But self-consciousness heightens existing characteristics and, where societies have never even arrived at general notions of law and order and have depended on instinctive and intuitive relationships, we shall sooner or later see the misuse and eventually the collapse of our institutional creations. The basic animal desire for a full belly may be common to all men and to satisfy it there may be an ever more clamant demand for 'capital', but capital creation will have ceased over a large part of the earth. For capital creation depended on European ideas of obligation, contract, and restraint and, like Europe's other creations, these had their origin in a rational acceptance of the dimension of time. No other group of mankind has yet developed this.

The illusion that it can be otherwise in a world of self-conscious human diversity has, perhaps, been stronger with the English because of their inability to appraise and reappraise general ideas. As pioneers they were ready enough to impose their will on others and could thereby imagine that they had also imposed their own dreams. But without acts of will there can only be wishful thinking. Political illusionism proves strongest of all over the notion of 'Commonwealth', although it is obvious to the outsider that 'Commonwealth' has no content as a political concept, while the diminution of British trade with overseas Commonwealth members underlines the changing realities of world trade. South African gold sales remain essential for the operations of the Exchange Equalization Fund, although politicians blandly affect to ignore this since the Republic left the Commonwealth. But when all the self-flattering phrases about 'North-South challenges', 'the moral duty to aid the underdeveloped' and 'world liquidity' are set aside and the African extravaganzas at UN conferences are dismissed for what they are, the reality remains that the creation of wealth depends on the economic growth of Europe, North America, and the few areas of European settlement. No international monetary or credit institutions could survive twenty-four hours in the face of a major collapse in North American or European economics.

It is not, therefore, to the aftermath of Empire that the City must look. Apart from the overseas areas of European settlement, such as Australia and South Africa, the next decade or so in the former British territories will be largely a tale of salvage of old assets, thinly disguised barter agreements and risks heavily insured by UK governmental agencies: this will offer little scope for expansion to the merchant banker or any other. The conflicts of self-consciousness in Latin America, which show no sign of abating after more than a century, make the area ever less attractive to commercial risks.

This points to the long-term field of activity of independent merchant banking, as well as of other British institutions concerned with credit creation, capital raising, and investment planning, as being in Europe and its overseas projections. There may be marginal risk ventures which can be undertaken in black Africa, south Asian and Latin American countries, and some bill business may still be undertaken in these regions, though its basis will shrink as the internal credit conditions become more chaotic; but these will be mainly theatres for commercial giants who can cover their own risks or for ventures based ultimately on state financing or insurance. Even as agents for organizing credit arrangements merchant banks are likely enough to become increasingly superfluous. Japan may be ready enough to authorize a quota of debenture and loan issues by her nationals on European markets yet she remains resolutely opposed to direct foreign investment within the country. Israel may offer a land of limited promise so long as the leadership remains of European origin; but as an Asian and African majority begins to dominate the

Israeli political scene there will be a lapse to more Levantine standards. Canada imposes ever fresh curbs on foreign investors, limiting their holdings and aiming at strengthening native institutions; the United States can take care of its own.

In spite of delays and occasional setbacks, the European Economic Community is moving towards a common economic policy, greater areas of trade are being freed and, whoever may happen to be the leaders in France or Germany, they are still bound, as are the governments of the other four signatories of the Treaty of Rome, to move automatically to the next stage of what will eventually be a single economy within a federal system. By 1970 all forms of discriminatory treatment of capital were to be removed and capital movements freed, as the Treaty puts it, 'to the extent appropriate to the functioning of the Common Market'. The merging of the three executives, the EEC Commission, the High Authority of the Coal and Steel Community, and Euratom, was followed at the end of 1966 by the merging of the Communities themselves and the central political problem became the method of control either by a new constitution of the Council of Ministers, or in a greater degree through the European Parliament, whose authority may well have to be enhanced by some form of direct election.

This is Europe's classical historical situation – debate over the control of some novel concentration of power and a new release of energies by an extension of privileges bringing in their train the formulation of new concepts, bursts of fresh creation, and new definitions of the frontiers between private sector and public interest. Such has been the evolution of the European mind: on one side the growth of national consciousness and of the nation state, the organization of central military power, the rise of large-scale industry and finance; on the other and confronting them, new geographical mobility for the men themselves, a struggle to consolidate individual privilege (or 'liberty' as we prefer to call it) and the assertion of the entrepreneur. In this situation new ideas and institutions are thrown up, new 'establishments' rise, and old ones vanish.

The vanity of British politicians and the narrow-mindedness of Whitehall clerks excluded the United Kingdom from the formative stages of this process. But the process still continues and not only do we remain part of Europe but the Common Market has become our biggest trading partner. If in the private sector our manufacturers have found ways to participate, it is at least as important that our financial agencies should play their part in shaping the future and exploring the new field for human energy.

As a nation of manufacturers, traders and bankers, it is for the British as vital to take part in this European venture as it was a hundred and fifty years ago to participate in reconstructing post-Napoleonic Europe, a century ago in opening up the West, and sixty years ago to profit by the European colonial ascendancy to expand world trade. All three chapters had profound repercussions on both the economy and society of the United Kingdom itself.

The British should not be blinded by the slow progress of the EEC in its search for a workable common economic policy, nor underestimate the potential worth of the long economic discussions between members which may be necessary to provide a sure foundation for something more than a customs union. In its first four years, EEC was perforce mainly concerned with the removal of internal barriers to trade, with establishing common rules for competition, and with guidelines for particular sectors such as agriculture. Until such lines had been drawn, there was little open pressure to formulate a general policy. But in 1960 a Monetary Committee was set up, then an Economic Policy Committee: the Ministers of Finance and then the Governors of Central Banks began to hold regular meetings. In 1962 the Commission presented its 'Action Programme' for the second stage from 1962 to 1966, stating that the time had come to move from a *zollverein* concept to the creation of a true economic union. For the third stage 1966–70 the Commission boldly stated that full monetary union should be the objective and that the Committee of the Governors of the Central Banks would become the central organ of a federal banking system.

In July 1963 the Commission was able to put forward 'Recommendations by the Commission to the Council: Medium-Term Economic Policy for the Community', which made a conscious effort to combine the concept of economic programming with that of maximum competition. So by January 1964, in making his annual report to the European Parliament, M. Marjolin could say that common economic action was now an accepted doctrine and recommend a joint policy to counter inflation in EEC countries. In 1970 the Werner Plan proposed that there should be parallel progress towards monetary union and a harmonisation of economic policies, and suggested that economic and monetary union within the Common Market could be achieved by 1980. The Werner Plan stressed that

211

changes in parities for EEC currencies will still be possible during the transition phase of monetary union, but proposed a move on to a narrowing of exchange margins within the Common Market as a first step towards fixed parities.

Throughout all EEC recommendations, proposals, debates and approvals runs the consistent theme that the free play of the market and adequate competition are to be regarded as the most effective instruments of progress. In no circumstances must programmes result in an increase in government economic intervention, and the rational framework of Community decisions is designed to decrease the need and scope for these. This may be an ideal, and in practice ideals tend to be obscured, but it is not too much to say that the hopes of EEC fulfilment must centre round the possibility of creating a European capital market, where the financial resources of the Community can be attracted and distributed in an orderly fashion by rates which are profitable and in the form of paper which is acceptable.

Europe's Main Need

Faith in a market is the foundation on which arose the first tenuous fabric of civilized settlement. The spectacle, in an African or Asian meeting place, of some wizened old figure sitting behind a few peppers laid out on a piece of sacking rightly brings an emotional catch in our throat. For round such exchanges began both settlement and civilization. In the April 1964 recommendations on restoring internal and external economic equilibrium, the Council of EEC paid tribute to the age-old concept when they declared: 'Fiscal and other obstacles to the export of capital, arising particularly from the investment rules for institutional investors, should be rescinded quickly.'* In October 1964 the panel of experts set up to study the integration of European capital markets held their first meeting under Dr Claudio Segré.

An efficient and flexible capital market, based on the finest rates of supply and demand, is precisely what Europe lacks. The various national traditions of banking and finance with their marked *dirigiste* features are, as we have seen in previous chapters, historically explicable and derive from specific needs and situations; it would be presumptuous to regard them as in themselves inferior to the customs of the Anglo-Saxon world. But they are not adapted to the needs of

* Recommendation of the Council of 15 April 1964, para. 13.

212

large-scale modern economies passing through vast technological and organizational transitions, nor sensitive enough to react to the shifting emphasis of emergent social and political entities. Regulations, however skillfully conceived and administered, are no substitute for the flexibility of human communication based on relationships of confidence.

The generous pump-priming of Marshall Aid, the post-war reconstruction programmes which created their own momentum, concealed how defective were the national mechanisms. The dislocations and desequilibria of 1962 and the evident inflationary pressures of 1963 showed how little designed were Europe's financial institutions to cope with the type of problems which in future the Continent must take in its stride. They also underlined how much work has to be done before the Community has become a community. There was no way of directing Germany's surplus of short-term funds to meet Italy's deficit, and German firms went on finding more attractive and flexible rates in London. Italy itself had to make its emergency arrangements with the US Federal Reserve authorities, while the balancing mechanism which lessened the strains in Europe was probably the London Euro-currency market.

In 1963 it was a retrograde step for the EEC countries to be using 'exchange control' not in its traditional, albeit clumsy, role of maintaining the balance of payments, but as an instrument of domestic monetary policy. In practice, the structural difference of the various European national capital markets proved the most effective restrictive weapon, something which further underlined the narrowness which was the main cause of their shortcomings, as Dr Segré himself has been the first to suggest.* Distortions in credit structures bring distorted prices and payments. Even exchange control and sliding customs scales, which form the main mechanism in the operation of the first stage of EEC, can be set at naught by depreciation in the value of negotiable paper. Resort to distress loans when other remedies fail is not calculated to create the basis of confidence required for the transition through the next two stages of European integration.

Much of the inflexibility results from the fact that savings do not flow to institutional investors and the latter are, in turn, controlled by regulations originally designed to maintain the ascendancy of royal and imperial treasuries with their mercantilist notions of a war chest.

* Quoted in a Brussels dispatch of 14 October 1964 in *The Times*.

213

The majority of Continental indirect taxation systems, which are basically forced public levies, are the progeny of the same philosophy. Dr Erhardt is thus not wrong in his 'social market' concept, and the new era in Europe calls consequently, not for centralization, nor even for 'decentralization', but for a mechanism, at once convenient and acceptable to investors, which can place loans up to the equivalent of $50 millions without strain on any one centre, and which can provide a market, both active and stable, for paper once placed.

Methods so far introduced mainly reflect attempts to maintain the conventional old instead of reaching for the orthodox new. Foreign currency loans, denominated in dollars, come up against existing currency regulations and are of limited value to institutional investors. European investors have no votes to protect the internal purchasing power of the dollar in the USA which is a prerequisite of the dollar holding its value in the world at large. The unit of account system may perhaps offer an instrument which could serve the future rather than the past since it gives a *de facto* exchange guarantee, and can adapt to an integrated market. The accounts of the High Authority are, after all, kept in units of account. 'This particular device presents a special interest to EEC', said Dr Claudio Segré, speaking in his function as a member of the EEC Directorate-General of Economic Affairs, 'and no effect should be spared to make it successful.'* In November 1970 the first loan ever denominated in all the currencies of the EEC, and with a fixed exchange rate guarantee, was announced by the European Coal and Steel Community. But whatever its virtues, a useful system requires not only a flexible marketing mechanism but also a good secondary market. Without this the entrenched German and French credit banks can continue to spread their old atavistic fears of the unknown.

The clearest symptoms of the underlying deficiency of the existing mechanism are shown by the disparity in interest rates between the European national systems on the one side and New York and London on the other, by the major part played by money of non-European origin in international issues, by the rigidity in financing the public sector, and by the fact that the short-term money market, as it exists in New York and London, can fluctuate independently of central banking attempts to regulate national economies by influencing long-term lending rates. So although Continental Europe

* Lecture on 22 July 1964 to the Second International Investment Symposium at Oxford.

has produced an imaginative concept for a future where, in some two decades, total EEC output will probably rise by eighty per cent above the 1964 figure, with a *per caput* output of seventy per cent higher and a working population of 145 millions (higher even than the United States), the main credit instrument for turning the concept into reality is still lacking. As Dr Segré has pointed out, the potential of the European markets could be gauged by the fact that outside sources had raised more money on them than Community institutions during the period from 1961 to mid-1966. The absorption capacity of these markets, if they were liberalized, would, he maintained, be far greater than the total of issues currently being floated on them.*

The growth of trade requires a market for 'excess' medium-term paper acquired by banks and other institutions for financing the export of capital goods. The liquidity requirements of banks place limits on what they themselves can hold, and the creation of national medium-term institutions only postpones the solution since they in turn have to make calls on other institutions and freeze their resources instead of releasing them. The existence of a market where paper can be traded from the longest term to that of a few days' maturity, and where the banks themselves supply a large part of the market's money, will be as essential for Europe's expansion as it was for Britain in the days of her outward thrust.

Neither the London merchant banks nor any other British houses need be under the illusion that they will find themselves warmly hailed throughout the European Economic Community. They will find jealousy, resentment, and opposition, just as their Euro-dollar transactions did initially. A French official ascendancy in the future Common Market financial bodies might result in the same determination to exclude outsiders as has been shown by the French Government itself in cutting down direct access by French industry and commerce to the London bill market. But the imponderables always work in the long run in favour of those who can reduce rates and restore equilibrium. The European central banks had to recognize and even encourage the London and Amsterdam Euro-currency markets, although their own commercial banks were still criticizing the traffic. The steering of dollars and Swiss francs through reputable houses to clients with genuine industrial and commercial requirements, and the encouragement of orderly arbitrage transactions to take advantage of higher interest rates, proved to be preferable to 'hot money' passing

* Address to the European Federation of Financial Analysts, January 1965.

between brokers and speculators. If their skills and their good name can bring profit, the merchant banks will find as many collaborators as opponents in Europe. If they continue to show the co-operation and human understanding, which unfortunately successive British Governments have too often lacked vis-à-vis Europe, their present head-start will carry them very far.

In Europe a 'new frontier' is opening up with a promise as fair as that of North America a century ago – that offered by the un-mistakable retreat and disintegration of the 'Iron Curtain'. Beyond this frontier are, not redskin camps and buffalo herds, but peoples of European stock with the same material and emotional needs as ourselves. After an era of building up basic industry and thwarting private consumption, their economies are approaching the stage where the rigid planning notions with a Marxist gloss are ceasing to have meaning. Tractor output and wheat acreage can be calculated centrally but not how to stock the counters of a five-and-ten-cent store. The expansion of trade with Eastern Europe will create an even more clamant demand for medium-term finance, something for which Western Europe is not yet prepared. The path pioneered by Lazards, in arranging finance for the supply of giant factories and plants for the Soviet Union, shows what perspectives of trade can be opened up by creative financial minds. Straddling frontiers and national systems with flexible methods and trained executives, the merchant banks should theoretically be best placed to realize these new European potentialities to the full. The restoration of balance within Europe by the reforged links with Slavs and Magyars, and the resultant expan-sion of trade should, as similar factors have achieved in past centuries, result in a fresh impetus to outward investment, and those who have been most creatively engaged will be in the forefront.

Except through the furtherance of European ideas there will be no great advance of creative economic activity in the world. The fallacy that by means of large-scale aid programmes it will be possible to start a 'take off' process in Asia and Africa, or even in Latin America, has been long in dying. It was mixed up with so many other superficial notions which have become the verbal stock-in-trade of the pedlars of political and journalistic cant, such as the advocacy of 'aid' to stop Communist penetration when it obviously does nothing of the sort, of 'aid' as a 'moral obligation' when the main practical outcome appears to be even more corruption, or of 'aid' as a means of preventing some global 'clash' which proves on examination to be little more than a projection of the inner neurosis of those who profess to foresee it. Outside the European conceptual framework the very notion of development has no validity and, even where the Chinese and Japanese, with their high instinctive endowment of skill, succeed in adapting our technology, their societies are likely to 'develop' along lines widely different from those of Europe and North America. Divergence and not convergence is inherent in a situation where self-consciousness is making men more Chinese, more Arab, more Bantu. Where existing temperamental characteristics are accentuated, possession of modern techniques may only foster aggressiveness or encourage innate tendencies to indulgence.

Meanwhile, European self-consciousness is also being heightened and requires that our ideas be continually recast and realized in new techniques and institutions. Europe's relationship with non-Europe can thus never be one of passivity or withdrawal, and the advance of the EEC countries to a stage where they can project common aims within a purposeful framework of concepts and institutions will engender a new outward thrust. A balance of payments surplus, resulting from economic expansion, will create the same potential as a century and a half ago when the shift of power and influence made London for a time the market of the world. That shift, it will be recalled, also brought its problems and its dangers. Unsound loans, excessive indebtedness, defects in the arrangements for negotiating commercial paper resulted in over-trading and default, particularly in the western hemisphere.* Skill and experience will therefore be demanded in the future as much as in the past.

Even while making a new bid for the future in Europe, the merchant banks will have to face up to the agonizing decision of whether to compete with the Americans or join them. This is in essence a vote of confidence or otherwise in Britain's own future. Like the rest of the City, the banks owe loyalty to the institutions which embody both our past history and our future purpose as a nation. The surrender of will and denigration of national character too often shown by Conservative and Labour politicians are a poor return from those who affect to play the role of political leaders and make claims on British loyalties. When trust and confidence die in a community, it

* This has already been pointed out by a former Secretary of ECGD, Sir Laurence Menzies, addressing the International Banking Summer School at Oxford on 28 July 1964 when he stressed that international over-trading on a large scale could lead to major defaults by some of the 'developing' countries and a collapse of confidence in international trade.

217

is only a matter of time before the pull of outside forces starts a process of disintegration.

The bans and prohibitions of an authority which no longer commands respect, but which fearfully concentrates on protecting its own position, have a way of transmitting its defects and weaknesses. Even merchant banks which have established their own footholds within the Common Market will be unable to develop a powerful enough momentum of business if they are continually limited by our own exchange control in the extent to which they can run open positions in foreign currencies. The chances of exploiting the best openings will in practice fall only to those who can count on the backing and trust of strong international allies.

If the EEC plans go forward a point will come in the next decade when the EEC countries will come to accept *de facto* that their national currencies, singly or jointly, or in the direct form of a backing for units of account, are in fact playing the role of reserve currencies.* At this point we shall have reached the end of the process highlighted by the $3,000 millions rescue action for sterling in November 1964 by the eleven major central banks of the world. The basic choice which Britain faces is whether to withdraw into a shabby insularity living resentfully on old dreams, or to face the realities of a new era where the financial mechanism of London would rise to new stimulating challenges. This is the real heart of the decision facing the merchant bankers.

---

* That this is primarily a question of will and recognition is illustrated by the statistical position of world currency reserves, (gold, SDRs, reserve at IMF, and foreign exchange)

$ millions at end of year

	1967	1968	1969
United States	14,830	15,710	16,964
United Kingdom	2,695	2,422	2,527
Germany	8,152	9,948	7,129
France	6,994	4,201	3,833
Italy	5,463	5,342	5,013
All countries	73,600	76,565	77,130

International Financial Statistics

A Task of Creation

The overseas operations of the merchant banks can in the last analysis only be a projection of Britain's own vigour and purpose. They can extend their range of services, they can be ready to try out new trade financing methods, they can seek fresh allies abroad to extend their placing power, but the limitations of domestic monetary policy can bring their hopes and plans to nought. Their foreign currency operations – as the post-election crisis of 1964 too vividly illustrated – depend on Britain having an active and expanding export trade. Their issue business is a facet of British industry's readiness to rationalize and modernize. As banks and issuing houses their responsibilities are in this respect at least as great as that of industry itself.

Similarly, if restriction of the private sector in the name of the public interest begins to place limits on their prospects, they must bear their share of responsibility for not making clear how they have served and can still serve the public interest. We live in an age of public pressures and, if the investor feels that he is not being protected, institutions concerned with investment will find themselves subject to increasing regulation. Half-hearted measures which can be only too easily represented politically as being defensive action by privilege – such as the watered down and apologetic monthly accounts of Stock Exchange transactions begun in September 1964 as a gesture to the demand for information – will only increase public clamour. When there is error, as there will always be in human actions, no mercy will be shown.

But there is no need for the merchant bankers either to apologize for themselves or to withdraw into selfishness. A bold example will find a popular response. For there is vigour enough in the nation itself. This is amply demonstrated by the two decades when, from a state of near bankruptcy in 1945, the United Kingdom could by 1965 estimate its overseas investments at £11,000 millions and, in spite of setbacks, was adding to them at a rate of over £200 millions per year and receiving from them annual earnings on capital of £490 millions. In addition, foreign industry had sufficient confidence over the same period to invest some £1,500 millions in Britain and draw annual earnings from it of some £160 millions.

Perhaps there would have been a stronger British economy if investment had been applied in greater proportion at home. But these figures do not reflect either stagnancy, idleness or lack of ingenuity

H

and competitiveness in trade. Our repeated balance of payments crises, warning calls and braking action just when industry and trade should have been moving forward into the type of fresh expansive phase which has characterized other economies, reflect rather some central misjudgement by those in charge. The effort and the vigour have thus been in great part wasted, with the resultant cry that sterling has 'weakened' again. But currency is still only a medium; the 'weakening' is a symptom, not a cause. The deficiency has been in the country's formulation of ideas and their application as valid principles of government and society by those who formed the British political and economic 'establishment'. The validity of a concept is demonstrated by the creation of power. Ingenuity by individuals can be no substitute for a guiding concept.

If our role for the sterling area is neither appreciated nor rewarded, and if in spite of the household skill of the Bank of England in handling its central reserve, sterling itself has ceased to be strong enough to play an effective role as a reserve currency, then it is certainly high time that we sought another role. The central issue has in fact always been a political one. What role do we want to play in the world? The heavy overseas government expenditure – on bases and commands, which are abandoned for reasons as obscure as those which led to their creation and which evidently failed to deter trouble-makers – on 'aid', which shows no return commensurate with the outlay and has to be continued under blackmail threats from the recipients – illustrates that whatever role we think we are playing is an ineffective one. At home, no group of politicians grapples with the problem of relating government expenditure, now the main inflationary and deflationary factor in the economy, to the need for productive growth. This has been the main cause of the continual under-investment, so that the rise in imports of capital goods and raw materials, which comes with each moment of 'go', precipitates the subsequent 'stop'. Planning comes down to being little more than exhortation with old clichés and the creation of committees and councils without powers.

The merchant bankers, therefore, face the same problem as the other British professions, from whom the top direction of national affairs is drawn. However widely they may distribute the material privileges of Victorian family ascendancies and of the Edwardian hey-day, they must now justify themselves by playing an active part in a new conscious formulation of the goals of society. What is required is the answer to the question: Are we Europeans and, if so, what sort of Europe do we hope to create? In working out the answer will come a clarification of their own role, whether an independent one, or one which exploits their special skills to gain a key position in some larger entity. The only outcome of evading the question will be retreat to insignificance.

Even to begin to answer is not easy. A whole series of British policy misjudgements since 1945 have to be made good. First each wartime European ally was dealt what seemed a stab in the back – the French in Syria, the Dutch in the East Indies, the Belgians in the Congo. Then we turned against our own kinsmen in dependencies still owing allegiance to the Crown, and set the applause of those who hated Europe higher than the maintenance of old loyalties. Finally the sturdy British working class, who always have to pay the price for the 'moral' narcissism of its presumed leaders, have been submitted to an apparently endless prospect of multi-racial tensions in the urban jungles of our time. It was almost as if we wished to destroy ourselves. Like Coriolanus we have stood: 'As if a man were author of himself and knew no other kin.'

Past history cannot, however, be rejected, for we are part of the European economy. This, fortunately, means that even as we depend on Europe, its plans for integration will always be uncertain of fulfilment without Britain. The mutual interaction of the peoples, ideas and societies of the western seaboard has lasted too many centuries for them to be able to ignore one another. They share the same unique historical conceptual process, and an idea engendered in one demands to be realized by all. The task of realization is presented ever anew to those who, like the City of London and its institutions, are both process and outcome. They can, of course, reject the task and fall out of the future stream of historical development: societies have perished in the past and will do so in the future. Or they can take up the task anew, and carry on their historical role of creation.

Accepting Houses Committee

Formed in 1914

MEMBERS*

The Rt Hon. Viscount Harcourt, K.C.M.G., O.B.E. (Chairman)	Morgan Grenfell & Co. Limited 23, Great Winchester Street London, EC2P 2AX
C.E.A. Hambro (Deputy Chairman)	Hambros Bank Limited 41, Bishopsgate London, EC2P 2AA
Hon. J.F.H. Baring	Baring Brothers & Co., Limited 8, Bishopsgate London, EC2N 4AE
Walter A. Brandt	Wm. Brandt's Sons & Co. Ltd. 36, Fenchurch Street London, EC3P 3AS
Hon. D.C. Campbell	Antony Gibbs & Sons, Ltd 22, Bishopsgate London, EC2N 4AQ
Hilton S. Clarke	Charterhouse Japhet Limited 1, Paternoster Row St Paul's London, EC4P 4HP
David R. Colville	N.M. Rothschild & Sons Limited New Court, St. Swithin's Lane London, EC4P 4DU
The Rt. Hon. Lord Farnham	Brown, Shipley & Co. Ltd Founders Court, Lothbury London, EC2R 7HE
Sir Kenneth Keith	Hill Samuel & Co. Limited 100, Wood Street London, EC2P 2AJ
Hon. R.H.M. Kindersley	Lazard Brothers & Co., Ltd 11, Old Broad Street P.O. Box 516, London, EC2P 2HT
Sir Cyril H. Kleinwort	Kleinwort, Benson Limited 20, Fenchurch Street London, EC3M 3DB

* As on 1 Jan 1971

Hon. David Montagu

Samuel Montagu & Co. Ltd
114, Old Broad Street
London, EC2P 2HY

H.H.-W. Pollard, O.B.E., T.D.

Guinness Mahon & Co. Ltd
3, Gracechurch Street
London, EC3V 0DP

N.J. Robson

Arbuthnot Latham & Co., Ltd
37, Queen Street
London, EC4R 1BY

Walter H. Salomon

Rea Brothers Limited
36–37, King Street
London, EC2V 8DR

Geoffrey C. Seligman

S.G. Warburg & Co. Limited
(incorporating
Seligman Brothers)
30, Gresham Street,
London, EC2P 2EB

Michael J. Verey, T.D.

J. Henry Schroder Wagg & Co. Ltd
120, Cheapside
London, EC2V 6DS

Banking Statistics of Accepting Houses

End of period

£ million

| | Total | Current and deposit accounts | | | | | | Coin, notes and balances with Bank of England | Balances with other United Kingdom banks | | Money at call and short notice | | Loans to United Kingdom local authorities |
| | | United Kingdom banks | | Other United Kingdom residents | | Overseas residents | | | | | | | |
		Sterling	Other currencies	Sterling	Other currencies	Sterling	Other currencies		Sterling	Other currencies	To discount market	To other borrowers	
1964	958.7	56.6	81.9	357.8	26.8	159.0	276.6	0.8	70.9	101.4	81.5	5.2	192.5
1965	1,030.5	87.2	103.2	422.8	19.3	141.3	256.7	0.8	93.5	84.9	67.9	6.6	242.2
1966	1,135.2	107.4	119.2	449.0	25.3	130.0	304.3	0.9	108.7	141.4	72.9	8.7	186.5
1967 March	1,284.0	136.6	167.8	451.6	23.7	183.4	320.9	0.9	126.4	156.1	74.9	8.0	248.1
June	1,317.5	127.5	166.2	492.9	28.0	156.2	346.7	1.1	120.0	145.3	86.3	22.4	254.5
September	1,372.1	118.0	151.4	583.0	30.8	136.3	352.6	0.8	136.4	136.9	94.6	10.7	301.7
December	1,464.0	118.7	201.3	557.9	34.6	150.9	400.6	0.9	148.6	149.7	66.2	13.9	271.8
1968 March	1,597.0	167.4	226.1	568.1	43.2	139.3	452.9	0.8	172.5	203.8	47.9	13.8	308.2
June	1,708.4	136.5	200.0	661.4	38.7	137.7	534.1	0.9	196.4	206.9	41.5	26.3	351.4
September	1,811.9	146.1	207.5	676.6	46.6	150.6	584.7	1.4	182.0	198.5	43.9	35.5	369.8
December	1,876.7	147.0	220.7	700.5	48.3	129.4	630.8	0.9	235.6	203.5	58.9	39.3	319.2
1969 March	2,155.2	233.9	275.1	730.3	60.4	113.5	742.0	0.8	259.7	364.0	53.0	24.5	365.8
June	2,259.7	194.4	283.9	760.2	67.5	107.9	845.8	1.5	240.7	436.7	47.5	32.2	380.2
September	2,391.9	209.6	296.2	817.0	76.9	100.8	891.4	1.3	297.2	423.2	51.8	47.5	359.0
December	2,446.0	222.4	318.7	815.8	75.1	117.3	896.7	1.7	319.4	398.5	60.5	35.8	336.9
1970 March	2,514.1	220.9	385.0	778.5	63.6	134.4	931.7	1.3	266.5	393.7	60.1	34.3	356.2
June	2,823.5	190.2	429.8	934.0	90.9	138.2	1,040.4	1.6	299.7	430.2	78.9	33.5	391.4
September	2,922.1	222.7	433.9	987.1	77.3	130.0	1,071.2	1.6	322.8	362.2	128.7	57.0	385.7

	Sterling bills discounted		British government securities		Total	Advances				Other assets		Acceptances	
						United Kingdom residents		Overseas residents					
	British Government Treasury bills	Other bills	Up to 5 years to maturity	Over 5 years and undated		Sterling	Other currencies	Sterling	Other currencies	Sterling	Other currencies	United Kingdom residents	Overseas residents
1964	11·5	14·2	50·8	10·3	469·2	205·8	15·2	22·3	225·9	45·5	26·2	189·1	41·7
1965	17·9	20·1	45·2	11·4	469·6	210·9	19·2	17·8	221·7	71·4	30·0	235·0	44·1
1966	14·0	19·3	63·4	12·0	529·0	217·3	23·6	15·8	272·3	104·1	32·3	220·7	50·5
1967 March	13·8	21·2	88·3	21·3	513·6	212·1	25·9	13·9	261·7	118·5	41·3	229·7	55·0
June	18·7	21·8	43·4	5·8	557·6	216·7	34·8	15·5	290·6	131·0	64·9	220·7	58·0
September	21·3	23·5	46·2	1·4	581·1	220·9	35·7	17·5	307·0	113·4	67·1	228·0	54·4
December	14·3	17·6	73·5	4·0	677·1	219·7	56·6	18·4	382·4	117·3	67·8	231·1	60·0
1968 March	18·1	18·7	66·1	5·7	685·3	212·5	58·2	13·7	400·9	112·4	79·2	235·4	64·9
June	19·4	16·8	37·2	2·1	761·6	232·8	80·3	19·4	429·1	129·0	77·1	240·9	67·7
September	11·4	19·2	61·5	10·7	822·3	233·1	73·1	27·4	488·7	134·4	93·9	226·9	68·0
December	13·9	14·2	39·1	4·4	899·9	233·2	88·3	27·8	550·6	141·7	78·0	260·6	67·9
1969 March	33·0	10·0	22·5	3·5	930·2	245·7	96·6	25·0	562·9	174·5	90·2	259·0	63·3
June	17·9	10·3	22·9	7·7	961·7	245·4	91·4	28·0	596·9	174·9	92·5	278·5	50·4
September	17·5	12·6	22·6	10·5	1,047·3	254·7	105·1	25·6	661·9	163·1	99·4	256·5	53·3
December	8·3	11·4	43·1	12·7	1,097·6	261·5	114·6	25·1	696·3	177·0	112·2	275·1	64·7
1970 March	17·2	16·2	35·3	26·2	1,164·4	265·9	120·9	16·5	761·1	209·6	122·3	275·5	67·0
June	4·7	14·2	15·5	19·9	1,349·6	298·1	137·9	21·1	892·4	253·3	125·3	296·1	69·5
September	7·2	8·4	15·7	12·4	1,430·3	300·4	152·2	21·5	956·3	244·3	146·2	290·0	65·0

Sources: Accepting Houses Committee
Bank of England

Extract from *Financial Statistics* (HMSO) No. 104. December 1970

Figures for Acceptances
(Members of the Accepting Houses Committee)

	Acceptances	Balance Sheet date
Hill, Samuel	68,220,000	31 March 1970
Hambros	60,763,370	31 March 1970
Kleinwort, Benson	59,978,000	31 December 1969
Schroder Wagg	40,317,000	31 December 1969
Warburgs	18,808,951	31 March 1970
Morgan Grenfell	15,417,138	31 December 1969
Barings	14,320,604	31 December 1969
Lazards	13,383,849	31 December 1969
Brown, Shipley	13,001,778	31 March 1970
Montagu	12,707,000	31 March 1970
Charterhouse Japhet	10,559,477	30 September 1969
Guinness Mahon	8,336,898	12 April 1970
Brandt's	7,504,000	31 December 1969
Arbuthnot Latham	5,583,371	31 March 1970
Anthony Gibbs	4,838,833	30 June 1970
Rea Brothers	4,808,487	31 December 1969

Note: Figures were not available for Rothschilds which was a partnership until 30 September 1970.
(Table compiled from figures available 1 December, 1970.)

Definitions of Credits and Bills

Documentary Credit

When a banker assumes liability to pay the price of goods or accept a bill for the invoiced amount, upon delivery to him of the invoices and shipping documents.

Irrevocable Credit

One which remains in force according to the period agreed in the Letter of Credit and cannot be revoked or cancelled unless the beneficiary is agreeable.

Refinance Credit

When an overseas importer makes an arrangement with London bankers to make an immediate payment to his suppliers and borrows the funds for this by drawing a time bill on an Accepting House which discounts it for him. This normally requires Exchange Control permission, particularly when the goods are invoiced in some other currency than sterling.

Fine Bank Bills

Drawn on and accepted by London banks and Accepting Houses of undoubted standing. Such bills command the finest rates of discount. Notice will also be taken of the name of the drawer, even though it is on the name of the acceptor that the bill is judged.

Agency Bills

Drawn on and accepted by the London branches of overseas banks, i.e. banks whose Head Offices are located abroad. A number of these banks enjoy the highest standing in the London Market and fine rates are quoted for their acceptances.

Trade Bills

Drawn by one trader on another. Trade Bills are well recognized in the Discount Market, though they are not so readily negotiable as Bank Bills and they do not command the same fine rates. Furthermore the total amount of Trade Bills that can be marketed on the strength of the name of any one Drawer or Acceptor is limited.

Foreign Domicile Bills

Drawn on and accepted by banks, companies or individuals abroad. These may obtain an advance for British banks but they will not normally be saleable in the discount market, unless endorsed by a London bank.

When the Bank of England is assisting the Houses either through Direct Assistance or loans at Bank Rate it will only buy or accept as collateral security Bank Bills or a limited number of those Trade Bills which have two good British names on them: in the latter case one of the names must be the acceptor and the other one can be the House which will have endorsed the bill on selling it to the Bank. This discrimination in favour of Bank Bills and against Trade Bills stems from the fact that the London banks and Accepting Houses who, by their undoubted standing, are able to give a bill 'Fine Bank Bill' status by accepting it, are within the discipline of the Bank of England – and consequently the Bank of England does not need to check the documentation of every bill – whereas the parties to a Trade Bill are not. In this way, the Bank of England restricts the volume of credit outside its control as Discount Houses cannot afford to commit too much of their resources to bills which although more profitable are only acceptable to the Bank of England in limited quantities. It will be seen, therefore, that Accepting Houses play a vital role in maintaining the quality of credit.

A Letter of Credit

This draft represents a simple facility letter. It is, of course, capable of amendment to include clauses covering any security which may be required, any embargo on the giving of security elsewhere during the currency of the credit and special requirements regarding insurance cover, etc.

Pinhead Banking Corporation
London, EC

Caledonian Assemblies Ltd,
Crowdieknowe,
Dumbrothshire.

Dear Sirs,

Following our recent discussions, we are now writing to place at your disposal revolving acceptance credit facilities of

£500,000 (say five hundred thousand pounds)

for the purpose of assisting in the finance of your purchases of steel.

The following terms and conditions will apply:

1. Availments will be made by means of your drafts drawn on us at 90 days' sight to your own order and blank endorsed. Individual drafts should not exceed £25,000 (i.e. a drawing of £100,000 would be accomplished by four drafts each at £25,000) and should bear a suitable clause, e.g. 'Drawn against purchases of steel'.

2. You will provide us each month with a certificate to the effect that your availments during the preceding month were not more than the amount of steel purchased by you.

3. We shall be pleased to arrange for the discounting of our acceptances in the London Discount Market, disposing of the proceeds, after deductions of your accepting commission, in accordance with your instructions which you will give us at the time of drawing.

4. Accepting commission will be charged at the rate of $x\%$ p.a., that is $y\%$ on each 90 days' draft. On this basis, the present all-in cost will total $z\%$ p.a., the current discount rate for Prime Bank acceptances being $w\%$ p.a.

230

5.   Remittances in cover of our acceptances should be in our hands in cash, London funds, not later than the maturity dates of the drafts, of which you will be advised at the time of acceptance. You may, of course, wish to make fresh drawings against new business, the proceeds of which are to serve against drafts maturing. In this event, you should let us have such drafts in our hands a few days before the maturity of the old drafts.

6.   This credit is revolving, that is to say it is intended to cover successive drawings provided the present agreed limit of drafts outstanding at any one time is not exceeded.

We shall be glad to receive your confirmation that the terms and conditions of this facility are acceptable to you.

Yours faithfully,

For Pinhead Banking Corporation

Issuing Houses Association

LIST OF MEMBERS*

Anglo-Scottish Amalgamated Corporation Ltd	68, Bishopsgate, EC2
Henry Ansbacher & Co. Ltd	1, Noble Street
	Gresham Street, EC2
Arbuthnot Latham & Co., Ltd	37, Queen Street
	EC4R 1BY
Baring Brothers & Co., Limited	8, Bishopsgate, EC2
Bentworth Trust Limited	41, Bishopsgate, EC2
First National Industrial Trust Limited	City Wall House
(incorporating Birmingham Industrial Trust Limited)	Finsbury Pavement, EC2
Wm. Brandt's Sons & Co., Ltd	36, Fenchurch Street
	EC3P 3AS
The British Empire Trust Co., Ltd	55, Bishopsgate EC2
British Trusts Association Ltd	39, King Street, EC2
Brown, Shipley & Co., Ltd	Founders Court
	Lothbury, EC2
Burston & Texas Commerce Bank Ltd	41, Moorgate, EC2
Charterhouse Japhet Limited	1, Paternoster Row
	St Paul's, EC4
Close Brothers Ltd	Gillett House
	55, Basinghall Street
	EC2
Dawnay, Day & Co., Limited	Garrard House
	31, Gresham Street
	EC2
Dawson & Forbes Limited	Sussex House
	38, Queen Street, EC4
Edward Bates, Mounthall Limited	16, Coleman Street
	EC2
Electric and General Industrial Trusts Ltd	8, Cleveland Row
	St James's, SW1

*As at December 1970

English Transcontinental Ltd	2, London Wall Buildings EC2
The Federated Trust and Finance Corporation Limited	1, Love Lane, EC2
Robert Fleming & Co., Limited	8, Crosby Square EC3
Robert Fraser & Partners Ltd	55, Grosvenor Street W1
Antony Gibbs & Sons, Ltd	22, Bishopsgate, EC2
Gray Dawes & Company Limited	40, St Mary Axe, EC3
Gresham Trust Limited	Barrington House Gresham Street, EC2
Guinness Mahon & Co. Ltd	3, Gracechurch Street EC3V 0DP
Gwent and West of England Enterprises Ltd	4th Floor Julian S. Hodge Building Newport Road, Cardiff Glam.
Hambros Bank Limited	41, Bishopsgate, EC2
Hill Samuel & Co. Limited	100, Wood Street, EC2
Industrial and Commercial Finance Corporation Ltd	7, Copthall Avenue EC2
Ionian Bank Limited	64, Coleman Street, EC2
Leopold Joseph & Sons Ltd	31–45, Gresham Street EC2
Keyser Ullman Limited	31, Throgmorton Street EC2
Kleinwort, Benson Limited	20, Fenchurch Street EC3
Lazard Brothers & Co., Ltd	11, Old Broad Street EC2
London and Yorkshire Trust Ltd	63, Brook Street, W1
Lothbury Assets Limited	52/54, Gracechurch Street EC3
Manchester and Liverpool Industrial Securities Ltd	63, Brook Street, W1
Matheson & Co. Ltd	3 Lombard Street, EC3
Midland Industrial Issues Limited	6th Floor King Edward House New Street, Birmingham, 2
Minster Trust Ltd	Minster House Arthur Street, EC4

Samuel Montagu & Co., Ltd	114, Old Broad Street EC2
Morgan Grenfell & Co. Ltd	23, Great Winchester Street EC2
J. F. Nash & Partners Limited	9, Station Road Kettering, Northants
Neville Industrial Securities Ltd	Neville House 42/46, Hagley Road Birmingham, 16
Northern Ireland Industrial Development and Finance Corporation Ltd	63, Brook Street W1
Old Broad Street Securities, Ltd	39, King Street, EC2
Rea Brothers Limited	36–37, King Street EC2
N. M. Rothschild & Sons Limited	New Court St Swithin's Lane EC4P 4DU
J. Henry Schroder Wagg & Co. Ltd	120, Cheapside, EC2
Scottish Industrial Finance Ltd	20, Blythswood Square Glasgow, C2
Securities Agency, Limited	117, Old Broad Street EC2
Seton Trust Ltd	Wardgate House 59A, London Wall EC2
Singer & Friedlander Ltd	20, Cannon Street EC4
Standard Industrial Trust Ltd	Shelley House Noble Street, EC2
Ufitec Trust Company Ltd	108, Cannon Street EC4
S. G. Warburg & Co. Limited (incorporating Seligman Brothers)	30, Gresham Street EC2
Williams, Glyn & Co.	67, Lombard Street EC3

Legal and Customary Requirements of Share Issues

1. *The Companies Act, 1948,* in which the prospectus requirements are set out in sections 37 to 55, combined with the Fourth Schedule. In addition, section 209 forms the backbone of all offers. This section provides that a minority can be compulsorily acquired, providing that acceptances have been received for at least 90 per cent, and the procedure for this is set out in the section.

2. Appendix 34 of *The Rules of the Stock Exchange* sets out the documents which have to be submitted to the Stock Exchange for quotation and the contents of those documents. The merchant bank will, of course, make itself responsible for compliance with these requirements.

3. *The Prevention of Fraud (Investments) Act, 1958,* and the *Licensed Dealers Rules, 1960.* Merchant banks in general are exempt from this legislation, as they are defined as 'exempted dealers', but they have a moral obligation to comply with certain requirements laid down by the Board of Trade as to the information given in offer documents.

4. *The Exchange Control Act, 1947,* and certain Bank of England orders made under that Act. Almost every issue and merger requires one or more consents from the Bank of England, and this is normally obtained by the merchant bank.

5. *The Control of Borrowing Order, 1958.* There used to be a very tight control on new issues, under which applications had to be made to the Capital Issues Committee. In 1959, however, the regulations were relaxed and for practical purposes all British companies can raise money without having to obtain consent. The issue of redeemable securities by bonus issue does, however, need consent, as do all issues by all foreign companies.

6. *The Income Tax Act, 1952,* in conjunction with all subsequent Finance Acts, needs careful scrutiny. Section 245 and the following sections of the 1952 Act relating to surtax are the ones which apply most frequently, and from time to time section 468, dealing with the transfer of trade abroad, also crops up. Of the subsequent Acts the most important is the *1960 Act,* and in particular section 28, whereby any transaction in securities which is not done in the ordinary course of making an

investment may be caught. The section is so all-embracing that clearance is necessary for any major deal, and it seems rather doubtful whether even the Inland Revenue know how the Act should be interpreted.

International interest rates

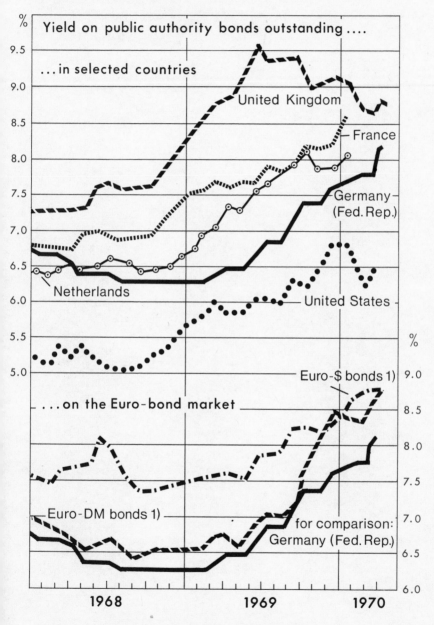

Yield on public authority bonds outstanding....

...in selected countries

United Kingdom

France

Germany (Fed. Rep.)

Netherlands

United States

Euro-$ bonds 1)

...on the Euro-bond market

Euro-DM bonds 1)

for comparison: Germany (Fed. Rep.)

1968   1969   1970

237

INDEX

239